Inquiry and the Common Core

INQUIRY
AND THE
COMMON CORE

Librarians and Teachers Designing Teaching for Learning

Violet H. Harada and
Sharon Coatney,
Editors

AN IMPRINT OF ABC-CLIO, LLC
Santa Barbara, California • Denver, Colorado • Oxford, England

Copyright 2014 by ABC-CLIO, LLC

Library of Congress Cataloging-in-Publication Data

Inquiry and the common core : librarians and teachers designing teaching for learning / Violet H. Harada and Sharon Coatney, editors.
    pages cm
  Includes bibliographical references and index.
  ISBN 978-1-61069-543-5 (pbk. : acid-free paper) — ISBN 978-1-61069-544-2 (ebook) 1. Inquiry-based learning—United States. 2. Education—Standards—United States. 3. School librarian participation in curriculum planning—United States. 4. Teaching teams—United States. 5. Lesson planning—United States. 6. Libraries and teachers—United States. I. Harada, Violet H., editor of compilation. II. Coatney, Sharon, editor of compilation.
  LB1027.23.I55 2014
  371.39—dc23   2013034976

ISBN: 978-1-61069-543-5
EISBN: 978-1-61069-544-2

18 17 16 15 14   1 2 3 4 5

This book is also available on the World Wide Web as an eBook. Visit www.abc-clio.com for details.

Libraries Unlimited
An Imprint of ABC-CLIO, LLC

ABC-CLIO, LLC
130 Cremona Drive, P.O. Box 1911
Santa Barbara, California 93116-1911

This book is printed on acid-free paper ∞
Manufactured in the United States of America

Contents

Foreword

Allison Zmuda

It is official. As educators, we have finally come to accept that the world we are training our students for is inherently unpredictable. We know that the students in our schools today need to be prepared to compete in a global marketplace, to tackle international policy issues, to create where there are little rules governing appropriateness and difficulty in standing out, and to contribute on behalf of their communities. More importantly, students want to engage with complex, meaningful problems as part of their schooling rather than it being relegated to after school or some day in the future.

Our schools are transforming because of more rigorous standards that are grounded in college, career, and citizen-ready skills. The writers of the Common Core State Standards outline a "portrait of students" capable of independently inquiring, evaluating, and producing texts for various purposes and audiences. Moving toward this powerful portrait requires significant shifts in the expectations we hold, assignments we design, and questions we ask of our students.

This volume is designed to inspire school librarians to create physical and virtual spaces that encourage inquiry. Through the creation and implementation of rich inquiry tasks both grounded in the CCSS and the AASL standards, librarians can rightfully regain their place as the original learning specialist focused on *every* student as they learn, discover, and engage in exploration. Whether it is a teacher-generated or student-inspired assignment, the job of a contemporary school librarian is to facilitate learning by sharing the wealth of resources to locate, synthesize, and create. Yes, librarians should be held accountable to demonstrate how inquiry and communication align with the CCSS, but the real challenge is how to elevate the rigor, creativity, and authenticity of the tasks facilitated in library physical and virtual spaces.

Editors Sharon Coatney and Violet Harada feature authors known throughout the school library world to describe the pedagogy and practice of the contemporary school librarian. Three prominent national initiatives are described in accessible and spirited prose that is relevant to any staff member working in the library space, including: looking at the core of the Common Core, focusing on project-based learning, and using inquiry as a classroom framework.

As educators, we all have a responsibility to create learning environments where students apply their knowledge to generate and pursue what they find fascinating. School librarians are uniquely poised to grow student capacity to pose powerful questions, access—and evaluate the credibility of—sources, and contribute information and ideas to an audience well beyond the walls of the school. By leveraging the CCSS and the AASL standards to promote new practice (or reinforce existing practice), the school librarian can inspire students and staff to enjoy the struggle that deep thought and sharing provide.

Introduction

Sharon Coatney

There is a critical need nationwide to create learning environments in K–12 schools that challenge and engage students in experiences that genuinely matter to them. This type of learning recognizes the importance of acquiring process-based skills along with disciplinary content. It demands deep thinking about underlying themes and issues rather than superficial curricular coverage and content.

This book is about how students learn best, how educators should teach to achieve engaged learning, how standards define the goals for that learning, and where the three must necessarily converge in schools. Central to the discussions and examples in this work are the Common Core State Standards (CCSS), a landmark effort of the National Association of Governors and the Council of Chief State School Officers to construct school-based standards that are consistent for students across the United States. These standards

- are aligned with college and work expectations;
- are clear, understandable, and consistent;
- include rigorous content and application of knowledge through high-order skills;
- build upon strengths and lessons of current state standards;
- are informed by other top-performing countries, so that all students are prepared to succeed in our global economy and society; and
- are evidence-based.[1]

Although the adoption of these standards is voluntary, most states have done so, and states that have not have standards of their own with similar goals. While these standards demand rigorous content and demonstration of knowledge through the application of higher-order skills, it is critical to recognize that they do not define or prescribe how educators should teach to achieve these standards. Research based on inquiry-focused teaching practices indicates the power of encouraging and guiding students to ask challenging questions, critically pursue answers, and create innovative representations of their new insights. This book focuses on the power of merging the rigorous CCSS with an inquiry approach to learning. It also stresses the unique opportunity the CCSS present for school librarians as major instructional partners, with its emphasis on student-driven research and close reading of informational resources at increasing levels of complexity.

ORGANIZATION OF THE BOOK

This volume would not have been possible without the invaluable contributions of a team of respected library educators and practitioners. They share their passionate beliefs and practices in the following chapters and exemplars and invite school librarians working with their school teams to approach the deep learning embedded in the standards through an inquiry approach. The chapters are arranged in four major sections.

In part I, "Integration of Inquiry and the CCSS," **Jean Donham** launches the book with a thoughtful discussion of inquiry as vital to meaningful learning and includes clear and relevant examples of how and why educators must promote inquiry learning in their schools. **Olga Nesi** follows with a deep examination of the core underlying the CCSS. She unpacks the standards and leads the reader to think seriously about the relationship between what the CCSS require and the inquiry learning that school librarians have traditionally promoted. **Deb Levitov** moves the discussion squarely to the role of the school librarian in the CCSS challenge and provokes readers to consider their present and future responsibilities, so vitally captured in both the AASL *Standards* and the CCSS. **Judi Moreillon** rounds out this section with a detailed description of the coteaching potential that the librarian must seize. She zeroes in on the importance of teaching reading comprehension strategies that significantly contribute to goals in the CCSS.

Part II, "Models for Inquiry-Based Learning," addresses the question, How should educators tackle a guided approach to inquiry learning? It then presents three possible answers. **Leslie Maniotes** carefully outlines the major features of the Guided Inquiry Design (GID), which is based on the ISP (information search process) created by Carol Kuhlthau. In their chapter, **Violet Harada and her colleagues** define the components of project-based learning (PBL) and major questions to consider when adopting PBL in a school. Finally, **Barbara Stripling** brings clarity to her inquiry model with particular emphasis on how digital learning must be part of educating today's learners.

All of these chapters address the CCSS and their relationship to inquiry in their respective models.

Part III, "Planning For Meaningful Learning," begins with **Kristin Fontichiaro** suggesting a friendly and sensible approach to taking existing units and lessons and "nudging" them a little at a time toward a full inquiry stance. Kristin's comments are anchored in her longtime column in *School Library Monthly*, "Nudging Toward Inquiry," and are particularly helpful to school librarians and educators as they work together to implement inquiry learning and the CCSS in their schools. This leads into Violet Harada's introduction to designing learning plans, which is followed by part IV, which showcases exemplars of K–12 lessons. Each learning plan reflects actual collaborative plans that have been successfully taught in schools using the CCSS and the inquiry process.

CONCLUSION

As editors, we feel the urgent need for a book of this nature. It not only defines inquiry learning as it relates to the CCSS, but recognizes the pervasiveness of these standards and the necessity for school librarians to actively embrace this priceless opportunity to make a difference as they work with teachers to implement dynamic ways to teach and learn. Jean Donham states that "inquiry prepares students to live in a rapidly changing world where no prescribed canon of knowledge will suffice." This is irrefutable. Olga Nesi confirms that the school librarian's contribution to the implementation of these new standards "is potentially limitless." We welcome you to dive into this book, explore the possibilities presented, and ultimately create your own footprints as learning leaders.

NOTES

1. Common Core State Standards Initiative, "About the Standards" (retrieved from http://www.corestandards.org/about-the-standards on July 23, 2013).

Part I

Integration of Inquiry and the CCSS

1

Inquiry

Jean Donham

Curiosity is the catalyst that sparks the inquiry process. We can be surrounded by information and ideas, but until our curiosity is piqued, we don't begin posing questions that project us into knowledge seeking or inquiry. Curiosity may be construed as an appetite for learning that arises when our attention is drawn to something that stimulates a desire to learn (Schmitt and Lahroodi 2008). Bruner asserted that curiosity is so important it "is essential to the survival not only of the individual but of the species" (1966, 115). Similarly, Gazzaniga (2005) linked curiosity to the human evolutionary drive to adapt and survive. Point to any discovery, any invention, any creation and ask, Could it have been realized without someone being curious and asking why? why not? how? what if?

Engendering such curiosity in students confronts educators with a number of challenges:

- *Unlearning certainty:* In school we too often teach students to expect that each question has a specific and often absolute answer, yet authentic inquiry may engage us in unanswered questions. What can we do to construct learning experiences that allow uncertainty and ambiguity to creep into the classroom?
- *Observation:* Nurturing skills to be observant is key to engendering curiosity; it is from observation that questions arise. Rendering visible the invisible by close observation and description is the precursor to posing authentic

Portions of this chapter were originally published in Jean Donham, "Deep Learning Through Concept-Based Inquiry," *School Library Monthly* 27, no. 1 (September/October 2010). Used with permission.

questions. Can we provide experiences that afford opportunities to observe in settings that will generate students' interest and cause them to raise their own questions? Can exploration of information in print and digital sources be a stimulus for curiosity and question raising, rather than question answering?

- *Substantive conversation:* Learning is social. How can we create learning communities that allow for interchange in which students articulate what they are wondering and refine their thoughts through conversation with one another?

- *Healthy skepticism:* Establishing a critical stance and challenging findings is central to authentic inquiry. Can we encourage in students a healthy degree of skepticism that causes them to wonder from various perspectives, not just their own? In school, students too often learn from a single source, a textbook. However, they need to have opportunities to examine information from various sources and wonder how and why perspectives are similar and how and why they differ. Instead of dismissing biased sources, should we encourage students to examine them as they adopt a critical and questioning stance? Can a questioning stance become a habit of mind?

- *Interdisciplinarity:* As students engage in study, we tend to compartmental-ize their learning into disciplinary boxes. However, in life they will need to engage in activities that integrate knowledge: the physician will find it neces-sary to discuss ethical, political, and legal issues and to formulate arguments in the context of such discourses; the artist will find it important to study structures of objects and beings in order to represent them artistically; the journalist will find it necessary to find voice in many disciplines. How can we design experiences that call for integration of knowledge?

As educators, we model the inquiry process. For example, modeling think-alouds can show our disposition of curiosity. When sharing resources with students, we need to hear ourselves pausing to say, "That makes me wonder. . . ." In examining resources from special interests, we need to hear ourselves saying, "I wonder about the background of this author or speaker or Web site. . . ." Similarly, encountering information from a distinctive or biased point of view requires us to ask, "I wonder whether we can find another viewpoint. . . ." By modeling close observation and wonder, we en-courage students to exhibit healthy skepticism by challenging information sources, and by expecting students to verify their findings.

Attention to detail yields questions worthy of further investigation. Can we look closely at an image and wonder why a bald eagle's beak is shaped the way it is? What does that tell us about its adaptation for food gathering? Modeling the value of interdisciplinarity can happen by asking in a science context how an artist would see symmetry or color or texture or. . . .

As we develop habits of inquiry in school, we serve our students best by approximating the experience of inquiry as it will be realized in their own lives. To the extent that we can create an authentic experience of wonder-ing, learning, and concluding or seeking further, we prepare students to be lifelong learners. Inquiry is a habit to be practiced throughout a life lived in a rapidly changing world.

While inquiry begins with wondering, wonder leads into a stage of exploration. In school settings, exploration is perhaps one of the most short-changed stages of the inquiry process. Often we allow students to short-circuit the inquiry process, accepting that they will gather factual information about a topic and be done. However, what we really need to do is encourage them to gain enough background knowledge in their information gathering that they can then pose real and substantive questions. Kuhlthau (1995) describes this exploration stage as that in which the learner simply reads and pokes around a topic of interest, becomes familiar with it, reflects and ponders, perhaps reconciles conflicting information, and generally invests in the line of inquiry—often without detailed note taking, but rather as an explorer. In school, we rarely allow time for this experience. Yet in college and in life, this is the nature of learning. Integral to this stage is reflecting on found information. The school librarian can intervene to provide scaffolding that asks students to record what they have learned from their exploration and what it makes them wonder. Kuhlthau (1995) also found that this is a particularly uncomfortable stage because of the uncertainty that accompanies a period when one is learning about something, but does not yet know exactly where that learning will lead. It may be at this stage that we implement the KWL (What do I know, what do I want to learn, what have I learned?) strategy, not at the very beginning, when what students know may be minimal. By waiting until they have begun to explore, the richness of what they know will provide the opportunity for better, deeper questions.

Inquiry in the context of the school curriculum requires students to engage in information seeking that may not originate from their own curiosity. Yet educators can create an environment wherein students develop background knowledge and enter into a mode of inquiry within curricular content. Even when we work in the context of imposed inquiry—questions that are raised in response to the demands of content curricula—we can simulate the inquiry experience. Inquiry engages students in a state of pursuing new knowledge. While we provide paths to information sources, help students develop strategies for information seeking, and develop in them standards of quality for the information sources they will trust, we also strive to extend their inquiry to questions of depth and opportunities to gain not only facts but also new insights. For example, they collect information about an animal, say the Canada goose: what it eats, where it lives, what threats to survival it faces, etc. The outcome is a report of factual learning. However, in an inquiry approach the result of that background knowledge is generation of questions about which students are curious now that they know something about the subject; it is now that they *begin* inquiry. What if migrating geese stop migrating southward because of climate changes and remain in more northerly habitats? How would the stay affect the geese? How would the change affect the new habitat? The generation of these research questions growing out of background knowledge distinguishes inquiry-based learning. These are authentic questions to which students have no answers and for which answers may be difficult to locate. These questions will require investigation into many subquestions and use of many sources. Students may need to investigate more deeply: Why do geese migrate? What are they seeking, and will they find it in a steady location? What resources do they consume, and what is their impact on an environment? What stimulates them to begin their travel? What are their nesting patterns, and how might staying put affect those behaviors?

Similarly, secondary school students might gather factual information about a country in Africa, then based on those facts pose a question such as, "What would it take for [Chad, Senegal, Nigeria, etc.] to become a significant participant in the world economy?" In short, inquiry does not end with a collection of facts. Factual findings lead to questions of interpretation, exploration, and speculation—all of which require deeper, more complex investigation.

THE IMPORTANCE OF A MENTAL MODEL

A mental model is an intellectual framework created by integrating what one knows or has experienced into a given concept or task. Pitts (1995) investigated the effects of mental models on students' information work. Her findings offer insight into their library use. She classified learners, based on their mental models of information processing, as either novices or experts. She describes the novice as one who has little prior knowledge of a topic; his or her personal understandings are fragmentary, based on a limited perspective. The expert has more connected understandings and a more global perspective. Pitts examined the work of high school student groups assigned to create video documentaries on topics in marine biology. For this project, there was no direct instruction about either the process or the content of the assignment. Pitts's assessment of the students' work revealed that they used very little information from libraries and were often unsuccessful in their search for information. She proposed several reasons for their lack of success. First, she suggested that students had incomplete subject-matter mental models and that this led to incomplete identification of their information needs. Her analysis of student searching revealed that most searches were very general in nature. In addition, she observed that students had limited mental models for information seeking and use. They nearly always looked in only one place, the online catalog. A final problem she identified was the inaccurate mental models that adults had of students' subject expertise or their information-seeking prowess. Adults tended to provide locational advice only, either assuming that students could identify the most appropriate resource or overestimating their expertise in the topic.

Pitts's findings raise our awareness of the shortcoming of students' mental models of research and suggest that more accurate mental models could improve their experiences and learning. In part, educators have helped students develop inaccurate mental models of research. When we consider what we ask of students in fact-gathering assignments, it is no wonder that they arrive at an understanding that research is an assembly process—that is, to gather some facts and assemble them into an organizational scheme surrounded by an introduction and a summarizing conclusion. Technology has facilitated the assembly process with copy-and-paste features. Overcoming such a model can begin with introducing students to the process of inquiry that starts with raising questions. Providing students with a model based on the work of Kuhlthau, Caspari, and Maniotes (2007) or Stripling (2010) can establish a new understanding of the task. However, supplying the model is only one step. Helping students (and teachers) appreciate the openness of inquiry, the importance of uncertainty, and the recursive nature of the inquiry process is central to replacing inaccurate mental models.

The American Association of School Librarians (AASL) *Standards for the 21st-Century Learner* (2007) provides a framework for creating an accurate mental model of the inquiry process. These standards begin with four powerful verbs that comprise the inquiry process:

- *inquire*, think critically, and gain knowledge;
- *draw conclusions*, make informed decisions and apply knowledge to new situations, and create new knowledge;
- *share* knowledge and participate ethically and productively as members of our democratic society; and
- *pursue* personal and aesthetic growth.

These student behaviors define a process that goes well beyond assembly of information toward constructing new understandings and insights. Further, the AASL *Standards* delineate skills, dispositions, responsibilities, and self-assessment strategies to be applied in the inquiry process. No other standards encompass all these dimensions of learning. Yet genuine inquiry clearly requires more than skills. It demands of students the dispositions of a learner, such as curiosity, open-mindedness, and perseverance. Beyond dispositions and skills, inquiry requires a sense of responsibility for ethical use of information. To be an independent person of inquiry, one must be metacognitive: able to self-assess and self-correct. Specific indicators in all these dimensions are defined in the AASL *Standards for the 21st-Century Learner*, which underpin the curriculum of inquiry for a library program and proffer a comprehensive mental model of inquiry that encompasses more than skills.

DEEP INQUIRY

Taba (1962) proposed teaching social studies by moving away from topical or chronological, fact-seeking tasks to conceptual understanding. She sought to deepen learning experiences by refocusing student explorations away from topics and toward concept-based inquiry. More recently, Erickson has advocated concept-based learning. She suggested that when students engage in a study, they should apply a *conceptual lens*. She defined concepts as having the following attributes (2008, 40):

- *Broad and abstract*: Because concepts are broad, they have the potential for transfer across settings. If students study the Pilgrims of the 1600s, they learn about them as a concrete and specific topic; if they study immigration, they learn about an abstract idea that has application across a variety of specific examples, including the Plymouth Pilgrims.
- *Universal in application*. Because concepts are universal, students construct understandings that apply in other settings and provide ways of seeing their world that will apply not only in school but also in life beyond school. If, for example, students study the Pilgrims, they take away factual knowledge about the 1600s. If they study the Pilgrims as one example of immigrants, along with the Irish, the Swedish, the Chinese, the Mexicans, the Hmong, and the Somalians, the conceptual lens of immigration gives them the opportunity to see the universality of the immigrant experience and the ensuing insights that can emerge from the comparisons across exemplars. What new attitudes and understandings might arise here that would not have arisen if they only studied the Pilgrims? Consider the universality of concepts like civil discourse, civil disobedience, extinction, and culture.
- *Timeless*. Concepts should carry through the ages. In social studies, for example, when students examine a concept rather than a specific event, the lessons of history become clearer. Consider such ideas as revolution, colonialism, or leadership as lenses for understanding history across eras and nations. What enduring understanding could emerge?
- *Represented by different examples that share common attributes*. By examining the characteristics of exemplars, students derive meaning from the concept. In adaptation, for example, as students consider various examples, new insights and understandings are likely to emerge when they consider the stimuli for various adaptations in living things: protection from predators, climate, food gathering, etc.

As another example, a middle school class might study Latin America. Each student investigates a country in Latin America. What questions do they pursue?

- What is the capital?
- What is the population?
- What natural resources does the country have?
- What are the major industries?
- What is the typical level of education of the people?

In addition, they probably try to find a picture of the national flag or a recording of the national anthem to decorate a poster or PowerPoint presentation.

Is this inquiry? It is fact gathering, but authentic inquiry should lead to new understanding and insights. Fact gathering can provide the background knowledge out of which inquiry arises.

Taba (1962) suggested that moving from this topical or factual focus to a conceptual focus would yield a different kind of thinking and questioning. She asked: How would learning change if the *topic* focus were replaced with a *conceptual* focus? For example, economic development could be a conceptual focus. When students consider sample Latin American countries in the context of the concept of economic development, several shifts occur. The level of complexity of their investigation is increased beyond knowing or understanding toward analyzing; with this conceptual focus, students now compare and contrast among the samples—an analytical process. They construct the meaning of economic development when they analyze the elements that constitute it and how they relate to one another.

The questions students pose immediately change. Now they are not only gathering facts, but also *interpreting* how their factual information relates to the concept of economic development. Now when they gather factual information, they are not merely preparing to report the facts; instead, they are applying that information for the purpose of analyzing economic development. Now they think about the role of government or education as factors in economic development and rise to more analytical and insightful inquiry, well beyond reporting found information. Another way to consider such a shift is that students may engage in fact finding in the particular, but then reflect on their findings as they apply to a more universal construct or idea.

National curricula in social studies and science, as well as the Common Core State Standards, support such a conceptual approach to student learning. For example, for the National Social Studies Standards, ten themes representing "big ideas" or concepts provide their organizing structure (National Council for the Social Studies 2010). These include such concepts as culture; power, authority, and governance; and individual development and identity. Similarly, in science, conceptual understanding focuses on ideas like patterns and stability and change (National Science Teachers Association 2013). Conceptual inquiry should be contextualized, then, around "big ideas" or concepts from these curricula. Making connections to these curriculum standards adds credence to the importance of engaging students in inquiry beyond fact gathering.

The school librarian may play an important role in moving toward deep inquiry and away from fact gathering by suggesting a slight shift when a teacher proposes to bring classes to the library to "do research." By reminding teachers that facts are easy to come by on the Web, the school librarian may consult with the teacher about designing deeper inquiry.

The most likely resistance will come from teachers worrying that the investigations will lead into the unknown, and for some this creates anxiety. The school librarian should step up to be the information adventurer who supports genuine inquiry and is willing to assert that sometimes research does not lead to answers, but rather to further questions. Boredom and disengagement in school are often attributed to the current generation's infatuation with media and technology—they need fast-paced experiences, we sometimes believe, as we observe them zipping around the Internet. However, another—perhaps more accurate—diagnosis is that they want more engaging, more interesting, and deeper work in school.

DEEP QUESTIONS

A particularly crucial aspect of inquiry is generating a research question that will lead to new understanding and insights, not merely to a summary of what the published literature says. Dahlgren and Öberg (2001) provide a taxonomy of questions that may be useful in encouraging students to generate a promising research query. They suggest five categories of questions:

- *Encyclopedic questions:* These are the general factual questions student might pose that would lead them to write a report analogous to an encyclopedia article. Examples: Who are the Hmong? What is causing global warming? Too often this is the kind of question students imagine as they begin an assignment. This kind of question will yield a report—but not a research paper; it will yield information but rarely insight.
- *Meaning-oriented:* These questions require students to construct the meaning of a concept, often within a particular context. Examples: What are the challenges inherent in cultural assimilation for the Hmong people? Why have certain states expressed particular concern about acid rain?
- *Relational:* These questions require the researcher to explore the relationship between or among phenomena. Examples: What factors have influenced women's opportunities from before the women's movement of the 1960s to today? What are the effects of climate change on sea lions?
- *Value-oriented:* These questions require the researcher to interpret events or phenomena in the context of a value system; this may encompass religious, political, social, gender, racial, or other social values. Examples: What has been the impact of the women's movement on men's family roles? What is the importance of animals being identified as endangered species?
- *Solution-oriented:* These questions require the researcher to examine a problem and seek solutions to that problem. Examples: How can prejudice toward nonwhite immigrants be reduced in the United States? How can the coral reefs be protected from further loss?

For younger students, alternative taxonomies may be useful. For example, questions may be classified with Bloom's Taxonomy in mind.

Knowing: What? When? Where?
> What is the pathway of monarch butterfly migration? What are they seeking when they migrate?

Analyzing: How? What evidence?
> How do the butterflies decide when to begin their travels?

Creating: What would . . . ? What should . . . ?
> What should be done to reduce the decline in the monarch butterfly population?

At the *knowing* level, students are engaging in exploration. Their questions build their background to underpin the questions they will later generate at the *analyzing* and *creating* levels. School librarians may give students a taxonomy of questions or recommend a specific type of question for a particular assignment. Such classification of questions can help to articulate the purpose of the inquiry and help students set a direction for their work.

PERSISTENCE

Inquiry that goes beyond fact finding can be difficult. Sometimes answers are elusive. Often, arriving at meaningful insights requires high-level thinking, integration of information from a variety of sources, speculation, inferential thinking, and further questioning. For authentic inquiry, students need a disposition of persistence that sees them through the challenges inquiry can pose. Educators can stand ready to intervene with alternatives when frustrations arise. Crow (2009) discovered the importance of relationships for supporting students engaged in inquiry. Her findings highlighted four themes: students' affinity for play, the point of passion experience, the presence of "anchor" relationships, and the social appeal of group work. To apply these factors to inquiry in school, they can be synthesized into the importance of relationships and deep interest in the inquiry. Relationships can support students' persistence as adults encourage and advise young researchers. Peers may serve as listeners and responders if we create peer response groups for inquiry projects. *Passion* or interest increases when young researchers have the power to determine their own line of inquiry and own their questions, and when the questions are deep or complex enough to ignite genuine interest. Simply raising awareness of the importance of perseverance for deep and insightful inquiry is an important step.

Students may be more likely to persevere when they hold an accurate mental model of the inquiry process, knowing that feelings of uncertainty are the norm, that inquiry is not linear, and that not all questions have readily available answers. Conversely, perceiving inquiry to be a straightforward, linear process or checklist threatens their fortitude to persist when roadblocks or frustrations arise.

AUTHENTICITY IN INQUIRY

An intended outcome for learning is the discovery of new insights as one interprets and integrates findings from a variety of sources, including one's prior knowledge. An insight is a clear and deep understanding of a complicated problem, phenomenon, or situation. An important word in that definition is *deep*. Deep understanding calls for students to "own" the ideas and information they take from their information searching. Wiggins and McTighe use the phrase "enduring understanding" to describe the important "big ideas" that educators want students to retain and apply to new settings or problems after they have forgotten many of the particular details (2005, 17). Students must have engaged themselves fully enough in their research to be conversant with the ideas and facts they have uncovered and be able to apply them to situations, problems, or decisions. This is the way adult information seekers work—they seek and gather information in order to apply it to situations or problems. These big ideas often result from insightful thinking.

For students to develop the ability to arrive at insights in a way that will be useful for lifelong learning, schools must present them with experiences that challenge them not only to collect and report information, but also to go beyond reporting to analyze, evaluate, and synthesize. Five attributes of inquiry can take students beyond collecting information to reaching insight. These are summarized in figure 1.1.

When teachers and librarians direct the questions that students will explore, students take on the role of answer seeker. They look for information

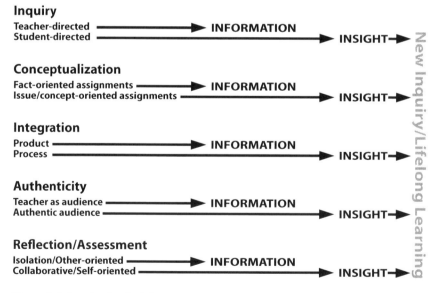

Figure 1.1. Inquiry for Insight

Source: J. Donham, *Enhancing Teaching and Learning: A Leadership Guide for School Librarians* (Chicago: ALA Editions/Neal Schuman, 2013).

to respond to the teacher's query—period. However, they do not own the inquiry, nor are they likely to reflect on their findings in ways that will lead them to insights. When students can direct their own inquiry, they are more likely to be vested in their quest and subsequently more likely to push themselves to ask the "so what?" questions that can lead to insight. Similarly, when students respond to fact-oriented assignments, they are collecting information to respond to largely closed-ended rather than open-ended queries. To the extent that assignments expect students to respond at the conceptual rather than the factual level or to address issues rather than information, students are more likely to arrive at insights.

The attraction of technology tools for creating products that impress can sometimes distract from the central purpose of inquiry: critical and creative thinking, problem solving, or decision making. School librarians may engage teachers and students to carefully integrate decisions about the product as part of the inquiry process. We may ask, "What product best serves the purpose of this inquiry for the intended audience?" This raises different questions about investing too much effort in a product's look rather than its substance and ultimately leads to recommendations for product design that enhances the content.

Authenticity is an important attribute of tasks that will engage students and lead them to be reflective and insightful. When students perceive that their work is aimed only at communicating with or pleasing the teacher, the likelihood of that engagement diminishes. When students can identify a more authentic audience for their work, it takes on new meaning and sets them up for thinking insightfully. Koechlin and Zwaan (2007) suggest challenging students to ask themselves, "What is really important about my findings? Why? To whom are they important?" Posing such questions during the inquiry process sets an expectation that students will think about audience and will see that their work should result in not only collected and assembled information, but also insights or new questions. Finally, when the assessment of student work is collaborative, students feel more ownership in the results. If at the end of an information quest students turn in a product to the teacher or the librarian who does nothing more than return it with a score or grade, the work is merely an exercise. When teachers, librarians, and students review the work together, that discussion is likely to bring students to a level of insight that might have been lost without the interchange of a collaborative assessment process. The teacher or librarian may pose questions that give students opportunities to think reflectively and consider what they might pursue further to enhance the work they have just completed. These five attributes of inquiry programs—student-directed inquiry, concept-oriented assignments, integration of the research process (as well as the end product) into content instruction, an authentic audience, and collaborative assessment—increase the meaningfulness of the inquiry experience for students and help them develop the intellectual processes that will make them insightful knowledge creators as adults.

CONCLUSION

Inquiry is complex. It develops out of curiosity, and educators have the important responsibility to create circumstances that generate and nurture curiosity. Inquiry requires commitment from educators and students—commitment to build on the known and to generate new insights and understandings based on deep and persistent questioning. Most important, inquiry prepares students to live in a rapidly changing world in which no prescribed canon of knowledge will suffice. Instead, students need accurate mental models of the inquiry process, curious dispositions, and skills that support their quest for knowledge.

REFERENCES

American Association of School Librarians (AASL). (2007). *Standards for the 21st-Century Learner*. Chicago: American Library Association.

Bruner, J. S. (1966). *Toward a Theory of Instruction*. Cambridge, MA: Belknap Press.

Crow, S. R. (2009). "Relationships That Foster Intrinsic Motivation for Information Seeking." *School Libraries Worldwide* 15 (2): 91–112.

Dahlgren, M. A., and G. Öberg. (2001). "Questioning to Learn and Learning to Question: Structure and Function of Problem-based Learning Scenarios in Environmental Science Education." *Higher Education* 44 (3): 263–282.

Erickson, H. L. (2008). *Stirring the Head, Heart, and Soul: Redefining Curriculum, Instruction, and Concept-based Learning*. Thousand Oaks, CA: Corwin Press.

Gazzaniga, M. S. (2005). *The Ethical Brain*. Washington, DC: Dana Press.

Koechlin, C., and S. Zwaan. (2007). "Assignments Worth the Effort: Questions Are Key." *Teacher Librarian* 34 (7): 14–19.

Kuhlthau, C. (1995). "The Process of Learning from Information." *School Libraries Worldwide* 1 (1): 1–12.

Kuhlthau, C. C., A. K. Caspari, and L. K. Maniotes. (2007). *Guided Inquiry: Learning in the 21st Century*. Westport, CT: Libraries Unlimited.

National Council for the Social Studies. (2010). *National Curriculum Standards for Social Studies: A Framework for Teaching, Learning, and Assessment*. Waldorf, MD: NCSS Publications.

National Science Teachers Association. (2013). *Next Generation Science Standards*. Retrieved from http://www.nextgenscience.org/next-generation-science-standards.

Pitts, J. M. (1995). "Mental Models of Information: The 1993–94 AASL/Highsmith Research Award Study." *School Library Media Quarterly* 23 (3): 177–184.

Schmitt, F. F., and R. Lahroodi. (2008). "The Epistemic Value of Curiosity." *Educational Theory* 58 (2): 125–148.

Stafford, T. (2009). "Teaching Students to Form Effective Questions." *Knowledge Quest* 38 (1): 48–55.

Stripling, B. (2010). "Teaching Students to Think in the Digital Environment: Digital Literacy and Digital Inquiry." *School Library Monthly* 26 (8): 16–19.

Taba, H. (1962). *Curriculum Development: Theory and Practice*. New York: Harcourt, Brace & World.

Wiggins, G., and J. McTighe. (2005). *Understanding by Design*. Exp. 2nd ed. Alexandria, VA: Association for Supervision and Curriculum Development.

2

What Is the "Core" of the Common Core State Standards?

Olga M. Nesi

In this time of tumultuous change precipitated by the Common Core State Standards (CCSS), school librarians have been given a gift of inconceivable value: an opportunity to make the strongest case ever for the indispensability of vibrant and deeply instructionally relevant library programs in all schools. Ironically, this opportunity is presenting itself concurrently with the suggestion that school libraries (and by extension, school librarians) are dispensable. With this added twist, making the case for our indispensability will require fierce and mighty work from each and every one of us. Simply staking a claim to these new learning standards only scratches the surface of what we need to convey. Doing the work involved in clearly demonstrating that claim is the only course of action that will convince others of our rightful place in the Common Core conversation.

It is in this very climate of suggested disposability that the CCSS have given us the opportunity to prove once and for all that our work is urgent and critical. What we teach in libraries is not the indefinitely postponable "library curriculum." Nor is it only marginally significant. We teach inquiry: the process of meaningful learning that transfers across *all* content areas. As it turns out, inquiry and the CCSS align seamlessly. Our success in demonstrating and clarifying this alignment to others will position our profession at the forefront of Common Core implementation. The opportunity to lead is ours for the taking, provided we fully accept both the scope of the work and the urgency with which it has to be performed.

INSTRUCTIONAL SHIFTS REQUIRED
BY THE COMMON CORE STATE STANDARDS

The framework on which all implementation efforts must be built is deeply dependent on identifying and meeting a set of instructional shifts that are central to the CCSS being met. The New York State Education Department (2012) has identified on its engageNY.org Web site the six ELA/Literacy shifts shown in table 2.1 as critical to the implementation of the CCSS.

Each of these shifts may require us to rethink a number of timeworn instructional approaches. To start, students will be asked to engage with informational text (both expository and narrative) far more than they have done in the past. Following directly from this shift are the next two. First, using increasingly complex text, students will learn about content through deep reading (as opposed to being spoon-fed content). Then, evidence-based argumentation takes a front row seat. Whether the text being read to create these arguments is fictional or informational, students will be expected to craft an evidence-based argument from the reading material. For their arguments to be well formed, evidence will have to be culled, analyzed, and synthesized from a variety of sources. Finally, as text complexity increases,

Table 2.1. Shifts in ELA/Literacy

Shift 1	Balancing Informational and Literary Text	Students read a true balance of informational and literary texts.
Shift 2	Knowledge in the Disciplines	Students build knowledge about the world (domains/content areas) through text rather than the teacher or activities.
Shift 3	Staircase of Complexity	Students read the central, grade-appropriate text around which instruction is centered. Teachers are patient, creating more time, space, and support in the curriculum for close reading.
Shift 4	Text-based Answers	Students engage in rich and rigorous evidence-based conversations about text.
Shift 5	Writing from Sources	Writing emphasizes use of evidence from sources to inform or make an argument.
Shift 6	Academic Vocabulary	Students constantly build the transferable vocabulary they need to access grade level complex texts. This can be done effectively by spiraling like content in increasingly complex texts.

students will build a critical mass of transferable vocabulary. In building this wide base of vocabulary, increasingly more complex texts will become accessible to them. In this new terrain, the proposal is that our students' deep and direct engagement with reading is no longer optional (if it ever was). And gone is the day when assignments could be completed without any reading whatsoever having occurred. What is of utmost importance here is the caliber of the tasks we create for our students to complete, for without a well-crafted task, not one of the identified shifts can take place.

THE IMPORTANCE OF RIGOROUS TASKS IN THE COMMON CORE LANDSCAPE

From the outset, the Common Core conversation has emphasized the necessity of well-crafted assignments that require students to engage deeply with content to produce new understandings and knowledge. This is a blessing for school librarians weary beyond comprehension of "copy-and-paste" assignments. For students to be directly involved with the creation of new knowledge, we must be sure to determine the following:

- What end product will students have to create as evidence that they have actually engaged deeply with the content?
- What inquiry skills will we have to teach them so that they can create the end product?
- How will we meaningfully teach them the necessary skills?
- What materials will we use to teach the skills?
- How will we assess that our teaching has been effective?

Thinking about instruction in this way is hardly anything new in education. Nor is the suggestion that we start with the end product and work backward to figure out what to teach. Struggling with actually shifting into this way of thinking, however, uncovers the extent of the paradigm shift the CCSS are precipitating. After all, teaching students how to think like and be historians is a distinctly different goal than teaching them history. Assessing the former requires us to create assignments that will serve as visible evidence that our students have actually thought about and used historical content to create new understanding and knowledge. Assessing that we have taught them history, on the other hand, merely requires that students regurgitate it.

Some framework for thinking about each of these questions follows. Multiple content areas are used as examples because inquiry applies to all content. Start with the understanding that "content" (e.g., history, science) did not "arrive" already digested for us to teach and our students to learn. All of what we traditionally consider teachable content was created (via inquiry) by historians, scientists, and others. Although there is some value in students knowing content, there is far more worth in teaching them how to think like the people who created the content in the first place. It is only in teaching them the thinking behind the creation of the content that they will ever learn it and be able to retain it beyond the moment in which they are tested on it.

What end product will students have to create as evidence that they have actually engaged deeply with the content?

When the sculptor Rodin was asked how he would go about sculpting an elephant, his reply was that he would start with a large enough piece of stone, then take away everything that was not an elephant. Implicit in this explanation is the notion that definition can be achieved by a process of almost Boolean removal. Where the crafting of rigorous tasks for students is concerned, it may be helpful to start by "taking away" tasks that are decidedly not rigorous. Fortunately, all tasks that are "not elephant" share a commonality of shallowness that makes them easy to remove: they only require students to move information around without doing anything meaningful with it. So, rather than being structured to prompt students to think about the content they are gathering, these tasks merely instruct: gather content, "put it in your own words," and be sure to say where you got it from. The question of what content is meaningful is irrelevant, because the content (in this assignment scenario) is completely interchangeable. Thus, we might ask students to "read about a scientist and write about that scientist." We might ask them to "read about a disease and write about that disease." We might ask them to "read about a Greek god and write about that god." Completely lacking are the analysis and synthesis of content that is imperative to the creation of new understanding.

Aside from analyzing and synthesizing content, rigorous tasks require students to express (and ideally even apply) their new understanding and knowledge in shareable ways. To limit the form this expression may take to writing alone is reductive at best and ridiculous at worst, if only because it excludes the suggestion that Van Gogh's paintings, Mozart's compositions, Martha Graham's choreography, and Alfred Hitchcock's films are not evidence of each of these artists' analysis, synthesis, and application of their particular "content," to say nothing of the notion that Albert Einstein expressed the new scientific knowledge he created (via inquiry) using a mathematical equation.

What inquiry skills will we have to teach them so that they will be able to create the end product?

Of course, if we expect students to create end products that serve as evidence of their thinking about particular content, we will have to teach them how to think about that content. Inquiry clarifies the "process" for creating new understanding and knowledge about content. A very short list of the skills in the process of creating history (as opposed to memorizing history) might include making observations about primary sources, making inferences from those observations, drawing conclusions and making claims based on observations and inferences, providing evidence for claims, interpreting evidence, and considering multiple perspectives. The students will have to be taught how to "do" all of the thinking steps in the process of inquiry, using, for example, historical content. At this point, it bears stating explicitly that the process of inquiry is highly recursive and not at all linear. Therefore, another large part of what students will have to be taught is that the "steps" in the process of creating new understanding and knowledge are not "performed" lockstep and to a definite conclusion. In fact, the landscape of true inquiry is littered with false starts and blind alleys and not at all a "neat" endeavor. As such, though it is critical to teach all of the inquiry skills the students will need, it is equally important to teach them how to determine when a skill they have already applied should be applied again to reframe their thinking and thereby deepen their understanding.

How will we meaningfully teach them the necessary skills?

The only way to teach students how to make a claim and support that claim with evidence from a text is to model our thinking for them as we read a text, make a claim, and support it with evidence. The rub, of course, is in the verbalization of our thinking process. Simply showing the students a claim and its supporting evidence will do nothing to teach them how we arrived at either. The extent to which we do all this with a degree of automaticity complicates the task further. There is no escaping the suggestion that we will have to become adept at clearly illustrating how we think and guiding and encouraging students to develop their own thinking style and skills. Thus, the most significant shift engendered by the CCSS implies that rather than teaching content, we are teaching our students how to think about content. And rather than teaching them that all questions have answers, we must teach them how to ask questions that do not yet have answers, with the expectation that they themselves can craft answers to them because we have taught them the skills they need to do so. The key is in the actual "doing" and creating rather than the passive transfer of content.

What materials will we use to teach the skills?

Our selection of particular material is very much dependent on precisely what we want students to "do" with it. As such, our instructional goals govern the choice of material (as opposed to the material dictating what we teach). By way of example, a piece of expository writing from an encyclopedia may be ideal for providing context, but may not be best for teaching students to consider multiple perspectives. To teach the latter, we may want to use an op-ed item or a piece of expository writing on a controversial topic. And while much of the material that is used in academic environments takes the form of writing, to exclude the use of other forms of "text" is to deny that in the creation of new knowledge, we "read" materials that take a variety of forms. As this is expressly not the case, we should be comfortable with the idea that a "text" might be any of the following: a photograph, the results of a scientific experiment, an interview, a poster, a painting, a physical artifact, a film, a performance, a piece of music, or anything else that conveys ideas, fosters observation and inferences, requires comprehension, and contributes to the creation of new knowledge.

How will we assess that our teaching has been effective?

Ideally our students are assessed formatively, so that we can determine the particular ways in which our instruction will need to be modified to achieve greater success. At each of the steps in the inquiry process, we assess our effectiveness by monitoring the thinking our students are doing. Our work is inextricably intertwined with that of our students. It is only in the close examination of what our students ultimately produce that we can ascertain the extent to which we have met our instructional goals. Where student work is concerned, the CCSS will cause yet another shift, away from the "one right answer" mentality to that of "many possible well-supported answers." For example, to meet Writing Standard 1 of the CCSS, students will have to produce writing that argues a claim and supports it with evidence from a number of texts. In a room full of students, more than one claim may be made. As long as each of these is clearly supported with evidence, it is "right." This is a shift that requires us to become comfortable with the ambiguity engendered by authentic thinking and learning. What is being assessed is not the "answer," but rather the thinking that produced it. Because there are as many different ways to think about content as there are students thinking about it, we will have to adjust to the idea that the "best" answer is the one that is the most well thought out. Testing, we are being told, will reflect this shift by providing for students all the content they will need to perform an authentic "task." For example, given three distinct pieces of text, students might be asked to craft an essay that makes a claim and supports that claim using evidence from all three. Writing will be assessed on whether or not students are able to make a claim, what evidence they use to support it, whether that evidence is the best available, and whether or not the students are able to conclude the "argument" in a way that follows obviously from the manner in which they presented the claim and the supporting evidence. Analysis, synthesis, and the application of inquiry skills are central to the task. This is distinctly different from assessments that test how much content a student has been able to memorize and regurgitate. In the end, this shift in assessment is meant to realign all K–12 instruction to the goal of preparing all students for college and careers.

A TRANSLATION TASK

To date, the greatest stumbling block to implementing the CCSS has been how to take even just one of the standards and determine *what*, precisely, should be taught. Even after one of these dense standards has been "unpacked," it continues to mystify. The language itself is largely foreign and threatens to remain so. Add the different languages of content area teachers,

and the situation is ripe for the exchange of loud babble. Our golden opportunity lies in figuring out how to translate all these languages simultaneously
for the various constituents we serve. To do this, we must first master the
language of the Common Core. If we stop at accepting the various crosswalks between inquiry and the CCSS, we will miss out on the opportunity
to incorporate our understanding of inquiry for others.

The commonality that will help us begin the task of translation lies in a
deep understanding of the inquiry process, its overlap with Common Core,
and how they both apply across a variety of content area standards. The
goal is to understand how inquiry skills have been used to unpack the Common Core. Finally, to be heard by teachers, we will need to complete the task
by translating the language of inquiry. Crosswalks created for us by others
are an excellent place to start, but until we walk some miles in the same
shoes and do the deep thinking ourselves, we will never arrive at the heart of
why we are claiming that the Common Core happens in the school library.
The more energy we devote to thinking about and actively participating in
the crosswalks, the clearer the following becomes: our work happens in *all*
of the Common Core standards for literacy (not only the standards that require students to complete research projects), as well as in all inquiry-based
content area standards. In our eagerness to "see ourselves" clearly in the
CCSS, we may be lunging headlong for the "research" standards of the
Common Core. They are, after all, where we are most comfortable. There is
in this comfort, however, a very real problem. The danger inherent in aligning ourselves only with the CCSS that require research is that our work will
continue to be marginalized. In this scenario, we address the research CCSS,
and teachers address all the other standards. Ideally, however, we can show
that the inquiry skills we teach align seamlessly with *all* of the literacy CCSS,
as well as with any content area standards that propose inquiry as the basis
for meaningful learning. It is in this latter scenario that the skills students
employ to navigate, for example, the scientific method, are clearly inquiry
skills and as worthy of our attention as the "research" standards of the
Common Core. Until we achieve full integration throughout the work our
colleagues are doing in their classrooms, our "curriculum" will continue to
be categorized as the "extra library thing" that happens only in the library
and independently of what happens in the classroom.

Fortuitously, the Common Core facilitates this integration for us. Embedded within the "research" CCSS (namely Writing Standards 7, 8, and
9) are references to the literacy ones (namely all the Reading Informational
Text Standards, as well as Writing Standards 1 and 2). This is precisely as
it should be. After all, wouldn't one be hard pressed to make the argument
that "research" can happen without reading and writing? And if inquiry
skills and libraries are all over the research standards, aren't they also, by
extension, all over the reading and writing standards? The correlation is
undeniable. (For two illustrations using several Grade 6 CCSS, see tables
2.2 and 2.3.)

Table 2.2. The Grade 6 "Research" CCSS W.6.8 as It Relates to CCSS Writing Standard 6.2

Common Core "Research" Learning Standard	Common Core Reading/Writing Standard Correlation	Because
If libraries are clearly here . . .	Then they *must also be* here . . .	
Research to Build and Present Knowledge	**Text Types and Purposes**	
W.6.8 Gather relevant information from multiple print and digital sources; assess the credibility of each source; and quote or paraphrase the data and conclusions of others while avoiding plagiarism and providing basic bibliographic information for sources.	W.6.2 Write informative/explanatory texts to examine a topic and convey ideas, concepts, and information through the selection, organization, and analysis of relevant content.	the skills embedded in W.6.2 (examining and developing a topic, organizing ideas, providing a conclusion) are the very skills students need to be able to "Present Knowledge" obtained from "gathering information."
	a) Introduce a topic; organize ideas, concepts, and information, using strategies such as definition, classification, comparison/contrast, and cause/effect; include formatting (e.g., headings), graphics (e.g., charts, tables), and multimedia when useful to aiding comprehension.	if we stop at teaching students how to gather information, paraphrase it, and provide bibliographic information, we have skipped two crucial steps in the inquiry process: the step that requires them to synthesize that information to create new knowledge and the step that enables them to present their newly acquired knowledge to others.
	b) Develop the topic with relevant facts, definitions, concrete details, quotations, or other information and examples.	
	c) Use appropriate transitions to clarify the relationships among ideas and concepts.	there is absolutely no point to students "gathering information" if they are not going to also be required to think about it and "do" something meaningful with it.
	d) Use precise language and domain-specific vocabulary to inform about or explain the topic.	
	e) Establish and maintain a formal style.	W.6.8 = "Copy and paste and change some of the words" unless students simultaneously apply the skills embedded in W.6.2 to the information gathered.
	f) Provide a concluding statement or section that follows from the information or explanation presented.	

Table 2.3. The Grade 6 "Research" CCSS W.6.9 as It Relates to CCSS Reading Informational Text Standard 6.1

Common Core "Research" Learning Standard	Common Core Reading Standard Correlation	Because
If libraries are clearly here . . .	then they *must also be* here . . .	
Research to Build and Present Knowledge	Key Ideas and Details	
W.6.9 Draw evidence from literary or informational texts to support analysis, reflection, and research. a) Apply Grade 6 Reading standards to literature (e.g., "compare and contrast texts in different forms or genres [e.g., stories and poems; historical novels and fantasy stories] in terms of their approaches to similar themes and topics"). a) Apply grade 6 Reading standards to literary nonfiction (e.g., "Trace and evaluate the argument, specific claims in a text, distinguishing claims that are supported by reasons and evidence from claims that are not").	RI.6.1 Cite textual evidence to support analysis of what the text says explicitly as well as inferences drawn from the text.	the reading skills embedded in RI.6.1 (knowing what the text says explicitly, inferring and analyzing) are the very skills students will need to achieve W.6.9: "Draw evidence from literary or informational texts to support analysis, reflection, and research." part b of the standard itself refers us to the reading informational text standard.

Even once we have made a strong case for the correlation between the Common Core research standards and the Common Core reading and writing standards, our work has barely begun, because we have not yet clarified the CCSS for our colleagues. As such, until we have used inquiry skills to fully "unpack" and "translate" each of the standards, our colleagues may not yet be willing to get on board. For a sample Sixth Grade Common Core Standard, "unpacked and fully translated" using inquiry skills, see table 2.4.

In the end, "unpacked and fully translated" standards will have to be followed by instruction. After all, while it is all well and good to firmly establish inquiry as the corollary that binds our library programs to the implementation of the CCSS, it is altogether something else to position ourselves to further translate that very correlation into actual instruction. Until instruction enters the scene, our assertion of our centrality to the process of implementing these new standards threatens to remain largely theoretical. More in-depth discussion appears in subsequent chapters of this book.

WHAT ABOUT THE CONTENT?

What has been most unnerving to content area teachers about the CCSS is their profound lack of content. Almost immediately, the verdict came in: "The Common Core is expecting us to throw out all content." Understandably, this misconception has raised a number of hackles, especially among teachers of science and history/social studies. In truth, however, there was no claim made that content would completely leave the educational stage in favor of process. Rather, much less content should be covered more deeply in the service of students being taught how to think deeply about content (as opposed to merely being taught the content itself). In a scenario in which students are being taught how to think about content, they cannot help but learn it, if only because they are being asked to "do" something with it: for example, make a claim about it and support that claim with evidence from the material they have read. This kind of learning is far more useful than the kind that "delivers" content with the expectation that the only thing students need to "do" with it is memorize and retain it just long enough to regurgitate it on an exam.

An analogy may help to clarify. Building a cabinet requires one to learn the process for doing so—namely, the recursive steps and discrete skills involved. Without wood, nails, glue, and stain, however, the cabinet cannot be built. Think of the actual building of the cabinet as the process and the materials used to build it as the content. One needs *both* the process *and* the materials. Librarians know this about learning. This is why we balk at assignments that ask students to gather material without requiring them to do anything significant with it. "Copy-and-paste" assignments ask students to simply move the content from one place (a resource) to another (a "report"). This does not a cabinet make. Similarly, teaching content without

Table 2.4. Common Core Writing Standard 1, Grade 6, Fully Unpacked and Translated

Common Core Writing Standard 1, Grade 6	Unpacked: Inquiry Skills That Align	Translated: Why?
Text Types and Purposes W.6.1 Write arguments to support claims with clear reasons and relevant evidence.	Use strategies to draw conclusions from information and apply knowledge to curricular areas, real-world situations, and further investigation. (AASL 2.1.3)	In order for students to be able to make claims from text they have read, they will need to be taught how to draw conclusions.
a) Introduce claim(s) and organize the reasons and evidence clearly.	Differentiate between relevant and irrelevant evidence. Interpret and organize evidence.	In order for students to know *what* textual evidence they should be using to support their claims, they need to be able to distinguish between evidence that is relevant to their claims and evidence that is not. In order for students to be able to "organize reasons and evidence clearly," they will need to be taught how to interpret the evidence they have chosen so that they can organize/categorize it to clearly support their claims.
b) Support claim(s) with clear reasons and relevant evidence, using credible sources and demonstrating an understanding of the topic or text.	Find, evaluate, and select appropriate sources to answer questions. (AASL 1.1.4) Evaluate information found in selected sources on the basis of accuracy, validity, appropriateness to needs, importance, and social and cultural context. (AASL 1.1.5)	The Common Core Standard requires students to use credible sources. In order for students to be able to do this, they need to be taught how to evaluate sources.

(continued)

Table 2.4. *Continued*

Common Core Writing Standard 1, Grade 6	Unpacked: Inquiry Skills That Align	Translated: Why?
c) Use words, phrases, and clauses to clarify the relationships among claim(s) and reasons.	Use the writing process, media and visual literacy, and technology skills to create products that express new understandings. (AASL 2.1.6)	The standard requires students to write an argument. If we expect them to be able to do so, we will have to teach them the process and skills necessary for writing a well-supported argument.
d) Establish and maintain a formal style.		
e) Provide a concluding statement or section that follows from the argument presented.	Employ a critical stance in drawing conclusions by demonstrating that the pattern of evidence leads to a decision or conclusion. (AASL 2.2.3)	In order for students to be able to provide a solid concluding statement, they will have to be taught how to evaluate the argument they have made for validity and how well it has been supported by the evidence they selected.

simultaneously teaching process yields the same results: materials are moved around, but nothing is "built."

Aside from the suggestion that students learn about the "material" from "working with it," there is the crucial advantage of the transferability of process. So, when school librarians are afforded the luxury to do so, we teach the transferable process of inquiry using whatever content/materials our colleagues ask us to use. It is only in the meaningful wedding of content and process that our students internalize the transferability of learning as a process. That is to say, if we teach the process for building a cabinet with oak, our students can transfer that process to building a cabinet with any number of materials. If a student understands how to craft an argument and support that argument with science as the material, he or she can also craft and support an argument using historical material. It is in the actual crafting of the argument that new knowledge is created and the proverbial cabinet is built. As the ultimate goal of all inquiry is the creation of new knowledge (rather than the regurgitation of established knowledge), it facilitates the shift from the learning of content to the creation of new knowledge *using* content.

Being liberated from having to teach excessive amounts of content implies that we will have to apply stringent instructional criteria to deciding *what* materials we will use to advance the teaching of inquiry. As accepted resource experts in our buildings, this presents yet another opportunity for us to be directly involved in the materials selection conversation.

COLLEGE AND CAREER READY

At the very center of the core of these new standards is the suggestion that all students should leave high school fully ready for college and careers. What this implies (by extension) is that they must be taught both problem-solving strategies and all the skills necessary to think deeply about content. On a more practical level, all colleges have libraries. Following is but a small sampling of the ways in which instructionally strong K–12 library programs prepare students for college and college library use. Strong K–12 library programs and librarians

- foster a love of independent reading and learning (both critical components to academic success in *any* educational environment);
- teach students how to locate and evaluate information (especially crucial in this time of easy access to vast and overwhelming amounts of information);
- teach students how to *think* about information by teaching them how to select it, organize/categorize/sort it to facilitate learning from it, and create new understandings about it;
- teach students how to make claims and draw conclusions from the information they are using;
- teach students how to consider multiple perspectives;

- teach students how to analyze, synthesize, and apply information; and
- teach students how to behave ethically in digital environments.

Even outside academic environments, inquiry and information literacy skills prepare students for life. Where lifelong work is concerned, students are career ready when they are able to independently use information to solve problems and complete tasks. As information is the new coin of the realm, it is only in knowing how to use it to solve problems and complete tasks that our students are ultimately employable in meaningful careers. Incidentally (and to further drive home the importance of moving away from the teaching of content independently of teaching process), consider the following: nowhere in the real world (with the exception of on the game show *Jeopardy*) is one given a problem to solve or task to complete without also being given unfettered access to all the information one may need to do so. In the career-ready scenario, the student who is most prepared to tackle tasks is the one who knows how and where to find good information and also knows how to apply that same information to completing given tasks. Simply knowing the information is no guarantee whatsoever that one will know how to *use* it.

IN CONCLUSION

As school librarians, we will never again be presented with so golden an opportunity to make a case for our indispensability, should we actually want to be indispensable. In order to be heard, however, we must reshape our work in wonderful new ways. We are not *only* resource providers, nor do we *only* teach bibliographic citation and how to use databases. We teach inquiry, and inquiry is the Common Core; our contribution to the implementation of these new standards is potentially limitless. If we are able to make this case well, perhaps one day all schools will have libraries, each will be fully staffed by a certified school librarian, and every librarian will be an instructional leader. This is just the magnitude of the opportunity before us. Are we ready for the challenging work ahead?

REFERENCES

American Association of School Librarians. (2010). "English Language Arts Crosswalk—Grade 6." In *AASL Learning Standards & Common Core State Standards Crosswalk*. Retrieved from http://www.ala.org/aasl/guidelinesandstandards/commoncorecrosswalk/ccelasixth on March 15, 2013.

New York State Education Department. (2012). "Shifts in ELA/Literacy in Pedagogical Shifts Demanded by the Common Core State Standards." Retrieved from www.engageny.org/resource/common-core-shifts on July 16, 2013.

3

School Librarians and the CCSS: Knowing, Claiming, and Acting on Their Expertise

Deborah D. Levitov

This chapter serves as an overview of how school librarians can prepare for the Common Core State Standards (CCSS) and identify manageable focal points within the standards and in relationship to school library programs. It addresses actions school librarians can take to be active partners with a legitimate seat at the CCSS table alongside other educators.

To be players in the CCSS, the starting point for school librarians is to realize their unique professional expertise that aligns with the learning expectations outlined in the CCSS. To prepare, school librarians should examine the CCSS and the six professional shifts (which outline the pedagogical changes demanded by the standards).

Librarians also need to access and evaluate their practices and the policies and mission of the school library to determine how they can best demonstrate alignment to the CCSS. Once they have gained needed background knowledge and have accomplished the professional and program reflection and self-awareness, school librarians will be poised to communicate the library program's connections to the CCSS.

HOW CAN SCHOOL LIBRARIANS PREPARE FOR THE CCSS?

Specifically, the basic starting point to understanding the CCSS is to read through the *Common Core State Standards for English Language Arts* (ELA) and become familiar with Appendix A, along with the "Six Shifts."

The Six Shifts

The following is a summary of the Six Shifts as they are found in the ELA CCSS, adapted from EngageNY (New York State Department of Education n.d.):

1. **Balancing Information and Literary Text:** 50 percent–50 percent balancing of literary and nonfiction texts.
2. **Content Area Literacy:** Building knowledge; deep analysis to make arguments from the texts read; students find their own meaning—create opportunities for students to experience learning for themselves.
3. **Staircase of Complexity/Increased Complexity of Texts:** Close reading for comprehension of complex text; scaffolding as needed.
4. **Text-based Questions and Answers:** Evidence-based conversation about text/writing to show comprehension of text (observable through students' work).
5. **Writing from Sources:** Deep analysis of the text; using evidence from the text to make an argument supported with evidence. This involves the students' response to text to show understanding.
6. **Vocabulary:** Academic language acquired through increasingly complex text. Vocabulary needed to understand and use complex texts.

An ideal example of connections for school librarians can be found in Shift 3, Text Complexity. School librarians (as information specialists and teachers via professional development) can explain text complexity, the role of Lexiles, and the larger picture of measuring text complexity using the Three Part Model provided in Appendix A of the CCSS (2010b) (e.g., qualitative and quantitative measure of text and reader and task considerations). In the process, school librarians (as information specialists) can then help locate resources already available or determine and acquire appropriate texts as needed. School librarians (as teachers) can also help students understand the role of Lexiles. They can (as teachers) incorporate reading comprehension strategies within the instructional work they do with students.

In connection with Shifts 2, 3, 4, and 5, school librarians (as teachers via professional development) can help others better understand the inquiry process (e.g., other educators, parents). They also can collaborate (as instructional partners and teachers) with other educators to design learning opportunities for students that will be inquiry based, while identifying appropriate resources (as information specialists) that are available for student learning.

There are other interpretations of the Six Shifts, but generally the emphasis is on the same content. Understanding these instructional shifts will help school librarians better identify how they can effectively link the CCSS to their roles.

Resources Related to the Six Shifts in the CCSS

Critical Thinking Works
"Common Core: Six Fundamental Shifts"
(http://criticalthinkingworks.com/?p=374).
This link provides an overview of the Six Shifts and an easily understandable visual and clear breakdown of each shift, with general statements of what it means for educators and students. It also has active links to inquiry.

Reading Rockets
"Common Core and ELLs: Key Shifts in Language Arts and Literacy (Part II)" by Susan Lafond
(http://www.readingrockets.org/article/51433/).
This article offers a very clear overview of what the Six Shifts mean for students and teachers.

New York State Department of Education
"Pedagogical Shifts Demanded by the Common Core Standards"
(http://www.engageny.org/sites/default/files/resource/attachments/common
-core-shifts.pdf).
This document provides an in-depth overview of the Six Shifts.

Arizona Department of Education
"Overview of the Six Instructional Shifts in the Implementation of the ELA Common Core"
(http://www.azed.gov/azcommoncore/files/2012/05/may17_elashifts.pdf).
This is an overview of the CCSS created by the Arizona Department of Education.

Revisiting Professional Roles and Standards

School librarians can also better integrate the CCSS into their practice by revisiting the roles of leader, instructional partner, information specialist, teacher, and program administrator outlined in *Empowering Learners: Guidelines for School Library Media Programs* (AASL 2009a). Other educators, or those outside the school community, do not innately understand how school librarians contribute to student learning and library program development and implementation, or how they fulfill unique responsibilities related to academic programs.

It is the ongoing responsibility of school librarians to educate others about their roles. They must show and tell what they do and how it impacts student learning and supports initiatives like the CCSS. This communication must be well informed and intentional, as well as systematic and systemic.

In order to educate others, school librarians must be able to clearly articulate their roles and their vision for the school library. So in addition to revisiting the roles outlined in *Empowering Learners*, school librarians should also reexamine the AASL *Standards for the 21st-Century Learner* (2007). These are a foundation for school library instructional programs and were developed in tandem with Partnership for 21st Century Skills (P21), a framework that

> presents a holistic view of 21st century teaching and learning that combines a discrete focus on 21st century student outcomes (a blending of specific skills, content knowledge, expertise and literacies) with innovative support systems to help students master the multi-dimensional abilities required of them in the 21st century. (http://www.p21.org/overview/skills-framework)

Many of the elements of P21 are reflected in the CCSS (e.g., critical thinking, inquiry, communication, collaboration, creativity, life and career skills, information technology skills, core subjects), and all are at the heart of the AASL standards.

With background information on the AASL standards, school librarians can examine the CCSS and identify how the library program they administer aligns. This requires taking the time, with the help of others, to examine and evaluate library programs, policies, and practices in order to adjust, modify, revise, revamp, and improve them. There are many resources available for school librarian and program evaluation that have been developed by AASL as well as at the state and district levels (see figure 3.1).

Through the reexamination of roles, program evaluation and modification, and raised self- and program awareness, school librarians will be well positioned to claim their authority and begin the process of identifying the areas of the CCSS through which they can best contribute to student learning.

IDENTIFYING FOCAL POINTS FOR SCHOOL LIBRARIANS IN THE CCSS

To make the CCSS manageable and significant within the mission of the school library, it will be helpful for school librarians to focus their efforts on particular elements of the standards. By focusing on specific areas within the CCSS relevant to their unique teaching role, school librarians will be able to build instructional partnerships with classroom teachers that result in deep learning experiences for students while addressing learning gaps in information skills and inquiry-based research. In this way the efforts of the school librarian relate directly to their expertise and build on the unique instructional planning and teaching role of the school library program. This also emphasizes for classroom teachers what the school librarian can best do to help them better meet the learning needs of students.

School Librarian Evaluation Examples

North Carolina Professional Standards for School Library Media Coordinators and Instructional Technology. http://it.ncwiseowl.org/standards/pro_standards

REACH Students. Chicago Public Schools Teacher-Librarian Evaluation Framework. http://cps.edu/Pages/reachstudents.aspx

New York State Teacher and Principal Practice Rubrics.* http://usny.nysed.gov /rttt/teachers-leaders/practicerubrics/#ATPR. Rubrics for school librarians:

- New York State Teacher Rubric: http://usny.nysed.gov/rttt/teachers-leaders /practicerubrics/Docs/nyla-rubric.pdf
- Rating Conversion: http://usny.nysed.gov/rttt/teachers-leaders/practice rubrics/Docs/Pearson_Conversion.pdf

*This is how the New York school librarian evaluation is listed.

School Library Program Evaluation Examples

A Planning Guide for Empowering Learners with School Library Program Assessment Rubric: http://www.ala.org/aasl/guidelinesandstandards/planningguide /planningguide. Available by subscription only from www.info.eb.com/aasl

Colorado's Highly Effective School Library Competencies: http://www.cde.state .co.us/cdelib/HighlyEffective/download/HighlyEffectiveSchoolLibraries.pdf

New York State's School Library Media Program Evaluation (SLMPE) Rubric: http://www.p12.nysed.gov/technology/library/SLMPE_rubric/home.html

The 21st-Century Approach to School Librarian Evaluation (AASL, 2012). [Book]

Figure 3.1. Examples of Evaluation Tools

Three focal points of the CCSS align well with the unique expertise of school librarians and the services and resources provided by the library program:

- Inquiry-based research
- Reading
- Complexity of text

To understand how to integrate each of these areas into the library program, it will be helpful for school librarians to make connections with the AASL *Standards for the 21st-Century Learner* (2007) and ascertain how the three focal points can be found throughout. In this way, the AASL standards will serve as a rich instructional resource for school librarians as they build their understanding of the CCSS and zero in on the instructional emphasis of the school library program.

Following is an explanation of the three focal points within the CCSS for school librarians to concentrate their efforts on and an explanation of the Six Shifts.

Focal Point: *Inquiry*

Throughout the CCSS the word *research* is used repeatedly, but it is explained in terms that school librarians have historically defined as *inquiry*. The "research" described in the CCSS is actually a shift to deeper, process-based learning. It differs from what has traditionally been presented as research in the K–12 setting. Instead of research that depends on predetermined questions and fact finding and reporting out of information, the inquiry-based research described in the CCSS requires students to generate meaningful questions, seek information, and show proof of new learning and understanding based on concepts, not topics.

In order to work well within the expectations of the CCSS, school librarians (as well as other educators) need a firm understanding of the inquiry-based research process. This is not new territory for school librarians. There is a rich history of research and literature available in the school library profession about inquiry learning:

> An inquiry approach to learning seeks to motivate students to take ownership of their ideas and to create something that matters to them. Inquiry stimulates learning in students from the youngest age by engaging their innate curiosity, through middle childhood by enabling their quest for independence, and on into their teen years, when they are gaining a sense of self through their developing knowledge and expertise, which prepare them for the challenges of work and daily living in adulthood. (Kuhlthau, Maniotes, and Caspari 2007, 25)

As Barbara Stripling explains through her research:

> Inquiry is a process of learning that is driven by questioning, thoughtful investigating, making sense of information, and developing new understandings. It is cyclical in nature because the result of inquiry is not simple answers but deep understanding that often lead to new questions and further pursuit of knowledge. The goal of inquiry is not the accumulation of information; it is the exploration of significant questions and deep learning. (2008a, 50)

See figure 7.1 (p. 95).

In *Standards for the 21st-Century Learner*, one of the Common Beliefs is that "inquiry provides a framework for learning" (AASL 2007). The statement elaborates:

To become independent learners, students must gain not only the skills but also the disposition to use those skills, along with an understanding of their own responsibilities and self-assessment strategies. Combined, these four elements build a learner who can thrive in a complex information environment. (AASL 2007)

(For further support and guidance, school librarians may access resources on Guided Inquiry (Kuhlthau, Maniotes, and Caspari 2007), the information process model (ISP) developed by Carol Kuhlthau and the inquiry model created by Barbara Stripling.)

Connections to inquiry are found throughout the CCSS. Judi Moreillon's "Matrix for School Librarians: Aligning Standards, Inquiry, Reading, and Instruction," developed for *School Library Monthly*, serves to illustrate these connections. (See chapter 4, pp. 49–66.) The matrix presents the CCSS College and Career Readiness Standards, which are identical across grade levels in the ELA standards. The columns in the matrix for "CCSS" and "Inquiry Process" demonstrate how inquiry is woven within the CCSS and shows how AASL *Standards for the 21st-Century Learner* align with both the CCSS and inquiry.

These connections provide school librarians with a combination of information that very few other educators have readily at their disposal. The AASL standards focus on information learning and multiple literacies and incorporate inquiry learning, all of which align with what is outlined in the CCSS. This information is most useful to school librarians as they formulate and act on their role in implementing the CCSS.

Focal Point: *Reading*

The next focal point for school librarians within the CCSS is reading, especially reading comprehension. Reading has always been a natural connection for school librarians and is well defined by the Common Beliefs found in the AASL *Standards for the 21st-Century Learner* (2007):

Reading is a window to the world. Reading is a foundational skill for learning, personal growth and enjoyment. The degree to which students can read and understand text in all formats (e.g., picture, video, print) and all contexts is a key indicator of success in school and in life. As a lifelong learning skill, reading goes beyond decoding and comprehension to interpretation and development of new understanding.

In the CCSS, the responsibility for all educators is to model and reinforce reading comprehension strategies. This includes school librarians as they engage students in teaching and learning. School librarians can also collaborate with and support classroom teachers to meet these requirements throughout the curriculum. Reading comprehension strategies can be aligned to the CCSS, the AASL standards, and the inquiry process, helping to demonstrate these important connections. See table 3.1 (p. 43).

The focus on reading also emphasizes the need for a rich collection of "fiction, literary nonfiction and informational texts" (Moreillon 2012, 7). To meet the expectations outlined in the CCSS requires the expertise of the school librarian to guide collection development to answer learning needs for all students while helping teachers identify the best resources in multiple formats.

Focal Point: *Complexity of Text*

The reading and writing gap between what is expected of high school graduates and their capabilities in college and in the workforce is one of the reasons that text complexity became a central issue in the CCSS (CCSS-ELA). This is a shift that calls for 50 percent literary and 50 percent nonfiction text. School librarians can play an active role in helping classroom teachers understand how to interpret the expectations of the CCSS related to complexity of text. But first it is important for the school librarian to know that determining appropriate texts requires more than quantitative or qualitative solutions. "Thoughtful qualitative analysis, paired with a quantitative measure of a text, cannot account for the specific needs of an individual student in a particular situation. This is the reason for the third dimension, reader and task considerations" (DelVecchio 2012, 10).

In addition to these three dimensions of text complexity, there are other criteria to be considered, as summarized by Jean Donham:

- Texts that range in complexity, style and genre, as well as various levels of reading proficiency.
- Conceptual texts offering the "big idea"; understanding that unifies text sets and provides examples in a variety of contexts.
- Cultural perspectives appropriate for specific contexts (e.g., civil rights) (2013, 6–7)

With this understanding of the CCSS and complexity of text, school librarians, in addition to helping others understand the process of identifying complex text, can play a unique role in the identification of existing resources and the acquisition of resources to provide appropriate texts matched to student needs. They can also help other educators as well as parents understand that Lexile levels alone are not the way to measure text complexity. School librarians can also work with their public library colleagues to help them understand this focal point within the CCSS.

PREPARATION, FOCAL POINTS, SIX SHIFTS

The three focal points—inquiry, reading, and complexity of text—call on the roles of the school librarian as a teacher and instructional partner, as well as an information specialist. All three areas will require the provision of resources (the role of information specialist), and each will require an emphasis on well-designed instructional strategies and learning experiences (the role of teacher) in collaboration with other educators (the role of instructional partner).

The Six Shifts provide further understanding, background knowledge, and an outline to which school librarians can attach their own expertise. This will result in connections to the CCSS aligned to the unique roles of school librarians, the library-related curricula, and the mission of the school library program.

Having prepared for the CCSS and identified the key focal points within them, school librarians are equipped to take action in relationship to the Standards as they relate to the school library and student learning.

TAKING ACTION: WHAT SCHOOL LIBRARIANS CAN DO

Effective involvement in the CCSS for school librarians includes proactive and active work in the following areas as they relate to the focal points identified (inquiry, reading, complexity of text) and six instructional shifts:

- leadership
- collaboration
- teaching
- program administration
- technology tools
- collection development
- professional development

Leadership

School librarians will be the ones to lead the effort to connect the school library program to the goals of the CCSS. This is not new for school librarians, but is an ongoing practice in relationship to the development of new curricula, new school initiatives, and academic standards. School librarians are champions of the library program and must work to continually educate others about the unique and important contributions made for students and staff, and in this case, the connections that are natural within the CCSS.

School librarians must take the lead in evaluating and improving library programs and to assess and evaluate their own performance. This is where advocacy and activism are key to making school libraries and school librarians an essential link to academic success for students while involving others in the process.

In a post to the blog *Leadership Development* on June 5, 2013, Ken Haycock provided the following definition of leadership:

It is associated with taking an organization into the future, finding opportunities that are coming at it faster and faster and successfully exploiting those opportunities. Leadership is about vision, about people buying in, about empowerment and, most of all, about producing useful change. *Leadership is not about attributes, it's about behavior* [emphasis added].

Key successful, behavioral strategies for leadership include

- serving on committees where the roles and mission of the library can be part of the discussion and planning and being part of the learning (and the CCSS) conversation;
- communicating information about the school library program in multiple ways on an ongoing basis (through, e.g., the library mission, resources, successful collaboration, stories of student learning, statistics);
- establishing ongoing communication with administrators (by, e.g., setting goals, providing reports, sharing results, informing, and educating);
- involving others in developing and defining the school library program (e.g., using surveys, polls, committees, advisory boards);
- modeling and communicating the unique professional expertise of the school librarian (e.g., providing professional development, writing articles, doing presentations, building instructional partnerships, showing learning results, referencing AASL standards and guidelines); and
- advocating for access to the best resources, be they in print, digital, online, or in terms of the availability of technology tools.

Collaboration

An excellent definition of *collaboration* can be found in a brochure published by AASL in 1996: "working together, having shared commitment and goals, developed in partnership. Leadership, resources, risk, control and results are shared. More is accomplished than could have been individually." In the same brochure, the following characteristics for collaboration were identified:

- Long term
- More pervasive relationship
- Commitment to a common mission
- Results in a new structure
- Comprehensive planning
- Well-defined communication channels at all levels
- Collaborative structure determines authority
- Resources are shared
- Greater risk: power in an issue
- Higher intensity (AASL 1996)

As effective players related to the CCSS, school librarians will embrace collaboration in multiple dimensions of library program planning and implementation. They will collaborate to

- redefine, develop, and strengthen the library program;
- build instructional links to the mission of the library;
- determine acquisitions and the best collection of varied resources needed;
- organize and curate the library collection;
- meet the learning needs of students;
- create an engaging learning environment;
- design and deliver meaningful learning opportunities for students;
- determine and help meet professional development needs; and
- make use of resources beyond the school walls.

Through collaboration, school librarians share ownership of the library with various groups of stakeholders and interested community members. This approach builds libraries that have investment and engagement from many people, at varied levels (students, teachers, administrators, parents, community individuals and groups, other agencies). This type of engagement will create understanding of why library programs are an essential part of the academic plan of all schools and why school librarians play a vital role in the success of that plan as important partners in the CCSS.

Teaching

School librarians will continue to be involved in teaching as they build instructional partnerships, plan instructional units, and help by delivering identified responsibilities for coteaching. This can be accomplished with individual students, groups of students, in the library, in the classroom, or online, depending on the objectives outlined and determined through communication, cooperation, coordination, and collaborative efforts. The unique roles and knowledge of school librarians will be at play in these teaching efforts, and evidence-based practice and learning assessment will be an essential part of what school librarians do related to the CCSS.

Following are guiding questions for the teacher role of school librarians:

What do we teach [that] truly matters?
How do we best teach it?
How do we know that students are actually learning what we teach?
How do we communicate these results to teachers and other stakeholder groups? (Zmuda and Harada 2008, xv)

School librarians can contribute an outside-the-classroom perspective that positions them to campaign for creativity and choice; encourages the use of complex texts; and offers solutions for inquiry-based, authentic, concept-based, problem-centered learning, higher level thinking, and that which fosters deep learning. School librarians can serve as a gauge for including some or all of these elements during the instructional planning process.

The AASL *Standards for the 21st-Century Learner* (2007) will serve as a foundation for school librarians collaborating with classroom teachers. These standards will be the background information for school librarians as they work to articulate the meaning of an inquiry-based research process. They will assist school librarians in identifying the skills, dispositions, responsibilities, and self-assessment strategies needed for students to be successful learners and meet the expectations reflected in the CCSS, especially in regard to the meaning of *research*.

School librarians also function as teachers as they are involved in identifying and providing professional development opportunities for other educators. This may be accomplished when working with large or small groups or one-on-one. It may entail helping other educators learn about such things as a new technology tool, database resources, concepts of complexity of text or inquiry, school library resources, and more.

Program Administration

School librarians are program administrators. This, however, is a role that is not always readily recognized by administrators or other teachers. Yet it is a vital role, because school librarians oversee and manage the implementation of a program that involves working with others to develop "program mission, strategic plan, and policies, as well as effective management of staff, program budget, and the physical and virtual spaces" (AASL 2009b).

As with any program administrator, it is the responsibility of school librarians to continually evaluate how the school library is functioning. This can be accomplished in many ways and should involve others. At the heart of the process should be the question, "What measurable difference do school library programs make in student learning?" (Zmuda 2011). This question then guides the development of a mission statement that is framed in terms of student learning goals, and it builds a program that encourages inquisitive and dynamic learners and supports the tenets of the CCSS.

A helpful tool to jump-start the examination of program and policy can be found in table 3.1. This guides school librarians, as administrators of programs, to examine such things as the mission statement, policy, assessment practices, instructional strategies, and philosophy with suggested actions (e.g., review, revise, implement change, and evaluate), with the help of guiding questions. This rubric is a resource that can involve others in critical decisions related to the library program that will result in making it an improved and evolving entity.

School librarians take the collaborative vision and developed mission for the library program and ensure that they translate into an engaging learning

Table 3.1. Six Steps: Saving Your School Library Program

1. To Do:	Review	Revise	Implement Changes	Evaluate
Mission Statement	What is the purpose? Is student learning the central focus?	What are the key words? What will students be able to do? Who will be involved?	Finalize. Share. Put it into action.	How is the mission statement used? How does it support student learning? What difference does it make?
2. To Do:	**Review**	**Revise**	**Implement Changes**	**Evaluate**
Program Alignment	What are the policies? What are the practices? What is the structure? How is student learning supported? Which policies are embraced/resisted by stakeholders?	How can learning be better supported? What is a learning commons? How can space be used differently/better? What kind of access and tools are needed?	Identify needs (e.g., time, money, revision, re-envisioning, professional development, resources, etc.) and act. Follow a timeline.	How do new policies and practices support student learning? How is space used differently and better? What changes have resulted in addressing access and use of tools?
3. To Do:	**Review**	**Revise**	**Implement Changes**	**Evaluate**
Student Learning	What student assessments are used? What is the nature of student learning via the library? What input do you receive?	How can assessments be improved to examine student learning? How is learning meaningful? What will be done to gather input?	Identify inquisitive and dynamic learning. Determine assessments. Arrange for professional evaluation and feedback.	What are the differences in student learning? How are assessments appropriate? How has input and feedback been used?
4. To Do:	**Review**	**Revise**	**Implement Changes**	**Evaluate**
Quality Tasks in the School Library	How are tasks supportive of student learning? How do tasks support the mission statement? How do tasks align with curriculum and national visioning documents?	How can learning be improved? What assessments can be used? What is the instructional intent? What are quality tasks?	Work with teachers to improve student learning. Use defined learning tasks as a guide. Use appropriate assessments.	Is student work authentic? How are definitions being met? How are tasks meaningful? What needs improvement?
5. To Do:	**Review**	**Revise**	**Implement Changes**	**Evaluate**
Instructional Time	What is the online presence? How does the library extend services beyond the school day?	What tools are available? What have others done? What resources will help? What online learning options are possible?	Identify possibilities. Know the purpose. Identify learning benefits. Follow a timeline.	What is the impact for students? What do colleagues think? What works? What can be improved?
6. To Do:	**Review**	**Revise**	**Implement Changes**	**Evaluate**
Know the Brain	What do you know about cognition and learning? How can you learn more? What resources will help?	How can students be more engaged? How can learning be more meaningful? How can students be helped to focus?	Identify expectations. Identify strategies. Work with others. Involve students. Get feedback.	In what ways are students more engaged? How is learning more meaningful? In what ways are students more focused?

Originally printed in *School Library Monthly*, "Use This Page," February 2011 based on an article by Allison Zmuda, "Six Steps to Saving Your School Library Program."

environment for students and staff that runs smoothly and operates effectively. In the end, it is up to the school librarian to be sure that the collective planning and policy development is put into action. Program administration is essential to creating the type of learning environment that is a prerequisite for successfully meeting the learning expectations of the CCSS.

Technology Tools

In the twenty-first century, the use of technology in meeting the CCSS is assumed and necessary for learning. On the Digital Learning Day Web

site (http://www.digitallearningday.org/learn-and-explore/what-is-digital
-learning/), digital learning is defined as

> any instructional practice that effectively uses technology to strengthen a stu-
> dent's learning experience. Much more than "online learning," digital learning
> encompasses a wide spectrum of tools and practice, digital learning empha-
> sizes high-quality instruction and provides access to challenging content, feed-
> back through formative assessment, opportunities for learning anytime and
> anywhere, and individualized instruction to ensure all students reach their full
> potential to succeed in college and a career.

The school librarian's role as a teacher is reflected throughout the AASL
Standards for the 21st-Century Learner as it relates to the use of technology
for student learning. In addition, school librarians can support teachers in
staying current with technology tools. "They [school librarians] can guide
teachers in the initial use of such applications, model use, provide professional development, and give ongoing support" (Young 2012). This is yet
another area in which school librarians must make their expertise known
and offer to share their knowledge.

In addition to embracing technology as a learning tool, school librarians
must also use technology to manage the library, make resources easily accessible, and communicate on an ongoing basis with the educational community (e.g., students, teachers, administrators, parents, and others). This
requires using an array of technology tools and remaining up to date about
what works best.

Collection Development

The CCSS provide a welcome emphasis on collection development and
allow the terminology to be part of the general education conversation and
not just in the school librarian's domain. They expand the traditional meaning of "collections" associated with print resources to embrace virtual, digital resources (e.g., blogs, presentations, eBooks, pod or video casts), and the
technology tools needed to access them all. They also encompass the idea of
curation, which Joyce Valenza explains as a unique qualification for school
librarians, "because they understand the curriculum and the specific needs
and interests of their own communities of teachers, administrators, learners
and parents" (2012). She defines curators as the people who "make sense
of the vast amounts of content that are continually produced. They are tal-
ented at scouting, identifying relevance, evaluating, classifying, organizing,
and presenting aggregated content for a targeted audience" (Valenza 2012,
page 20).

Curation is part of the fabric of school libraries, so it is natural to incorporate this skill within the process of collection development to make
the school library a "go to" place for information in all forms and formats,

24/7. "Libraries are about facilitating physical and intellectual access to information and learning . . . [and] to represent the presence of an information professional" (Valenza 2012, page 21). In this way school librarians can capitalize on the many and ever-increasing technology tools available.

At the same time, school librarians can help students become curators of their own learning. This will be on a different scale than curation done for the library program, but it will empower students to organize and share their own information (Valenza 2012, page 22). The expertise of school librarians can extend to teachers by helping them gather and organize the resources needed for their classrooms, their own continued education, or personal interests. Once again, school librarians can bring their unique expertise to their learning community and show how it is a valuable addition to the academic program.

Professional Development

Professional development proposed, organized, and/or delivered by school librarians is mentioned throughout the "Taking Action" section of this chapter. This subsection presents the multiple ways school librarians provide information, support, and instruction for other educators. Offering professional development matches their unique expertise; school librarians are meant to empower students and teachers with information and resources.

The CCSS embody critical and higher level thinking, inquiry, and problem solving. The Six Shifts show that instructional emphasis must be on student learning that involves deep analysis and makes arguments from texts read. It is also stressed that students must be given opportunities to find their own meaning—opportunities to experience learning for themselves. For school librarians to become part of the CCSS effort, professional development is a good place to start. Through presentations, workshops, and sharing of information, teachers leave these encounters "knowing that they can turn to librarians for support in identifying materials for instruction and developing assessments" (Ellis 2013).

SUMMARY

Once school librarians study the CCSS and the Six Shifts and reexamine their roles and the mission and practices of their library program, they can zero in on the three focal points for school library involvement (inquiry-based research, reading, and complexity of text). They will be prepared to bring their expertise to the CCSS table in a significant way.

As the "Taking Action" section of this chapter shows, there are many avenues for school librarians to be activists in the process of bringing the CCSS to life for students and teachers and making the school library the answer to information and learning needs on many levels.

The CCSS do not prescribe how teachers should teach, all that should be taught, interventions to meet special learning needs, or all that is needed to prepare students to be college and career ready (CCSS 2010a). Nevertheless, within them there is a great deal of room for participation by well-informed and -prepared school librarians to partner with others to shape the library learning environment in a way that positions it to be an integral and essential part of the CCSS picture. The result will be empowered school librarians and dynamic school library learning environments that will meet the present and future needs of students as well as others in the learning community.

REFERENCES

American Association of School Librarians. (1996). *Lessons Learned: Collaboration*. [brochure].

American Association of School Librarians. (2007). *Standards for the 21st-Century Learner*. Chicago: American Library Association. Available at http://www.ala.org /aasl/standards.

American Association of School Librarians. (2009a). *Empowering Learners: Guidelines for School Library Media Programs*. Chicago: American Library Association.

American Association of School Librarians. (2009b). *Standards for the 21st-Century Learner in Action*. Chicago: American Library Association.

Common Core State Standards Initiative (CCSS). (2010a). *Common Core State Standards*. Retrieved from http://www.corestandards.org/the-standards on June 7, 2013.

Common Core State Standards Initiative (CCSS). (2010b). *Common Core State Standards for English Language Arts* (ELA). Retrieved from http://www.core standards.org/assets/Appendix_A.pdf on June 7, 2013.

DelVecchio, Steve. (2012). "Text Complexity: School Librarians Have a Role." *School Library Monthly* 29 (2) (November): 9–10.

Donham, Jean. (2013). "Text Sets, Deep Learning, and the Common Core." *School Library Monthly* 29 (6) (March): 5–7.

Ellis, Leanne. (2013). "College Readiness: Librarians Can Help the Transition/On Common Core." *School Library Journal* (May 21). Retrieved from http://www .slj.com/2013/05/opinion/on-common-core/college-readiness-librarians -can-help-the-transition-on-common-core/ on June 8, 2013.

Haycock, Ken. (2013). "Leadership vs. Management." *Leadership Development* (blog), June 5. Retrieved from http://kenhaycock.com/leadership-vs-management/ on June 7, 2013.

Kuhlthau, Carol C., Leslie K. Maniotes, and Ann K. Caspari. (2007). *Guided Inquiry: Learning in the 21st Century*. Westport, CT: Libraries Unlimited.

Moreillon, Judi. (2012). "Reading Comprehension at the Core of the Library Progam." *School Library Monthly* 29 (2) (November): 5–7.

Moreillon, Judi. (2013). "A Matrix for School Librarians: Aligning Standards, Inquiry, Reading, and Instruction." *School Library Monthly* 29 (4) (January): 29–32.

New York State Department of Education. (n.d.). "Pedagogical Shifts Demanded by the Common Core Standards." Retrieved from www.wi.k12.ny.us/curriculum /common-core-shifts.pdf on July 20, 2013.

Stripling, Barbara. (2008a). "Inquiry: Inquiring Minds Want to Know." *School Library Media Activities Monthly* 25 (1) (September): 50–52.

Stripling, Barbara. (2008b). "Inquiry-based Teaching and Learning—The Role of the Library Media Specialist." *School Library Media Activities Monthly* 25 (1) (September): 2.

Use This Page. (2011). "Taking Action: Saving School Libraries." *School Library Monthly* 28 (5) (February): 2.

Valenza, Joyce Kasman. (2012). "Curation." *School Library Monthly* 29 (1) (September/October): 20–23.

Young, Robin. (2012). "Digital Learning: The Role of the School Librarian." *School Library Monthly* 29 (1) (September/October): 33–35.

Zmuda, Allison. (2011). "Six Steps to Saving Your School Library Program." *School Library Monthly* 28 (5) (February): 45–48.

Zmuda, Allison, and Violet H. Harada. (2008). *Librarians as Learning Specialists: Meeting the Learning Imperative for the 21st Century.* Westport, CT: Libraries Unlimited.

4

Putting the Pieces Together: Connecting to the Core Through Coteaching Curriculum Standards

Judi Moreillon

CONNECTION DEVELOPMENT

It is time for a new librarianship, one centered on learning and knowledge, not on books and materials, where the community is the collection, and we spend much more time in *connection development* instead of collection development" [emphasis added]. (Lankes 2011, 9)

Twenty-first-century school librarians must be adept at making connections. As leaders in our schools, our global view of the learning community positions us to see the big picture. Like our principals, we are challenged to identify and capitalize on these connections in order to create learning environments in which students and educators can thrive. In this culture of collaboration, meeting the professional development needs of classroom teachers and specialists and the learning needs of students is at the heart of the school librarian's daily work.

While the collection of library resources is a foundation on which we build lessons and units of instruction, it is the connections we make between resources and curriculum that shape the impact of the school library program on the academic program in our schools. Resources that languish in the library or remain unused online do not make a difference in student learning. To meaningfully integrate these resources and use them to improve teaching and learning, school librarians must enact instructional partnerships. As Lankes notes, it is time for school librarians to focus on "connection development" rather than collection development.

Figure 4.1 shows how coteaching can be the starting point that connects the pieces of the Common Core State Standards (CCSS) with the work of school librarians. With the advent of the CCSS, the school librarian's role as an instructional partner has never been more important. When states, districts, and principals are rolling out new initiatives, they should be able to look to librarians as key players who can help teachers and students successfully meet new requirements. Coteaching is a key component in the CCSS puzzle.

"When school librarians are asked, 'who do you serve?' most would answer 'students,' yet the primary clientele in terms of power, impact, and effect would be teachers" (Haycock 2010, 3). Coteaching with our colleagues is the most effective way for school librarians to collect and share data to demonstrate how the school library program contributes to student achievement. When school librarians coplan, coteach, and coassess student learning outcomes, we are part of the implementation team that helps spread innovations throughout the building, district, and state.

When school reform efforts are underway, the amount of information and the knowledge needed to comply are extensive. In *The Tipping Point*, Gladwell (2000) explained that "connectors" are needed to help people deal with the vast options of information and knowledge accessible through electronic media. "Connector" librarians excel at putting the pieces of the

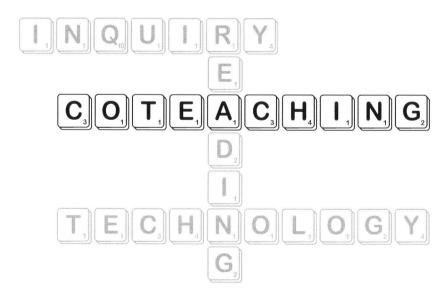

Figure 4.1. CCSS Connections

CCSS puzzle together through the word-of-mouth that results from successful standards-based coteaching, which integrates reading, inquiry, and technology into instruction. These connections help position us to maximize the impact of the work of the school librarian and of the library program on student learning outcomes.

Aligning the CCSS and the AASL *Standards for the 21st-Century Learner* is one important piece of the puzzle. As school librarians, we must not lose sight of our mission as educators who guide students in becoming effective users and producers of ideas and information. Still, the primacy of the CCSS in most states cannot and should not be denied. The librarian's collaborative lesson plans should focus on classroom curriculum standards. Noting how these standards align with the AASL standards may be most important for us and our administrators, but perhaps not as important for our classroom teachers and specialist colleagues, who are already overwhelmed with new standards requirements.

The CCSS specify the outcomes that are expected rather than the means educators will use to help students achieve those results. School librarians who align instructional partnership work with the AASL standards, inquiry, reading, and technology integration offer essential components to meet these standards. The CCSS College and Career Readiness (CCR) Anchor Standards "define the cross-disciplinary literacy expectations that must be met for students to be prepared to enter college and workforce training programs ready to succeed" (CCSS 2010, 4). With the goal of developing lifelong learners, school library program goals can work in tandem with the CCR Anchor Standards to prepare students for continuing their postsecondary education and living, working, and participating in twenty-first-century economic and civic life.

In the introduction to the English language arts standards, the CCSS (2010) offer seven key points, which paint a portrait of college- and career-ready students who

- demonstrate independence;
- build strong content knowledge;
- respond to demands of audience, task, purpose, and discipline;
- comprehend as well as critique;
- value evidence;
- use technology and digital media strategically and capably; and
- come to understand other perspectives and cultures.

These are precisely the types of knowledge and skills that are at the heart of what school librarians teach and school library programs strengthen on a daily basis. Keeping our goals focused on the big picture, school librarians can position our collaborative work in relationship to these seven key points and the broad CCR Anchor Standards while we address grade-level-specific standards when we coteach with our colleagues.

COTEACHING

In *Empowering Learners: Guidelines for School Library Media Programs*, AASL describes "leaders" as educators who build relationships and partnerships, integrate twenty-first-century skills throughout the school environment, demonstrate professional commitment and knowledge, and take a global view in the learning community (2009, 17). The school librarian who takes a leadership role in the school helps build and sustain a culture of collaboration in which these behaviors and responsibilities can be enacted. Working alongside principals, school librarians align our work with administrators' priorities and play a key role in spreading innovations throughout the school environment. "Instructional partnerships are one pathway to achieving the leader role in our schools—a path that has been proven to positively impact student learning" (Moreillon and Ballard 2012, 7).

The implementation of new initiatives is difficult, and change reminds administrators and teachers that in order to achieve school-wide goals, educators must work collaboratively. In April 2013, the Literacy in Learning Exchange released the findings of a national survey, the "NCLE Report: Remodeling Literacy Learning." The report states that although "working together is working smarter, schools are not structured to facilitate educators working together" (NCLE 2013, 5). It also noted that "effective collaboration needs systemic support" (6). The report recommends embedding collaboration in the school day. "The most effective school systems in the world design their schools so that teachers spend substantial portions of their day working alongside other educators to think through challenges together" (29).

Coteaching provides the best kind of professional development. When educators coteach, they are developing their expertise through job-embedded practice in the actual school day, with real students, curriculum, and resources, and with the supports and constraints inherent in their daily work. This model respects the principles of adult learning, including self-direction, internal motivation, individualization, a sense of equality with the learning facilitator, and a problem-solving orientation to the learning event (Knowles 1978). When administrators and educators have a shared commitment to adult learning as well as student learning, they can build a true learning community for all.

Researchers have found positive correlations between classroom-library collaboration and student achievement. Kachel and colleagues (2011) summarized the research findings of the School Library Impact Studies (Library Research Service 2013) and identified a positive correlation between classroom-library collaboration for instruction and increased student achievement in fifteen of the twenty-one studies they reviewed. Comprehensive collaboration includes coplanning, coteaching, and coimplementing standards-based lessons. Other studies show the value classroom teachers and principals place on the collaborative work of school librarians (Kimmel 2012; Lance and Hofshire 2012; Todd, Gordon, and Lu 2011).

When educators collaboratively plan and coteach standards-based lessons, we are practicing "distributed cognition" (Lave and Wenger 1991). While both classroom teachers and librarians bring their knowledge of curriculum and instructional strategies to the collaboration table, classroom teachers and specialists bring their knowledge of individual students and each student's learning needs. School librarians bring a deep knowledge of resources, including technology tools. Individually, educators know bits and pieces, but when we combine our knowledge, skills, and actions, we co-construct educational programs that connect curriculum with student learning needs and relevant, engaging resources.

Through building relationships with colleagues, we set the table for our collaborative work and support our principals in sustaining a culture of collaboration. Through coteaching, we strive to share and develop our expertise and take turns leading and following. Donaldson notes, "Great schools grow when educators understand that the power of their leadership lies in the strength of their relationships. Strong leadership in schools results from the participation of many people, each leading in his or her own way" (2007, 29). With shared leadership, all members of the learning community will have opportunities for professional growth while providing children and youths with dynamic learning experiences.

STANDARDS ALIGNMENT

The CCSS do not use the terms "library" or "information literacy." However, "connector" school librarians can easily translate the CCSS based on an understanding of the underlying alignment among standards, processes, and strategies. Key concepts such as comprehending text while engaged in independent reading, identifying relevant information, using diverse and digital media, determining resource credibility and accuracy, citing evidence, making logical inferences, analyzing, and summarizing are part and parcel of the CCSS *and* the AASL *Standards for the 21st-Century Learner*. When school librarians serve as connectors who quickly see how literacy practices can be applied across disciplines, we become invaluable instructional partners who contribute to student learning outcomes as well as the culture of collaboration in our schools.

Table 4.1 shows the alignment among the CCSS CCR Anchor Standards, AASL standards indicators, inquiry learning, and reading comprehension as well as some application tools to support student learning in each of these standards, processes, and strategies. This matrix, originally published in the January 2013 issue of *School Library Monthly*, is a reference guide that can be useful to school librarians when coplanning with colleagues. It serves to pull together the pieces of the puzzle to align library programs

Table 4.1. A Matrix for School Librarians: Aligning Standards, Inquiry, Reading, and Instruction

CCSS*	AASL Standards Indicators**	Inquiry Process	Reading Comprehension Strategy	Applications
Key Ideas and Details: 1. Read closely to determine what the text says explicitly and to make logical inferences from it [the text plus background knowledge].	Use prior and background knowledge as context for new learning. (1.1.2)	Constructivist approach—building on learner's background knowledge	Activating background knowledge	Using brainstorms, K-W-Ls, mind maps, webs, discussions, journaling, sketching, to activate prior knowledge
Cont. 1. . . . make logical inferences from it [the text plus background knowledge].	Connect ideas to own interests and previous knowledge and experience. (4.1.5)	Motivation—Tapping into what is personally meaningful, relevant	Activating background knowledge	Using student interest inventories to generate topics
Range of Reading and Level of Text Complexity 10. Read and comprehend complex literary and informational texts independently and proficiently.	Read widely and fluently to make connections with own self, the world, and previous reading. (4.1.2)	Negotiation—Initiating school-based learning experiences that connect outside-of-school interests and school curriculum	Building background knowledge	Using text sets of resources in multiple formats on a broad topic to build background knowledge and focus interest
Research to Build and Present Knowledge 8. Gather relevant information from multiple print and digital sources, assess the credibility and accuracy of each source, and integrate the information while avoiding plagiarism.	Find, evaluate, and select appropriate sources to answer questions. (1.1.4)	Plan—Locating, evaluating, and using appropriate resources throughout the process	Using fix-up options (ask a new question)	Using Web site evaluation graphic organizers/tools, meeting bibliography criteria for accessing information in various formats

Research to Build and Present Knowledge 7. Conduct short as well as more sustained research projects **based on focused questions**, demonstrating understanding of the subject under investigation.	**Develop and refine a range of questions** to frame search for new understanding. (1.1.3)	**Formulation**—Developing and refining questions throughout the process	Questioning	Developing questions, revising and refining questions, testing hypotheses
Comprehension and Collaboration 2. Integrate and evaluate information presented in **diverse media and formats**, including visually, quantitatively, and orally.	Display initiative and engagement by posing questions and investigating the answers **beyond the collection of superficial facts.** (1.2.1)	**Investigation**—Collecting and responding to ideas and information	Questioning	Using Cornell note-making format to record questions during investigation
Key Ideas and Details 2. Determine **central ideas** or themes of a text and **analyze** their development; **summarize** the key supporting details and ideas.	**Organize** knowledge so it is useful. (2.1.2)	**Investigation**—Collecting and responding to ideas and information	Determining main ideas	Note-making graphic organizers that show relative importance, summary paragraphs
Key Ideas and Details 1. Read closely to determine what the text says explicitly and to make **logical inferences** from it.	Read, view, and listen for information presented in any format (e.g., textual, visual, media, digital) in order to make inferences and gather meaning. (1.1.6)	**Construction of new knowledge**—Providing a rationale for drawing inferences	Drawing inferences	Taking a stance or position, refining a thesis statement or hypothesis

(*continued*)

Table 4.1. *Continued*

CCSS*	AASL Standards Indicators**	Inquiry Process	Reading Comprehension Strategy	Applications
Craft and Structure 6. **Assess** how point of view or purpose shapes the content and style of a text.	Employ a critical stance in drawing conclusions by demonstrating that the **pattern of evidence leads to a decision or conclusion.** (2.2.3)	**Construction of new knowledge**—Demonstrating the ability to provide evidence from texts	Using fix-up options (make an inference)	Using graphic organizers that categorize information in terms of point of view, purpose, style, or bias
Integration of Knowledge and Ideas 9. **Analyze** how **two or more texts** address similar themes or topics in order to build knowledge or to compare the approaches the authors take.	**Make sense of information gathered from diverse sources** by identifying misconceptions, main and supporting ideas, conflicting information, and point of view or bias. (1.1.7)	**Construction of new knowledge**—Demonstrating comprehension through negotiating conflicting information or bias	Using fix-up options (write about the confusing parts)	Recording and resolving discrepancies, conflicting information, tensions
Integration of Knowledge and Ideas 7. **Integrate and evaluate** content presented in **diverse media and formats**, including visually and quantitatively and quantitatively, as well as in words.	Continue an inquiry-based research process by applying **critical-thinking skills** (analysis, synthesis, evaluation, organization) to information and knowledge in order to **construct new understandings, draw conclusions, and create new knowledge.** (2.1.1)	**Construction of new knowledge**—Developing a framework for expressing conclusions and new understandings	Synthesizing	Composing outlines, flow charts, storyboards, drafts, or using other strategies to demonstrate new understandings

Presentation of Knowledge and Ideas 5. Make **strategic use of digital media and visual displays of data** to express information and enhance understanding of presentations.	Use strategies to **draw conclusions** from information and **apply knowledge** to curricular areas, real-world situations, and further investigations. (2.1.3)	**Presentation**—Demonstrating ability to integrate knowledge and apply it to answer inquiry questions	Synthesizing	Using multiple literacies to create and share final products that inform, persuade, or explain new understandings
Research to Build and Present Knowledge 9. Draw evidence from literary or informational texts to support analysis, **reflection, and research.**	**Reflect** on systematic process and assess for completeness of investigation. (2.4.2)	**Reflection**—Assessing the learning process and outcomes	Using fix-up options (define/refine the purpose for reading the text)	Using exit slips, oral or written reflections, and other self-assessment instruments to reflect on process and product
Production and Distribution of Writing 6. Use technology, including the Internet, to **produce and publish** writing and to interact and collaborate with others.	Use writing process, media and visual literacy, and technology skills to **create products** that express new understandings. (2.1.6)	**Presentation**—Demonstrating ability to integrate knowledge and apply it to answer inquiry questions	Synthesizing	Using multiple literacies to create and share final products that inform, persuade, or explain new understandings

*Selected College and Career Readiness Anchor Standards for English Language Arts in K-5 and 6-12 Cited in the Common Core State Standards (CCSS). Available at http://www.corestandards.org/assets/CCSSI_ELA%20Standards.pdf.

**Excerpted from *Standards for the 21st-Century Learner* by the American Association of School Librarians, a division of the American Library Association, copyright © 2007 American Library Association. Available at www.ala.org/aasl/standards. Used with permission.

Source: This matrix was originally published in *School Library Monthly* (January 2013) and is used with permission: http://schoollibrarymonthly.com /articles/pdf/Moreillon2013-v29n4p29.pdf.

with standards initiatives (CCSS and AASL). This is not a comprehensive document; there are other examples that could be included in each category. But the matrix offers librarians a place to start collaborative conversations with classroom teachers and specialists. Being able to see the connections is a first step toward fully integrating the library program into the classroom curriculum.

INQUIRY AND READING IN THE CCSS

Improving students' reading proficiency is a central focus of the CCSS CCR Anchor Standards. The ability to comprehend text in all formats is similar to the position of "reading," as shown in figure 4.1 (p. 54). Reading holds the other parts of the puzzle together. Students who cannot make sense of text cannot be successful inquirers, and they cannot use technology effectively to produce new knowledge. The CCSS acknowledge the central role of reading in student achievement in all content areas.

What is inquiry learning? Inquiry is a student-centered approach to learning in which students immerse themselves in ideas, information, and resources in order to develop personally meaningful questions. It requires students to take ownership of their learning. In the process, students practice habits of mind (Costa and Kallick 2008) and dispositions (AASL 2007) and experience a range of emotions (Kuhlthau 1985), from excitement to frustration, from being overwhelmed to the exhilaration of discovery.

Inquiry learning positions educators as guides who encourage learners' curiosity and facilitate their learning process. Educators provide interventions throughout the inquiry process to help students negotiate the various stages of the process, answer their own questions or solve a problem, produce knowledge, and share their learning. Throughout the process and again at the final stage, students reflect on the processes and product(s) of their learning. They practice metacognition. Learners who are able to employ metacognitive skills are more confident about what they know and are more successful at independent learning (Coffield, Moseley, Hall, and Ecclestone 2004; Marzano 1998).

School librarians have a leadership role to play in supporting classroom teachers, who may still structure students' information-seeking assignments on fact-based research. As educators move to an inquiry model, they need support for facilitating a less linear, less predictable process that offers students more choices and autonomy. The CCSS and the AASL *Standards for the 21st-Century Learner* are aligned in suggesting that students have more learning experiences that involve accessing, evaluating, analyzing, and synthesizing information from multiple sources in a variety of formats and genres.

In many schools, the CCSS require a renewed commitment to teaching reading comprehension across content areas. The American College Testing

Corporation *Condition of College & Career Readiness 2012* report found that only 52 percent of high school graduates met the reading benchmark. Although this percentage has remained steady from 2010 to 2012 and is down from 53 percent in 2008 and 2009, students, educators, parents, and decision makers should not be satisfied with this level of proficiency. Even if students are not pursuing postsecondary education, they must be proficient readers in order to contribute to the workforce and to civic and political life.

Learning and applying reading comprehension strategies is one way to support readers at all levels of proficiency to improve their reading skills. Applying these strategies is a problem-solving, metacognitive activity. Once they have learned the strategies, readers must recognize when they lack or have lost comprehension and must select from a menu of strategies to gain or regain comprehension. When readers are conscious of these strategies and can apply them appropriately and effectively, they are more confident and successful in independent reading. Students who are successful with inquiry learning must be proficient at reading independently.

As table 4.1 shows, reading comprehension strategies are aligned with AASL standards indicators. This alignment shows school librarians that when we coteach reading strategies, we can have a positive impact on students' reading proficiency while keeping our commitment to facilitating inquiry learning and teaching information problem-solving skills. Through our collaboration with math, science, social studies/history, and technology classroom teachers, we can coteach reading strategies in the content areas where they have not been consistently addressed.

WRITER-CENTERED PERSPECTIVE IN READING AND SIX SHIFTS IN THE ENGLISH LANGUAGE ARTS

The Common Core requires that students and teachers shift the focus to a "writer-centered" perspective. Rather than a "teacher-centered" approach that asks students to learn what the teacher already knows, the writer-centered model requires learners to independently apply strategies to determine how authors position readers to draw conclusions from texts. This goal aligns with the school librarian's objective of developing independent readers. The most effective strategy instruction involves educators using think-alouds to model close reading and deep investigations with mentor texts. This model supports students as they develop the behaviors of active, strategic readers and inquirers. School librarians are perfectly positioned to coteach these strategies alongside classroom teachers and, if need be, in stand-alone library lessons as well.

Through direct instruction using think-alouds, educators teach reading comprehension strategies so that developing readers learn to apply them as needed in various combinations in their independent interactions with texts (Keene and Zimmermann 2007; Moreillon 2012, 2013; Zimmermann and

Hutchins 2003). While each discipline has a unique perspective on ideas and information, as well as specialized vocabulary, there are seven strategies that readers can apply to gain or regain comprehension regardless of the discipline or type of text:

- activating or building background knowledge;
- using sensory images, including visualization;
- questioning before, during, and after reading;
- making predictions and drawing inferences;
- determining main ideas;
- using "fix-up options" to regain comprehension; and
- and synthesizing.

Readers can apply these strategies to any reading event. Increasing the complexity of the text only increases the reader's opportunity to monitor and "fix up" comprehension as needed. With practice, these strategies become skills that readers use without conscious effort.

School librarians can integrate comprehension strategies through close reading as part of inquiry learning mini-lessons or interventions. Close reading requires think-aloud modeling with a small chunk of text from a mentor text in order to investigate how the writer used words or the illustrator used images to lead readers to draw conclusions. For example, when school librarians teach note making with a sample text, we use think-alouds, in which we share our thought processes to help students learn how to determine main ideas and distinguish them from supporting details. We do this with both traditional print and digital texts. As students matriculate through the grades, they continue to benefit from applying reading comprehension strategies to various genres and formats and from close reading with increasingly complex texts in all disciplines.

Whether students are reading a history or science text, in print or online, they must recognize when they have lost comprehension and use strategies to regain it. They need to activate their background knowledge or build it if they lack it, make predictions and draw inferences, ask questions, determine main ideas, and synthesize across texts. All of these reading comprehension processes must be applied during inquiry learning. Active, strategic readers are active, strategic inquirers.

In addition to the writer-centered focus, the changes in the CCSS English language arts (ELA) have been characterized by "Six Shifts." Each of these shifts describes a pedagogical change that classroom teachers are expected to follow. The first shift is an increased use of informational text as students matriculate through the grades. Unfortunately, the CCSS are not consistent in the use of terminology to describe the types of texts required to address this shift. Scholars who have studied the features of these texts seem to agree that the intent of the authors of the CCSS is for students to read more texts with analytical expository structures. The CCSS use the term "literary non-fiction" for other types of texts that have a more creative narrative frame, such as speeches, essays, autobiographies, and biographies. It is important for school librarians who have long used the general term "nonfiction" to make finer distinctions in this broad category. (For a complete investigation into the challenges of this terminology in the research literature and the CCSS, see Maloch and Bomer 2013.)

To address the first shift, school librarians can increase the focus of both our instruction and reading promotion efforts on informational texts with expository frames. While studies show that elementary classroom libraries and classroom engagements with texts focus primarily on fiction (Duke 2000; Jeong, Gaffney, and Choi 2010), our school library–based inquiry units of instruction tend to center on topical informational texts. These resources have text features to support information seeking such as indexes, tables of contents, headings and subheadings, boldfaced words, graphics and charts, glossaries, and more. To further our attention to this shift, integrating more literary nonfiction (essays and speeches in particular) into our teaching is one way school librarians can contribute. Promoting the work of informational book and literary nonfiction authors and illustrators through book displays, book trailers, and author-illustrator visits are other activities to consider.

The second shift is a commitment to teach the four language arts skills—reading, writing, speaking, and listening—across content areas rather than in ELA classes alone. Traditionally, reading comprehension strategy instruction has been centered on fictional texts in ELA classes. While teaching reading across the curriculum is not a new idea, it is one that proactive school librarians should support. Many elementary teachers have not practiced strategy instruction with science and social studies texts, and many secondary teachers, who teach exclusively in the content areas, have not considered strategy instruction one of their responsibilities. In fact, many classroom teachers have not been trained to teach reading comprehension strategies in the disciplines. School librarians can serve as instructional leaders who teach these strategies simultaneously to students and content-area teachers.

The third shift requires that students be challenged by analyzing increasingly more complex texts. When we provide graphic organizers to help readers activate their background knowledge and combine it with evidence in a text to determine a theme, we are scaffolding readers' analysis of texts. When we teach students to determine accuracy, authority, and bias in resources, we are teaching them to analyze texts. When inquirers make notes, they are analyzing texts for main ideas and supporting details. We can help learners make sense of ideas and information in multiple resources. We guide them as they apply research-based instructional strategies such as determining similarities and differences (Dean, Hubbell, Pitler, and Stone 2012) and support students in analyzing texts with graphic organizers such as category matrices and webs and Venn diagrams. Analysis is part and parcel of a school librarian's teaching.

1. Increase in Informational and Literary Nonfiction Texts

❏ Students read topical informational books and electronic resources.

❏ Students read literary nonfiction (essays, speeches, biographies, and autobiographies).

2. Reading, Writing, Listening, Speaking Across Content Areas

❏ Students read topical informational books and electronic resources in non-ELA content areas.

❏ Students read literary nonfiction in non-ELA content areas.

❏ Students applied the writing process in non-ELA content areas.

❏ Students engaged in speaking and listening in non-ELA content areas.

3. Text Complexity

❏ Educators considered the complexity of the texts (Lexile levels and content) and the tasks students were asked to perform with complex texts when designing the lesson or unit of instruction.

❏ Students engaged with texts beyond their proficient reading level.

❏ Students were asked to use these texts for specific purposes and effectively completed tasks.

❏ Students applied reading comprehension strategies to make sense of difficult texts.

4. Text-based Answers

❏ Educators provided graphic organizers to scaffold students' note making and citing evidence.

❏ Students applied the "determining main ideas" reading comprehension strategy to make notes and answer questions.

❏ Students quoted and cited portions of the text to support their answers to questions.

5. Writing Arguments

❏ Students wrote to describe, inform, or argue.

❏ Students quoted or paraphrased and cited portions of texts to support their arguments and expository writing.

6. Academic Vocabulary

❏ Educators defined and used academic vocabulary in the lesson objectives, which were shared with the students, and reinforced these terms throughout the lesson. List them:

❏ Students learned/applied interdisciplinary academic vocabulary during this lesson. List the terms:

Figure 4.2. Six Shifts Checklist for Inquiry and Reading Comprehension Strategy Lessons

The fourth shift concerns students' ability to identify and cite specific evidence in the text to support answers to questions. Teaching students to quote and cite, paraphrase, and avoid plagiarism has long been a staple of library lessons. School librarians can increase our attention to this shift by comodeling these processes during cotaught literature and inquiry lessons. Supporting our classroom teacher and specialist colleagues in assessing student learning outcomes in this area and using these data to improve our instruction are essential.

The fifth shift involves students using facts and evidence in writing arguments. This shift is closely connected to the fourth, citing evidence. Writing in the CCSS CCR Anchor Standards takes a decided turn away from writing that conveys personal experiences and opinions, toward writing that requires students to persuade with evidence and explain information with facts. Though we do not want to discount the importance of personal response to ideas and information, we can increase our focus on persuasive writing that is heavily grounded in data and established facts. Coupled with an increased focus on the ethical use of information, our teaching and school library resources are integral to student achievement in writing arguments.

The final shift requires that students learn and are able to apply academic vocabulary that crosses content areas. Before they engage in learning tasks, students must be able to comprehend and apply concepts such as "state a thesis," "generate a hypothesis," "determine bias," or "identify assumptions." The *Visual Thesaurus* ("Word Lists" 2013) offers an extensive list of "general academic words."

Many of the keywords in the AASL *Standards for the 21st-Century Learner* are on that list, including *analyze, apply, assess, authentic, context, debate, evidence, genre, infer, inquire, modify, opinion, organize, perspective, research, solve, stance, synthesis,* and *viewpoint.*

When classroom teachers, specialists, and school librarians coplan and coteach, we can use a checklist such as the one provided in figure 4.2 to note how our instruction addresses the Six Shifts.

If school librarians organize instruction around the CCSS CCR Anchor Standards, the AASL standards, inquiry, and reading, we will position our coteaching efforts at the center of the CCSS implementation puzzle. Applying the inquiry process and reading comprehension strategies involves learners in critical thinking. When we scaffold their learning with graphic organizers and comonitor students' guided practice, assess student learning outcomes, and adjust instruction to support students' success, the school librarian can lead in enacting improved literacy instruction.

TECHNOLOGY TOOLS INTEGRATION: THE MISSING PIECE?

Some believe that technology tools are a missing piece in the CCSS puzzle. Prensky, who writes books and a blog related to innovative uses of twenty-first-century tools for learning, states that "many of the 'new' Common Core State Standards serve only the needs of the 19th and 20th centuries" (2013, 24). His call for a new curriculum focused on effective thinking, actions, relationships, and accomplishments would involve students in using technology tools to "extend their brains" while they are engaged in interdisciplinary learning. Many applaud Prensky and others whose ideas call for starting from zero and completely reframing schooling as we know it today.

That said, most educators will be required to enact the changes necessary to implement the CCSS and will need support for stretching the standards to engage students in the kinds of deep learning proposed by visionaries such as Prensky. To achieve this, it will be necessary for educators to apply our considerable creativity to innovating within the CCSS framework. The fact is that these standards are structured around disciplinary teaching and lack the technology tools foundation many educators know is necessary for success in the twenty-first century. "Connector" school librarians, serving in the roles of information specialist and instructional partner, will continue, as we have done in the past, to coplan and coteach interdisciplinary lessons and units of study that integrate technology tools. We can capitalize on standards that ask students to access, use, and synthesize information from multiple sources in multiple formats to think critically, solve problems, work collaboratively, and produce new knowledge. We will increase our commitment to making sure students have opportunities to employ technology tools for creative as well as functional purposes.

School librarians can use what we know and continue to learn about the skills needed for effective transliteracy. In our collaborative lessons, we can make sure that students practice reading, writing, and interacting across platforms. We can integrate technology tools and devices into student learning engagements. We can bring our knowledge of various media and digital social networks to the collaboration table to ensure that students use twenty-first-century tools to learn, produce knowledge, and communicate. In combination with the AASL *Standards for the 21st-Century Learner* and technology tools, the CCSS can be extended to address the skill set we know students need to succeed.

PUTTING IT ALL TOGETHER

In the twenty-first century, the art of school librarianship involves leading through making connections. While the implementation puzzle may seem daunting to our colleagues, school librarians can rise to the challenge and reach out to help everyone in our learning communities succeed. When we make connections beyond the walls of the library to connect our work with classroom teachers and specialists and content-area standards, we have the opportunity to become full members of our schools' literacy teams. The implementation of the CCSS provides school librarians with an opportunity to bring together our various areas of expertise—collaborative teaching, inquiry, reading comprehension strategies, and technology tools integration—to ensure that our colleagues and students engage with a curriculum that is relevant to the needs of today and, with a bit of luck, tomorrow.

REFERENCES

ACT. (2012). "College Readiness Benchmarks Over Time." *The Condition of College & Career Readiness 2012*. Retrieved from http://www.act.org/research/policy makers/cccr12/readiness2.html ond May 30, 2013.

American Association of School Librarians. (2007). *Standards for the 21st-Century Learner*. Chicago: American Association of School Librarians. Retrieved from http://ala.org/aasl/standards on May 30, 2013.

American Association of School Librarians.(2009). *Empowering Learners: Guidelines for School Library Media Programs*. Chicago: American Library Association.

Coffield, Frank, David Moseley, Elaine Hall, and Kathryn Eccleston. (2004). *Should We Be Using Learning Styles? What Research Has to Say about Practice*. London: Learning and Skills Research Center.

Common Core State Standards Initiative (CCSS). (2010). *Common Core State Standards*. Retrieved from http://www.corestandards.org/the-standards on May 30, 2013.

Costa, Arthur L., and Bena Kallick, eds. (2008). *Learning and Leading with Habits of Mind: 16 Essential Characteristics for Success*. Alexandria, VA: Association for Supervision and Curriculum Development.

Dean, Ceri B., Elizabeth Ross Hubbell, Howard Pitler, and Bj Stone. (2012). *Classroom Instruction That Works: Research-based Strategies for Increasing Student Achievement*. 2nd ed. Alexandria, VA: Association of Supervision and Curriculum Development.

Donaldson, Gordon A. (2007). "What Do Teachers Bring to Leadership?" *Educational Leadership* 65 (1): 26–29.

Duke, Nell. (2000). "3.6 Minutes per Day: The Scarcity of Informational Texts in First Grade." *Reading Research Quarterly* 35 (2): 202–224.

Gladwell, Malcolm. 2000. *The Tipping Point: How Little Things Can Make a Big Difference*. Boston: Little, Brown.

Haycock, Ken. (2010). "Leadership from the Middle: Building Influence for Change." In *The Many Faces of School Library Leadership*, edited by Sharon Coatney, 1–12. Santa Barbara, CA: Libraries Unlimited.

Jeong, Jongeseong, Janet Gaffney, and Jin-Oh Choi. (2010). "Availability and Use of Information Texts in Second-, Third-, and Fourth-grade Classrooms." *Research in the Teaching of English* 44 (4): 435–456.

Kachel, Debra E., et al. (2011). *School Library Research Summarized: A Graduate Class Project*. Mansfield, PA: School of Library & Information Technologies Department, Mansfield University. Retrieved from http://libweb.mansfield.edu /upload/kachel/ImpactStudy.pdf on May 30, 2013.

Keene, Ellin Oliver, and Susan Zimmermann. (2007). *Mosaic of Thought, Second Edition: The Power of Comprehension Strategy Instruction*. Portsmouth, NH: Heinemann.

Kimmel, Sue C. (2012). "Seeing the Clouds: Teacher Librarian as Broker in Collaborative Planning with Teachers." *School Libraries Worldwide* 18 (1): 87–96.

Knowles, Malcolm. (1978). *The Adult Learner: A Neglected Species.* 2nd ed. Boston: Gulf.

Kuhlthau, Carol C. (1985). *Teaching the Research Process.* New York: The Center for Applied Research in Education.

Lance, Keith Curry, and Linda Hofshire. (2012). "Report: A Closer Look: Change in School Library Staffing Linked to Change in CSAP Reading Performance, 2005–2011." Denver, CO: Library Research Service. Retrieved from http://www.lrs.org/documents/closer_look/CO4_2012_Closer_Look_Report.pdf on May 30, 2013.

Lankes, R. David. (2011). *The Atlas of New Librarianship.* Cambridge, MA: MIT Press.

Lave, Jean, and Etienne Wenger. (1991). *Situated Learning: Legitimate Peripheral Participation.* Cambridge, UK: Cambridge University Press.

Library Research Service. (2013). *School Library Impact Studies.* Retrieved from http://www.lrs.org/data-tools/school-libraries/impact-studies on May 30, 2013.

Maloch, Beth, and Randy Bomer. (2013). "Informational Texts and the Common Core Standards: What Are We Talking About, Anyway?" *Language Arts* 90 (3): 205–211.

Marzano, Robert. (1998). *A Theory-based Meta-analysis of Research on Instruction.* Aurora, CO: Mid-continental Regional Educational Laboratory.

Moreillon, Judi. (2012). *Coteaching Reading Comprehension Strategies in Secondary School Libraries: Maximizing Your Impact.* Chicago: ALA Editions.

Moreillon, Judi. (2013). *Coteaching Reading Comprehension Strategies in Elementary School Libraries: Maximizing Your Impact.* Chicago: ALA Editions.

Moreillon, Judi, and Susan Ballard. (2012). "Coteaching: A Pathway to Leadership." *Knowledge Quest* 40 (4): 6–9.

National Center for Literacy Education (NCLE). (2013). "NCLE Report: Remodeling Literacy Learning." March 19. Retrieved from http://www.literacyinlearning exchange.org/remodeling on May 30, 2013.

Pattison, Darcy. (2013). *Making the Common Core Practical: 6 Shifts in Learning: CCSS Style.* Retrieved from http://commoncorestandards.com/ela/6-shifts-in -learning-ccss-style on May 30, 2013.

Prensky, Marc. (2013). "Our Brains Extended." *Educational Leadership* 70 (6): 23–27.

Todd, Ross J., Carol A. Gordon, and Ya-Ling Lu. (2011). "One Common Goal: Student Learning." Report of Findings and Recommendations of the New Jersey Library Survey, Phase 2. New Brunswick, NJ: Rutgers Center for International Scholarship in School Libraries. Retrieved from http://cissl.rutgers.edu/images /stories/docs/njasl_phase%20_2_final.pdf on May 30, 2013.

"Word Lists: General Academic Vocabulary." (2013). *Visual Thesaurus.* Retrieved from http://www.visualthesaurus.com/wordlists/144473 on May 30, 2013.

Zimmermann, Susan, and Chryse Hutchins. (2003). *7 Keys to Comprehension: How to Help Your Kids Read It and Get It!* New York: Three Rivers.

Part II

Models for Inquiry-Based Learning

5

Guided Inquiry Design and the Common Core

Leslie K. Maniotes

Through Guided Inquiry, students ask their own real questions and investigate problems relevant to their lives. As they investigate, they construct new understandings and articulate what they learned as they share their learning with others. Inquiry is at the core of well-designed problem-based learning, expeditionary learning, project-based learning, experiential learning, flipped classrooms, traditional research assignments, blended learning, and integrated approaches used in schools today to address the needs of students in the digital age. Through Guided Inquiry, students learn many complex and integrated skills and content, including the essential skills of how to find and use information within a meaningful context.

The Common Core State Standards (CCSS) assume an inquiry approach through the emphasis on research from the youngest children up through high school as students prepare for college and careers. This chapter explains how Guided Inquiry Design builds a purposeful approach to support learning to accomplish proficiency in the Common Core.

WHAT IS GUIDED INQUIRY?

Guided Inquiry is a practical way of implementing an inquiry approach to improve learning for students in schools in grades K–12. Guided Inquiry Design is a framework that facilitates students' learning through inquiry. It was created to provide teachers with a framework to design units of inquiry learning, based on what we know from our research about the learner's experience.

Guided Inquiry is based on extensive studies of the information search process (ISP) in assigned research projects (Kuhlthau1985, 2004). These studies clearly show that learning through research is more than simply collecting information. The ISP research explains that inquiry learning is complex and requires guidance, instruction, modeling, and coaching through "zones of intervention" (Kuhlthau 2004).

Because of its complexity and the challenges of moving theory into practice, the ISP is translated into an instructional design framework called Guided Inquiry Design (Kuhlthau, Maniotes, and Caspari 2012). This design framework was created to help teachers use what we know about the ISP research in a practical design process to scaffold inquiry learning in school projects.

Guided Inquiry Design requires that teams of teachers use backward design, beginning with the standards, to identify a theme, essential question, or big idea for study (Wiggins and McTighe 1998). Through this theme students engage their own interests and understandings to come up with an aspect of the learning or a question that particularly interests them within that topic. Guided Inquiry is also informed by the concept of third space (Maniotes 2005; Gutierrez, Rymes, and Larson 1995). It engages students in the third space, where they connect their sociocultural knowledge from outside of school with the official, formalized elements of the curriculum. These connections push students to construct new understandings, otherwise out of their reach, in a "zone of proximal development" (Vygotsky 1978), which engages them deeply in relevant work.

The types of big-theme questions addressed through Guided Inquiry in grades K–12 are limitless. Inquiry can include questions of science, humanities, history, mathematics, social/ethical issues, economics, and so forth. The following are examples from teams that I have worked with:

- What are the ways we can stay healthy?
- How does violence in the media desensitize the viewers?
- What social issue are you passionate about? In what ways can you effect a change in a social issue?
- What are the ways that people's actions shape history?
- What are the possible motivations for people to choose a side?
- How do we (in our school and in our town) dispose of our garbage? How does this impact the environment? What is currently being done to reduce the environmental impact from our trash? What can I do to help?
- Bottled water: Is it worth it?
- What is the best energy source for us to use?
- In what ways does the past inform the present?
- How do changes in city neighborhoods or economics impact street art?

As these questions suggest, inquiry is cross-disciplinary. Through an inquiry unit of study, students learn across disciplines and integrate and apply concepts among multiple subjects. Science, mathematics, technology, and social studies topics can be addressed through inquiry. Accomplishing the Common Core will require an integrated approach in the rich context for learning that Guided Inquiry Design provides.

THE GUIDED INQUIRY DESIGN FRAMEWORK

Guided Inquiry is a way of teaching students the core concepts from the CCSS while engaging content and perspectives that are personally relevant and interesting. It is a process of creating something new out of multiple sources of information. Teachers design Guided Inquiry by knowing the inquiry process and structuring the sessions to support student learning through each phase. The process is based on the ISP (Kuhlthau 2004). The following section is an introduction to Guided Inquiry Design based on the stages of the ISP model.

Information Search Process and Guided Inquiry Design

The Guided Inquiry Design framework (see figure 5.1.) begins with **Open**: that is, to open students' minds and capture their attention, to get them thinking and wondering, and to help them make connections to their sociocultural knowledge and the world outside of school. Next is **Immerse**, which is to build enough background knowledge to generate some interesting ideas to investigate. **Explore** then gives students time to look around and find ideas for an important and interesting, authentic inquiry question. Next, students pause to **Identify** and clearly articulate the inquiry question before moving on to **Gather** information. After gathering, students **Create** and **Share** what they have learned. Finally, they **Evaluate**, reflecting on content and process and evaluating achievement of learning. The process is not a linear one: inquiry is a "messy" process, but it does move sequentially across time, and the model reflects that movement. Guided Inquiry Design encourages collaborative construction of knowledge, with reflection and assessment occurring throughout the process.

INQUIRY TOOLS TO ACHIEVE THE COMMON CORE

"The information search process (ISP) research shows that inquiry learning is more than simply identifying a task, collecting information, and accomplishing the task. It is a complicated holistic process of thinking and learning from a variety of sources that involves constructing a personal understanding" (Kuhlthau, Maniotes, and Caspari 2012, 37). It is for this reason that we have embedded tools within Guided Inquiry Design to help students think, construct understanding, and engage deeply throughout the process. These tools work to accomplish the literacy, discipline-specific

Model of the Information Search Process

Tasks	Initiation	Selection	Exploration	Formulation	Collection	Presentation
Feelings (affective)	uncertainly	optimism	confusion frustration doubt	clarity	sense of direction/ confidence	satisfaction or disappointment
Thoughts (cognitive)	vague ························· → focused					
					increased interest	
Actions (physical)	seeking relevant information ···········→ seeking pertinent information					
	exploring				documenting	

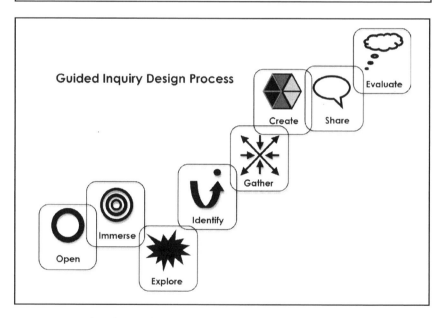

Figure 5.1. Model of the Information Search Process and the Guided Inquiry Design Process

Kuhlthau, C. C., L. Maniotes, and A. Caspari. (2012). *Guided Inquiry Design: A Framework for Inquiry in Your School.* Westport, CT: Libraries Unlimited

language, and high level content knowledge that students need to become proficient in the Common Core at each grade level.

Much of learning through inquiry is becoming self-aware of how we learn and what we can do to help ourselves progress through each phase to come to a successful conclusion with our investigation. The tools are designed to help students strengthen their awareness of how they learn as well as to provide them with strategies employing literacy skills and to engage in content area study. Inquiry tools help students in each phase to think, question, innovate new ideas, construct new meaning, and share with others.

Inquiry Circles/Pair Share Protocols: Working in Small Groups and Pairs

The CCSS require students to work in a variety of groups and encourage small group collaborative work. The inquiry circle and pair shares are two structures in Guided Inquiry Design that support learning in small groups through inquiry.

An inquiry circle (Kuhlthau, Maniotes, and Caspari 2012) is a structure designed to help students think about ideas, collaborate on a narrowed topic, and share resources. Students meet with their small group, called an inquiry circle, throughout the inquiry process. It is a mutually informing group. Members may challenge one another's sources, ideas, and perspective, or they may share resources and use the conversation to build a stronger argument. They are there to help one another, critique one another's work, and support one another's thinking. Each student comes to the meeting prepared and ready to engage in discussion with the others. This structure enables collaboration and sharing, giving students opportunities to discuss in academic language, try out using evidence to back up their arguments, and get feedback from peers, as required in the CCSS.

Another structure in Guided Inquiry that supports thinking, questioning, and reflection is the "pair share protocol" (Kuhlthau, Maniotes, and Caspari 2012). Through the Common Core, students are expected to have opportunities to build their spoken language as well as written communication skills. Inquiry is a creative process that requires built-in reflection and discussion time. In Guided Inquiry, we recognize the power of reflection and talking through ideas in preparation for composing or creating something. The pair share protocol supports students talking, thinking, and writing throughout Guided Inquiry Design.

The pair share increases reflection time through its simple structure. Students have opportunities to talk and get ideas from each other, use academic language as they practice applying discipline-specific vocabulary they are learning through the inquiry, and try out ideas before committing them to paper. Each phase of the inquiry has a pair share protocol that helps facilitate just the right conversation between pairs of students needed for that phase of learning, as indicated by the ISP studies.

Composing in Inquiry Journals

The CCSS increase the amount of expository reading and writing, including writing to persuade. Guided Inquiry provides an authentic environment for students to write well-informed, persuasive essays and expository texts. In order to write a well-informed, persuasive piece, one must first have done some research. This research occurs through the Guided Inquiry process.

The journal is a structure for writing that supports learning throughout the inquiry. Using the inquiry journal, students build arguments over time, connect notes, synthesize ideas, provide evidence for their claims, and reflect on the process. The structure of journaling in Guided Inquiry is most effective for reflection and learning when used regularly and throughout the inquiry process.

Inquiry Logs

In the CCSS, students are expected as early as fourth grade to begin to collect a list of sources for research. In Guided Inquiry, the inquiry log is a systematic structure for collecting the necessary information on sources throughout an inquiry.

In Guided Inquiry Design, we have expanded the inquiry log to be used, not only as a tool to gather sources, but also to track the journey of learning. Through the structure of the inquiry log, students raise their awareness of how they are reading texts, how they are making choices through inquiry, and how to use the tool to organize their work.

Through the use of the log, students see that they may not use all the resources that they read, view, or scan in their final piece. The inquiry log helps students learn that through documenting all their sources, they can more easily go back to the sources they think might be useful at a later time. When students don't use a log, they can get unnecessarily frustrated when they lose track of a resource or quote that would have been perfect to accentuate the point they wanted to make as they craft their synthesis. The inquiry log in Guided Inquiry Design extends the CCSS expectation of collecting a list of sources into use of a learning tool.

Inquiry Community

The inquiry community supports the rigor of the CCSS in a structure for regular sharing and learning as a community. The inquiry community functions as a resource in Guided Inquiry, similar to the pair share protocol that is used to share learning along the way. The inquiry community is the whole group of students (or class) that regularly share their progress. Here, they test out ideas within a group of people investigating a component of the larger theme. They gain support in an academic community, share the discipline-specific language they are learning, and build on conceptual understandings together.

Inquiry Charts

The CCSS require students to synthesize and apply information at high levels across content areas. Charts, diagrams, and graphic organizers help students visualize their learning. They are used to assist students in reading and analyzing texts as well as organizing and composing written text.

Inquiry charts are a key strategy for student learning in inquiry. They have two key functions in Guided Inquiry Design. They help students make decisions and incorporate many ideas into a cohesive whole. Guided Inquiry Design uses inquiry charts at strategic points in the process to facilitate decision making and thinking. First, when students are identifying a direction for the inquiry in Identify, they use a chart to decide. Later, when they are trying to synthesize disparate information in Create, charts are used to help students visualize and create something new with the information they have found. Through engagement in Guided Inquiry Design, students learn when and how charting ideas can help them in various situations.

ACCOMPLISHING THE CCSS USING THE GUIDED INQUIRY APPROACH

The Common Core State Standards (CCSS) are a description of what students need to know and be able to do, to develop skills across their K–12 years so that they will become college and career ready. In general, the standards are proficiency based, in that they describe what students should master by the end of each grade. The standards are spiraled so that the same core skills are built upon and grow every year as students develop competence in each of the areas.

The standards are drawn from a national perspective, ensuring high academic rigor for all of our students across the United States. They work toward equity in public education. Traditionally, it has been left up to states and in some places local school districts to decide what is taught in schools. Because of the variation in expectations depending upon locale, there has generally been a lack of consistency and a wide variation of rigor from school to school, district to district. The CCSS were created to increase equity and rigor in what is taught in schools across the nation.

The CCSS offer a great opportunity to rethink how we are meeting the needs of today's students. These standards describe what students must know and be able to do, yet they do not describe how these abilities are to be accomplished or assessed. Therein lies a large gap and potential for change and redefining how we teach. Within the language of the CCSS, we can examine the possible intent, notice the patterns, and draw our own conclusions about how the standards can best be met.

There are many tools schools might consider using to accomplish the Common Core. As Kuhlthau, Maniotes, and Caspari (2007, 94) stated while looking at the national standards from subject area disciplines, not *all* standards, but most, can be accomplished through an inquiry approach. Likewise, the lion's share of the Common Core can be accomplished through inquiry learning, and Guided Inquiry is well suited to fulfill the high level thinking, composing, and analyzing that is required in the Core. *Guided Inquiry Design* (Kuhlthau, Maniotes, and Caspari, 2012) is a practical framework for schools to adopt to accomplish the *CCSS English Language Arts and Literacy in History/Social Studies, Science and Technical Subjects.*

The standards emphasize academic skills, close reading, and literacy embedded in content area study. The English Language Arts CCSS require heightened rigor for students that matches the learning of Guided Inquiry in a number of key areas:

- Integrated learning literacy through content area study
- Increased nonfiction reading and writing
- Emphasis on research

INTEGRATED LEARNING IN GUIDED INQUIRY DESIGN

The Common Core requires integrating literacy through content area study. The CCSS language arts standards are framed in a new way. The language arts are not skills taught in isolation, but reading, writing, speaking, viewing, and listening are used to make meaning of disciplinary subjects. The Common Core recognizes that students use and develop literacy skills as they communicate on a variety of topics from the youngest ages.

The CCSS present an opportunity to purposefully and intentionally integrate learning as students learn about content through reading and writing by interacting with resources on the topics of history, social studies, science, and technical subjects. Conversely, students increase their sophistication and skill in reading, writing, listening, and talking as they engage with this content of the disciplines. As the standards are articulated in this way, teachers must consider how to teach content, language, and reading at the same time.

In Guided Inquiry, integrating learning is a core component intentionally scaffolded through the design. The inquiry tools provide a structured means to help students develop their literacy skills as they move through inquiry. As students engage in inquiry learning, they build concepts about content within the discipline of study. Finally, students intentionally use the language of the discipline as they learn about the content and engage in discourse. Guided Inquiry Design helps educators plan for intentional literacy learning and content learning at the same time.

Students are not only learning literacy skills while they engage in inquiry; they are learning many overlapping and critical skills necessary for college and career readiness. Perhaps this is why research and inquiry are embedded in the language of the CCSS.

Five Kinds of Learning in Guided Inquiry

When inquiry is guided, students accomplish five interwoven, integrated kinds of learning:

- Curriculum content
- Information literacy
- Learning how to learn
- Literacy competency
- Social skills

(Kuhlthau, Maniotes, and Caspari 2007, 2012, 8).

Through Guided Inquiry, students engage in all five kinds of learning. They learn curriculum content through questioning, wondering, reading, exploring, and interpreting various texts as they find facts and synthesize ideas in discipline-specific areas while investigating their questions. Students learn the concepts of information literacy as they engage in locating, evaluating, and using information within a meaningful context. They learn how to learn as they reflect on the inquiry process and develop a personal learning identity. They use literacy competency as they apply reading, writing, speaking, listening, viewing, and presenting skills to think, interact, and construct ideas. Guided Inquiry occurs within the social context of a learning community. Social skills include the ability to collaborate and share in successful sustained group work and within a wide variety of contexts (pairs, small groups, and large groups).

These five kinds of learning are essential for developing academic competency, career readiness, and life skills. Within the Guided Inquiry approach, it is recognized that all of these are happening at once because of the nature of inquiry learning. Each of these types of learning needs attention, scaffolding, and instruction at certain points during the inquiry process.

Designing sophisticated inquiry units that facilitate learning in all five areas requires a collaborative approach. As educators use inquiry to accomplish the CCSS, there will be a great need for schools to develop collaborative learning teams. In *Guided Inquiry Design* Kuhlthau, Maniotes, and Caspari describe a learning team that works together to accomplish the five kinds of learning that occur in inquiry (2012, 11). The learning team of collaborating teachers designs the learning experience so that students build their skill in each of the five areas through the Guided Inquiry Design and use of inquiry tools.

Within Guided Inquiry, students develop skills, knowledge, and awareness in all of the five kinds of learning. The members of the learning team structure learning goals for each of these areas and are attuned to all five kinds of learning so that they assess each as they confer with students and interact across the inquiry process (Kuhlthau and Maniotes 2010).

As described previously, Guided Inquiry meets the CCSS assumption of integrated learning, and the design process, systems, and structures embedded within the approach can help educators plan for and intentionally impact student learning. This isn't the only area of the CCSS that Guided Inquiry addresses. The next sections discuss the key areas of increased nonfiction texts and how and when students read closely during Guided Inquiry.

INCREASED NONFICTION READING AND WRITING

The Common Core requires a shift in current educational practice to increase the amount of nonfiction reading and writing. Because of the rich information world in which we live, students have a need to become more proficient in reading and writing nonfiction texts. Teachers could do this by adding nonfiction to their books and units. However, the potential of the CCSS is in the opportunity that they provide to rethink how we are doing things to better meet the learning needs of our students.

Inquiry learning requires reading all kinds of nonfiction texts. Through Guided Inquiry, students ask and investigate their own questions. They seek pertinent information through a variety of sources, including the many types of nonfiction texts. They persist in this challenging endeavor because they have an interest in making meaning of an engaging concept or idea. Through the engagement of third space, students seek to create meaning, because of the nature of the process and the relevance of the topic.

Fiction texts also play a role in Guided Inquiry. Fiction can be used skillfully to fill in contextual details or enrich a concept during or prior to study. However, through Guided Inquiry, students are learning about a topic, asking questions, and finding information about that topic in order to synthesize the information and create something new to share with others. Increasing the amount of inquiry in a school will naturally increase the amount of nonfiction reading for a purpose, to explain and to inform others about an interesting topic.

The CCSS writing expectation includes more expository writing to explain and persuade. Guided Inquiry matches that call for more expository writing with more rigorous inquiry projects undertaken for a clear purpose that will increase the level of expertise in these written genres over the course of schooling.

The outcome of a Guided Inquiry Design, or sharing of the learning in the Share phase, is most often an expository product. For example, when students investigate social issues, a persuasive essay is a natural outcome that will help them to articulate the problem to an audience that can make a difference. At other times, the outcome is sharing information with others through a variety of media and formats, but usually requiring the creation of some explanatory text to do so. The change of emphasis on nonfiction texts in the CCSS points to inquiry as a highly useful approach to accomplishing integrated learning using nonfiction texts to simultaneously develop content knowledge and literacy skills.

Close Reading

Readers read in different ways depending on the context and purpose of the reading. Inquiry provides an authentic context for students to read with an authentic purpose. As described in *Guided Inquiry Design* (Kuhlthau, Maniotes, and Caspari 2012), in the early phases, Open, Immerse, and Explore, before students have identified a direction for the inquiry, they skim and scan information as they read widely to help them find a focus. Once they have a question or direction for the inquiry in the Identify phase, they must engage in close reading and analysis of text. In order to synthesize, summarize, evaluate, and create, students read deeply in the Gather and Create phases. The Common Core requires this close reading, which naturally occurs in the later phases of Guided Inquiry, when students are inspired to dig deeply to find and synthesize information from a variety of texts to learn about their topic and share with others.

Through Guided Inquiry, we recognize that students may not be aware of these different approaches to reading that occur in the various phases of the process. Explicit in the Guided Inquiry Design is how the purposes of reading are closely connected to the phase of the inquiry process, as indicated in the research on the ISP. Awareness of these phases and strategies, or purposes for reading and working within these phases, is critical to students' success with the inquiry.

For example, reading closely or deeply too soon can halt the exploration necessary to identifying an interesting inquiry focus or question. Students benefit when they know that at the beginning of inquiry, they should read lightly as they explore ideas in the Immerse and Explore phases. Conversely, reading lightly or scanning materials in the latter stages of inquiry would result in a shallow reporting of facts. Connecting reading to the purpose of the task is authentic when set in an inquiry context. If the purpose of reading is not addressed with students, the learning is greatly impacted.

Therefore, using Guided Inquiry Design, the learning team can structure the learning so that students gain awareness of and understand reading for a variety of purposes. Through inquiry, students begin to learn that when they are in the beginning phases of inquiry, they read widely, skimming and scanning for ideas that they are interested in learning more about. They learn that once they have their topic, they read closely and deeply to gather information pertinent to their specific topics. They learn how to take notes on their reading and how to keep track of all their sources as they synthesize the information into an essay, project, or letter at the end of inquiry. They provide relevant quotes to back up their ideas with evidence from the non-fiction texts that they find through their search for information.

In the Common Core, this type of reading and writing begins as early as the fourth grade. Preparation for providing textual evidence to back up ideas begins even earlier than that and increases in complexity as students advance in grades. Students become aware of the need for different kinds of reading at different phases of the inquiry. They build their skills, increasing the complexity with which they can engage in the process and gathering evidence with which to support their claims. The more practice they have in authentic learning environments, the more independent they become in using these skills on their own and applying them to real-world situations.

Writing to Persuade and Explain

The Common Core requires that students write less personal narrative and more to persuade and explain. The Guided Inquiry process develops persuasive and explanatory essay writing. Through inquiry, students become informed on issues they care about. Their writing progresses across the unit of study and builds as they construct understandings of the topic. As students research the multiple sides of an issue, they create their own cases with which to persuade others. Just as professional writers do, students, through Guided Inquiry, become informed and create opinion pieces that are thoughtful and well researched. Guided Inquiry places students in an authentic writing environment in which research and writing go hand in hand in mutually informing ways.

Likewise, students are expected to compose explanatory writing with increasing complexity beginning in third grade. Teachers could routinely assign a book report to meet this task. However, Guided Inquiry Design scaffolds the learning to increase rigor and relevance by allowing students time to dig into research, use multiple sources to gather information, and create their own explanation of what they have discovered. Guided Inquiry is an authentic context that supports a deeper understanding and level of engagement in which to write an expository text. As students are investigating a topic within the third space relevant to the curriculum and to their lives, learning and application to their daily lives increase dramatically.

EMPHASIS ON RESEARCH

The CCSS emphasize the importance of students learning through inquiry and require students to become competent in research in order to be college and career ready. In each grade, the CCSS indicate research through the use of nonfiction texts as a means to construct understanding, gain literacy skill, and compose expository texts. Research and inquiry is infused throughout the literacy standards as a necessary component of the CCSS.

CONCLUSION

Guided Inquiry helps educators pull all the pieces together, integrate all five kinds of learning, and collaborate to accomplish rigorous instruction. Guided Inquiry Design supports teachers in designing inquiry units and supports students in learning through inquiry. The structures embedded within Guided Inquiry Design provide an authentic context for students to learn. Using the language in the standards, our students will have the "wide, deep and thoughtful engagement" (CCSS 2010, 3) necessary to broaden their worldviews, participate thoughtfully in civic engagement, and prepare for their lives when they accomplish the CCSS through Guided Inquiry.

REFERENCES

Baltimore Country Schools Research Symposium. http://www.bcps.org/news/articles/article3250.html. Accessed May 16, 2013.

Common Core State Standards Initiative. (2010). *Common Core State Standards*. Retrieved from http://www.corestandards.org/ on July 29, 2011.

Gutierrez, K., B. Rymes, and J. Larson. (1995). "Script, Counterscript and Underlife in the Classroom: James Brown versus Brown v. the Board of Education." *Harvard Educational Review* 65 (3): 445–471.

Kuhlthau, C. C. (1985). *Teaching the Research Process*. New York: The Center for Applied Research in Education.

Kuhlthau, C. C. (2004). *Seeking Meaning: A Process Approach to Library and Information Services*. 2nd ed. Westport, CT: Libraries Unlimited.

Kuhlthau C. C., and L. K. Maniotes. (2010). "Building Guided Inquiry Teams for 21st Century Learners." *School Library Monthly* 26 (5): 18–21.

Kuhlthau, C. C., L. Maniotes, and A. Caspari. (2007). *Guided Inquiry: Learning in the 21st Century*. Westport, CT: Libraries Unlimited.

Kuhlthau, C. C., L. Maniotes, and A. Caspari. (2012). *Guided Inquiry Design: A Framework for Inquiry in Your School*. Westport, CT: Libraries Unlimited.

Maniotes, L. K. (2005). "The Transformative Power of Literary Third Space." PhD diss., School of Education, University of Colorado, Boulder.

Maniotes, L. K. (2010). "Teaching in the Zone: Formative Assessments for Critical Thinking." *Library Media Connections* 29 (1): 36–39.

Vygotsky, L. E. (1978). *Mind in Society: The Development of Higher Psychological Processes*. Edited and translated by M. Cole, V. John-Steiner, S. Scribner, and E. Soubermen. Cambridge, MA: Harvard University Press. (Originally published 1934).

Wiggins, G., and J. McTighe. (1998). *Understanding by Design*. Alexandria, VA: Association for Supervision and Curriculum Development.

6

Engaging Students Through Project-Based Learning

Violet H. Harada, Carolyn Kirio,
Sandy Yamamoto, and Elodie Arellano

Project-based learning (PBL) focuses on the process of learning rather than simply the content that has been learned. It requires a major mind shift, from mastery of factual information and text-based exercises to projects that stress higher-order thinking and performance-based, authentic assessments. For this reason, PBL moves away from isolated, teacher-directed lessons to learning that is student centered and integrated with real-world issues and practices (Bell 2010).

Why embrace PBL? The Buck Institute for Education (2013) cites the following as critical benefits of implementing PBL:

- It merges thinking and knowledge by helping students master both the content and the process.
- It acknowledges and meets the needs of learners with a range of learning styles and needs.
- It emphasizes real-world skills, including problem solving, communication, and self-management.
- It integrates disciplines by focusing on themes, issues, and deeper investigation of topics.
- It capitalizes on concerns and skills valued in the community.

In PBL, students actively engage in project planning, collaborative problem solving, and disciplined thinking. They construct knowledge that combines facts with the analysis, synthesis, and evaluation of relevant information.

In the process, students demonstrate mastery of current standards, including the *Standards for the 21st-Century Learner* (American Association of School Librarians 2007) and the Common Core State Standards (CCSS; Common Core State Standards Initiative 2012). In short, students apply understanding and practices that are critical to succeed in today's changing world (Costa and Kallick 2010).

MAJOR FEATURES OF PBL

PBL is an approach to teaching and learning that brings curriculum in line with the way the world really works. It challenges students to wrestle with issues and problems in the community and to work collaboratively in understanding them and moving toward thoughtful solutions (Newell 2003). The attributes discussed below enable PBL (Markham 2011; Larmer and Mergendoller 2010; Harada, Kirio, and Yamamoto 2008).

Learning is applied and authentic.

Learning emerges from the in-depth study of issues, themes, or problems. There are no simple right or wrong answers or quick solutions to these complex situations. The issues or themes are directly related to content standards in the various disciplines and require that students closely read and understand increasingly complex texts (Moreillon, Luhtala, and Russo 2011).

Students are at the center of PBL.

PBL allows students to shape the learning experience in ways not always possible in traditional school environments. They develop a sense of ownership and responsibility by identifying critical questions to investigate that are personally relevant to them. They work with their instructors to agree on goals, decide on critical tasks and appropriate resources, and create workable timelines for accomplishing the work. These dispositions and responsibilities are highlighted in the *Standards for the 21st-Century Learner* (American Association of School Librarians 2007) and the CCSS (Common Core State Standards Initiative 2012).

PBL demands academic rigor.

PBL challenges students to move from *memorized* learning to *memorable* learning (Kist 2013; Marzano 2003). It leads to the acquisition of knowledge in many disciplines and challenges students to use modes of inquiry that are central to the disciplines (e.g., scientific inquiry, historical investigation). The process requires students to apply higher-order thinking skills that are crucial aspects of the CCSS, such as

- asking and refining questions,
- debating ideas,
- making predictions,

- designing plans and/or experiments,
- collecting and analyzing data,
- drawing conclusions based on evidence,
- communicating ideas and findings in creative ways, and
- asking new questions.

Learning is facilitated.

Instructors do not relinquish control of the learning situation; instead, they share it with the students. While they still directly teach new and difficult skills, they spend more time guiding students and providing support as the learners experience difficulties.

Learning is collaboratively constructed.

An important aspect of PBL is collaborating with peers. Students partner with colleagues in face-to-face and virtual situations to exchange ideas and points of view. They engage in field-based investigations in which they share various research methods and resources. They form teams that design and execute projects together.

Adults and students are colearners.

Adults and students view themselves as part of a learning community in which everyone contributes to the development of fresh perspectives on content knowledge and everyone experiments with new techniques, strategies, and technologies. PBL encourages dialogue with adults, not just in school but also in the larger community. The students discuss their progress and products with adults outside the school as well as with their instructors. Some actually work side by side with adults in the community through internships and community service activities. Community volunteers, who serve on judging panels, also value the knowledge they gain by evaluating final products and performances.

Self-reflection is ongoing.

Self-reflection is essential for both student and instructor (Harada and Yoshina 2010). PBL requires both formative and summative assessments, in which students and instructors use a range of methods to reflect on works in progress. Key questions they must ask themselves include the following: What is my goal? How well am I achieving this goal? What is working well? What problems am I having? How might I deal with these problems? What are possible solutions? By thoughtfully reflecting on these questions, students grow in their ability to regulate and improve their performance.

READINESS FOR PBL

School librarians may be eager to embrace PBL. Before moving forward, however, it is important to consider the following questions relating to students and the school community as well as one's personal readiness for PBL (Harada, Kirio, and Yamamoto 2008).

Are the students ready?

Students can help to make decisions throughout the PBL process, from the creation of the overarching questions that frame the project to the final product. Realistically speaking, however, the degree of student involvement will depend on students' experience and proficiency in such areas as problem solving, communication, and self-management. Critical questions that PBL teams must ask include the following:

- What cognitive skills do students demonstrate?
- What reflective skills do they practice?
- What background knowledge do they possess?
- What skills in collaborative teamwork do they demonstrate?
- What degree of independence and self-choice do they practice?

Are the teachers and administrators ready?

The practices already embedded in the school community determine whether the school is ready to embrace PBL. Questions that require honest responses include the following:

- Are classroom teaching and the curriculum focused on the testing?
- Do teachers work collaboratively by grades or departments?
- Are they familiar and comfortable with the current standards (i.e., CCSS)?
- Do administrators provide release time for team planning?
- Do administrators support librarian engagement in team planning with teachers?
- Is the school day structured so that students have flexible blocks to work on projects?

Are you ready?

As the school librarian, you must also examine your own expertise and skills. Consider the following questions:

- Are you familiar with the school's curriculum priorities?
- What instructional partnerships have you developed with teachers?
- Are you able to integrate current standards (i.e., CCSS and AASL *Standards for the 21st-Century Learner*) in your instruction?
- Do you possess a repertoire of teaching strategies for a diverse range of students?
- Are you able to contribute a range of resources in many formats for use in PBL?
- Are you able to adapt your teaching to the various planning and working styles of your faculty?

PLANNING FOR PBL

Effective planning for PBL starts with an idea of what the students must be able to do *at the end of the learning experience*. Wiggins and McTighe (1998) popularized the term "backward design" to describe this concept in curriculum planning. This notion of planning with the end in mind is crucial for PBL. Start with the project concept; that is, consider the dispositions you want students to develop and the concepts and understanding students will need to master. A possible sequence in planning might include the following (Harada, Kirio, and Yamamoto 2008):

- Articulate key student outcomes and learning standards to be addressed.
- Brainstorm project ideas and select a project that targets the outcomes and standards desired.
- Identify prerequisite skills and knowledge students must already possess to work effectively in this project.
- Agree on the essential or overarching question for the project.
- Determine criteria to assess the final project/performance.
- Develop criteria to assess progress at key checkpoints in the process.
- Create tools to perform the assessment.
- Outline the process/procedure: include a project timeline and identify where students focus on different standards as they move through the project.
- Collaborate on the instructional team's roles and responsibilities in the project.

In this process, it is important to make expectations and criteria for achieving the goals as explicit as possible (Harada and Yoshina 2010). Ask yourself: Are the guidelines clear for students? Do students know how their work will be assessed? Better still, will students be involved in the establishment of the criteria for assessment (Louis and Harada 2012)? Not only must teachers and students clearly understand what is expected and how learning will be assessed, but these expectations should also be communicated to parents so that they will support the relevance of the projects and assist as appropriate.

It is critical to establish milestones in PBL. Students can lose interest and become mired in projects that extend over a lengthy period of time. By grouping the assignments and tasks, instructors make the project more manageable for students. The students also experience a sense of progress and achievement if they receive feedback and encouragement at checkpoints in the process.

TIPS FOR GETTING STARTED

Teams that have worked on projects offer the following practical advice based on their own successes and challenges (Harada, Kirio, and Yamamoto 2008).

Start planning early.

The earlier the team starts, the greater their possibility for success. Dialogue and negotiation are necessary for all team members to understand and accept their roles. The sequence and flow of the learning experience should also be mapped. More careful planning up front yields orderly administration of the project and a process that is more clearly understood by all partners.

Things will take longer than you anticipate.

Students must gather and interpret the data to create projects that demonstrate their understanding. This requires not only hands-on sessions but also opportunities for conferencing with the instructors. A reasonable length of time is also needed for students to prepare quality projects and presentations.

Acknowledge that the process will be nonlinear and spiraling.

At many points within PBL, students may need to backtrack and reexamine concepts and information to generate deeper thinking. In turn, instructors go back and forth as they clarify or elaborate on previous work. The learning spirals as students continually reflect and experiment to gain proficiency in certain areas and move on to more rigorous challenges.

The instructor must be both the sage on the stage and a guide on the side.

There is a continual balancing act between teacher direction and student independence. At times, instructors must do more direct teaching and modeling, because the concepts or tasks are new and difficult for the students. At other points in the process, however, instructors may be pleasantly surprised to discover that students can initiate suggestions for their work and demonstrate their independence.

What to cut or minimize remains a challenge.

There is also tension between breadth and depth in the program. Giving up content for the sake of in-depth knowledge is not easy when teachers are faced with curriculum guidelines that mandate specific content be covered within the year. There are no best solutions to this challenge; PBL recognizes that teams must carefully examine "what's important to learn" in making decisions. With states adopting the CCSS, there has been a push to focus more deeply on fewer topics or themes. This emphasis on rigor fits well with the inquiry approach embedded in PBL.

Assessment must be a continuous activity.

Because of the length of projects and the diversity of learners, there must be checkpoints to assess student performance. The data collected will also determine the modifications needed to adjust the learning pace and to facilitate students' progress. For teachers, who are accustomed to traditional modes of assessment (i.e., quizzes and tests), the development of alternate assessment strategies that are performance based will be a new learning experience (Harada and Yoshina 2010). This presents a great opportunity for librarians to examine the bountiful literature on authentic assessment with their faculties and to participate in the workshops and webinars available through various state and national professional organizations.

Motivating students will remain a challenge.

Students must select themes and issues to investigate that they find personally relevant. The project itself must be one that is intrinsically rewarding, because much of the work depends on their ability to function independently. Instructors and peers must provide frequent feedback and encouragement. Everyone must celebrate small successes that provide incentives to continue the work.

Allow time to learn new technical skills or technologies.

If students are not familiar with the technologies they plan to use, they need time and assistance to master the necessary skills. Because the use of technology is tremendously appealing to students, they are often willing to invest extra time outside of the classroom to perfect their skills. Depending on the skills required, this is an area in which students of different ages can teach their peers to effectively use a range of tech tools and applications.

PBL IN ACTION

PBL is an exciting approach that naturally builds upon an inquiry frame for learning. It challenges students to be inquisitive and to ask questions that result in personal meaning making, not just regurgitating a collection of found facts. It encourages them to solve problems based on experimentation and reflection. Following are snapshots of PBL at the elementary, middle, and high school levels.

Eating Healthier: Elementary Project

Fifth-grade students are concerned about obesity and healthy eating habits. They want to know if all popular snack foods are bad for them and how to compare the nutritional value of various snacks. They ask the following questions: What snacks do we like to eat? What's in our snacks? How healthy are the snacks? What snacks might be healthier?

The teacher and school librarian collaborate on this project focusing on nutrition and healthy eating. Students conduct a survey among their peers to identify the most popular snacks, and they get tips for healthy eating by interviewing the cafeteria manager and the school dietitian. The school librarian teaches students how to organize and synthesize the information they collect. Students prepare e-brochures and digital posters to communicate messages about the importance of healthier eating habits for a community wellness fair. (A description of this project is available in the AASL Lesson Database at http://aasl.jesandco.org/content/what-makes-snack-healthy.)

Examples of the CCSS that the project addresses include the following:

- Reading informational. Integration of knowledge and ideas. 5.RI.7 Draw on information from multiple print or digital sources, demonstrating the ability to locate an answer to a question quickly or to solve a problem efficiently.
- Writing. Research to build and present knowledge. 5.W.7 Conduct short research projects that use several sources to build knowledge through investigation of different aspects of a topic.

Building Greener Communities: Middle School Project

Eighth-grade students receive an invitation to participate in a district fair focusing on the sustainable future of the community. This piques their curiosity about the issue of sustainability. With guided assistance from their teacher and the school librarian, students explore various areas of community life and the importance of using existing resources in effective and efficient ways. In their investigations, they address the following essential questions: What is involved in greening a community? How green is our community at this time? How can we build a greener community? Students explore a range of strategies to maintain a healthy and eco-friendly environment. As teams, they focus on different aspects of community life and how to use existing resources more efficiently. They collect and evaluate information from diverse and timely primary and secondary sources and devise methods to communicate their findings. Researched topics include saving energy in our homes, reducing and recycling waste in our community, growing and eating locally produced foods, adopting transportation that is less dependent on fossil fuel, and creating a greener school. The teacher monitors the daily progress of the teams, while the school librarian helps students in locating and using relevant resources. Students ultimately produce infographic displays that integrate visuals, graphs, and text. (A description of this project is available in the AASL Lesson Database at http://aasl.jesandco.org/content/building-greener-community.)

Examples of the CCSS that the project addresses include the following:

- Reading science and technical. Integration of knowledge and ideas. 6-8.RST.7 Integrate quantitative or technical information expressed in words in a text with a version of that information expressed visually (e.g., in a flow-chart, diagram, model, graph, or table).
- Writing history. Production and distribution of writing. 6-8.WHST.6 Use technology, including the Internet, to produce and publish writing and present the relationships between information and ideas clearly and efficiently.

Transforming Society Through Social Action: High School Project

How can an individual make an impact in his or her community? Students in tenth grade seek to improve their community by actively participating in local projects that focus on current social issues. They ask: What issues reflect critical needs or problems in my community? How do they affect people and the environment? What has been done in the past? How can I address these needs? How will serving others demonstrate my civic responsibility?

Students explore diverse social issues impacting the local community before they individually select an issue to which they feel a personal connection. The school librarian helps students develop more effective search techniques and best strategies to organize, evaluate, and synthesize found information. The instructional team works with students to build their skills in critical thinking and assists them in finding suitable service projects as well as volunteer organizations to help. Students reflect on their progress through journals and periodic exit passes. They showcase their projects at a social issues fair, with community members judging the final presentations.

Examples of the CCSS that the project addresses include the following:

- Writing. Production and distribution of writing. 9-10.W.4 Produce clear and coherent writing in which the development, organization, and style are appropriate to task, purpose, and audience.
- Writing. Research to build and present knowledge. 9-10.W.8 Gather relevant information from multiple authoritative print and digital sources, using advanced searches effectively; assess the usefulness of each source in answering the research question; integrate information into the text selectively to maintain the flow of ideas, avoiding plagiarism and following a standard format for citation.

SUMMARY

PBL is an approach to learning that actively engages students in deeper levels of comprehension and interpretation about what and how they study (Levin and Schrum 2013). It does not polarize process and content, but views them as major elements in a holistic learning experience (Newell 2003). School librarians fully agree with this stance. As teaching partners, they strongly advocate for incorporating information skills and classroom content. PBL provides an ideal platform for learning that focuses on creative solutions to real-world problems and authentic challenges.

REFERENCES

American Association of School Librarians. (2007). *Standards for the 21st-Century Learner.* Retrieved from http://www.ala.org/aasl/standards on March 29, 2013.

Bell, Stephanie. (2010). "Project Based Learning for the 21st Century: Skills for the Future." *Clearing House* 83 (2) (January): 39–43.

Buck Institute for Education. (2013). *Project Based Learning for the 21st Century.* Retrieved from http://www.bie.org/tools/ on March 28, 2013.

Common Core State Standards Initiative. (2012). *Common Core State Standards.* Retrieved from http://www.corestandards.org/ on March 29, 2013.

Costa, Arthur L., and Bena Kallick. (2010). "It Takes Some Getting Used To: Rethinking Curriculum for the 21st Century." In *Curriculum 21: Essential Education for a Changing World*, edited by Heidi Hayes Jacobs, 210–226. Alexandria, VA: Association for Supervision and Curriculum Development.

Harada, Violet H., Carolyn K. Kirio, and Sandy H. Yamamoto. (2008). *Collaborating for Project-Based Learning in Grades 9–12.* Columbus, OH: Linworth Publishing, Inc.

Harada, Violet H., and Joan M. Yoshina. (2010). *Assessing for Learning: Librarians and Teachers as Partners.* 2nd ed. Santa Barbara, CA: Libraries Unlimited.

Kist, William. (2013). "New Literacies and the Common Core." *Educational Leadership* 70 (6) (March): 38–43.

Larmer, John, and John R. Mergendoller. (2010). "7 Essentials for Project Based Learning." *Educational Leadership* 68 (1) (September): 34–37.

Levin, Barbara B., and Lynne Schrum. (2013). "Technology-Rich Schools Up Close." *Educational Leadership* 70 (6) (March): 51–55.

Louis, Patricia, and Violet H. Harada. (2012). "Did Students Get It? Self-Assessment as Key to Learning." *School Library Monthly* 29 (3) (December): 13–16.

Markham, Thom. (2011). "Project Based Learning." *Teacher Librarian* 39 (2) (December): 38–42.

Marzano, Robert. (2003). *What Works in Schools: Translating Research into Action.* Alexandria, VA: Association for Supervision and Curriculum Development.

Moreillon, Judi, Michelle Luhtala, and Christina T. Russo. (2011). "Learning that Sticks: Engaged Educators + Engaged Learners." *School Library Monthly* 28 (1) (September/October): 17–20.

Newell, Ronald J. (2003). *Passion for Learning: How Project-Based Learning Meets the Needs of 21st Century Students.* Lanham, MD: Scarecrow Press.

Wiggins, Grant, and Jay McTighe. (1998). *Understanding by Design.* Alexandria, VA: Association for Supervision and Curriculum Development.

7

Inquiry in the Digital Age

Barbara Stripling

A group of friends is gathered around the table at a restaurant in Sioux Falls, South Dakota, and they start talking about the local Walk to Cure Diabetes. They know that diabetes is a serious health problem, partly because so many cases are undiagnosed until real damage has been done. But what are the symptoms that are so easily missed? Immediately, Taylor pulls out her cell phone, searches, and finds the Mayo Clinic site on diabetes symptoms. The conversation continues, but with solid information, not just conjecture.

We live in a society that is surrounded, permeated, and inundated with information. Digital tools have opened the door to 24/7, fingertip access to finding, using, and creating information. But is collecting information all there is to learning? These friends actually went beyond information gathering; they were engaged in authentic inquiry, facilitated by their digital tools. They had some background knowledge about diabetes, which led them to ask a critical question. They were able to investigate right then, and Taylor knew enough about inquiry to seek an authoritative source for the answers. Then the group followed up by talking about the new information and drawing conclusions together.

The mission of librarians is to empower all the Taylors whom we serve to develop the skills and attitudes to make inquiry a natural part of daily life, ensuring that they do not drown in the overabundance of information and can turn information into learning. Taylor and her friends were certainly in line with the 47 percent of American adults who use a mobile device to get local news and information (Pew Internet 2011). They were, however, vastly different from most of those adults, because they sought substantive information to answer a question, rather than simply accessing the weather (42 percent), local restaurants/businesses (37 percent), and general local news (30 percent) (Pew Internet 2011).

Our unique contribution to the information age we make as school librarians is to teach and guide our students to look beyond the "what," the information itself, to the "so what." Why do they need information? What are they planning to do with it? What questions are driving their inquiry? What problems are they trying to solve? What do they want to discover? How can we, then, enable them to accomplish their goals?

To understand the "so what," we need to understand the nature and role of inquiry, especially in today's diffused and disorganized information environment. Inquiry is certainly not a new concept, but research about learning has led to a growing interest in inquiry as a door to deep and active learning. The new science of learning focuses on students' understanding and applying ideas to new contexts rather than simply knowing, doing rather than receiving (active instead of passive learning), and constructing new understandings rather than memorizing facts (Bransford et al. 2000). The roots of this type of learning, called *constructivism*, extend back to John Dewey, who theorized that learning is a combination of acting and reflecting on the thoughts, actions, and feelings. Dewey's philosophy was that meaningful learning emerges from a series of coherent experiences that enable learners to engage actively, reflect, and organize ideas to derive their own meaning (Dewey 1938).

Although the foundation of constructivism can be traced back to Dewey, it has emerged as a prominent educational theory during the last twenty to thirty years. Although there are numerous and varied interpretations, its four main characteristics transform thinking about teaching and learning in the library: 1) learners are responsible for *constructing their own meaning*; 2) learners build new *understanding on their prior knowledge*; 3) learning is *social* and formed through *social interaction*; and 4) the most meaningful learning emerges from *authentic tasks* (Applefield, Huber, and Moallem 2000/2001; Bruning, Schraw, and Ronning 1995; Pressley, Harris, and Marks 1992).

INQUIRY-BASED LEARNING

Inquiry captures those characteristics. It is a more authentic, active, and thoughtful approach to learning than traditional teacher-controlled classrooms. The ability to solve problems and use information literacy skills to pursue inquiry-based learning has increasingly been identified as critical in the twenty-first century, not just by educators, but also by business leaders and professionals in every content area.

Based on research about constructivist learning and inquiry, I developed a six-phase model for the inquiry cycle (Stripling 2003), known in the professional literature as the Stripling Model of Inquiry (see figure 7.1). The

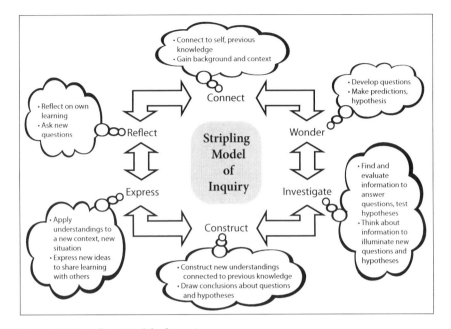

Figure 7.1. Stripling Model of Inquiry

Source: Barbara Stripling, "Teaching Students to Think in the Digital Environment: Digital Literacy and Digital Inquiry," *School Library Monthly* 26, no. 8 (April 2010): 17.

model incorporates the thinking skills of inquiry in a six-phase, recursive process that encompasses a full definition of inquiry.

The Stripling Model of Inquiry is a frame for learning that involves *connecting* to personal interests and a desire to know, asking *questions* that probe beyond simple fact gathering, *investigating* answers from multiple perspectives, *constructing* new understandings and conclusions, *expressing* the new ideas through a variety of formats, and *reflecting* on both the process and product of learning. Inquiry is recursive and cyclical, with learners going back and forth between the phases to ask new questions and pursue new avenues of investigation as they arise. True inquiry should result in new understandings for learners, but not final answers, because learners should naturally discover intriguing areas to pursue in future investigations.

Inquiry is a good model for research in the library, but if school librarians are going to collaborate with classroom teachers to design and teach inquiry-based learning units, then the same model must fit naturally with different discipline areas. Science has a solid connection to inquiry. The scientific process is very much aligned to the Stripling model: defining the problem, generating a hypothesis, designing an experiment, observing and collecting data, analyzing and interpreting the data, drawing conclusions, and reporting results.

The history/social studies curriculum is another good fit for an inquiry model because history is an inquiry- and interpretation-based discipline. Surprisingly, though, a model of inquiry has not been proposed for the history field by educators, historians, or researchers. In the history education literature, what has been investigated and described is an array of discipline-specific skills and habits of mind, not an overall process of inquiry. Students may be expected to *do* historical inquiry, but often not to learn the underlying process behind it.

Why does this matter for school librarians? First, if classroom teachers do not consider the inquiry process, their assignments may be structured to guarantee that students simply grab information, any information, to complete them. Students may come into the library with an assigned topic, but they do not have any context or background to be able to ask questions or develop a search strategy. Students could spend hours clicking on Web sites, finding nothing of value, because they do not know to start with defining what they really want to know. If we, as librarians, are mindful of the inquiry process, we can help teachers effectively transform instructional design and delivery to enable students to be successful at every phase of their inquiry investigations.

Of course, the inquiry experience is much more complex than simply following a process. It involves both skills and attitudes; its special characteristics set it apart from rote learning, direct instruction, or even traditional research. Let's look at those characteristics. Inquiry learning is all of the following:

- *Intellectually active*—Students are making conscious and deliberative decisions and engaging with ideas and text using a critical eye. ["Mrs. Stripling, did you know that that Web site has a mistake? It has the totally wrong date for the invention I'm researching."]
- *Question-based*—Good questions lead to explorations of the unknown, in which the answers cannot be copied from one source. [Finally, Jerry, known as the "what-if" student because he constantly interrupts class time to ask hypothetical questions, has a chance to follow his curiosity to wherever it leads.]
- *Personalized*—Inquiry depends on an individual's pursuing ideas that connect to his or her own interests or prior knowledge. [The little first graders clustered around the insect books, still out of breath from hurrying into the library from the playground. They had to find out: What are those white things the ants are pulling across the sidewalk?]
- *Authentic*—The result of an inquiry exploration should be the application of the learning to a new situation or a connection to the real world. [Derek, the sophomore who never connected with anything he was supposed to be learning at school, cried out with delightful surprise when he was researching the Renaissance, "Oh, so that's where the Teenage Mutant Ninja Turtles got their names!"]

- *Open-ended*—The answers or solutions are discovered and formed by the inquirer during his or her investigation. It is not a process of the inquirer's looking for the one right answer that the teacher already knows. ["You mean I'm supposed to draw my own conclusions? But what if I'm wrong?"]
- *Divergent and convergent*—Inquiry investigations push against the accepted frames by asking Why? What else? Why not? They also bring together disparate points of view to lead to new ideas and understandings. ["I never thought I would understand the points of view of both the slaves and the slave owners."]
- *Transformative*—During inquiry, mental models are brought to the surface, examined, compared to new evidence, and rejected or revised based on new understandings. ["I always thought the Civil War was just about slavery, but now I see so many other factors that played a part in the war."]

IMPLICATIONS OF THE COMMON CORE FOR INQUIRY-BASED LEARNING

The vision of the Common Core State Standards (CCSS) is to ensure that every student develops the knowledge and skills to succeed in college and career. Inquiry-based learning is integral to the Common Core, not only in the research strand of the writing standards, but also in the critical thinking, literacy, inquiry, and technology skills that form the basis of the standards.

A close examination of the Common Core reveals that the type of learning envisioned is completely aligned with the characteristics of inquiry-based learning; in fact, the Common Core opens the door for librarians to lead school-wide implementation of inquiry. The learning outlined in the Common Core is constructivist; students are expected to read text with deep comprehension, make inferences, form opinions and conclusions based on evidence, develop a line of argument, and produce and present their own understandings through multiple formats. Both the Common Core and inquiry are predicated on deep-level thinking, depth of content knowledge rather than breadth, the application of learning strategies and skills across the disciplines, and the continuing development of skills across the grades.

The difficulty that many educators are finding as they try to implement the Common Core into everyday teaching practice is that the CCSS are extremely complex and dense. Each standard and each grade-level indicator actually contains a number of skills that must be taught before the student develops mastery of the standard. That process of breaking the CCSS apart into their component skills is what some school library systems have done in aligning the inquiry skills that school librarians teach with the Common Core. One good example of that alignment can be found in New York's Empire State Information Fluency Continuum (http://schools.nyc.gov/Academics/LibraryServices/StandardsandCurriculum/default.htm).

IMPLICATIONS OF THE DIGITAL ENVIRONMENT FOR INQUIRY-BASED LEARNING

In addition to Common Core alignment, an important consideration in integrating inquiry-based learning throughout the curriculum is the effect of the digital environment, because that is increasingly where our students live in their personal time. If they are to integrate inquiry successfully into their personal and academic lives, we must identify the new skills, thinking strategies, dispositions, resources, and learning environments that frame inquiry in the digital information world. Librarians should particularly pay attention to the impact on inquiry of three aspects of the digital environment: the nature of digital resources, access, and interactivity.

The Nature of Digital Resources and Impact on Inquiry

Electronic resources are assuming an ever more important role in the information world. eBooks, digitized collections, digital libraries, and open-source and proprietary databases have all become increasingly important as resources that our students need for their investigations. Primary sources are becoming increasingly available. Not only are organizations, cultural institutions, and libraries digitizing their long-held collections of primary-source documents, but increasingly libraries are digitizing and curating local cultural artifacts.

Digital resources, including those on the World Wide Web, have the potential to lend authenticity to inquiry. The information is created and published by individuals and organizations to communicate directly with the reader. Real voices come through; real-world and current issues surface.

But with that authenticity come bias and questions of credibility. Evaluating the authority and validity of digital information now must be done by the inquirer, and sometimes finding the elusive "who" behind a Web site is a little like playing "Where's Waldo?"

Digital resources also offer more global and multifaceted perspectives. That's great for robust inquiry. The challenges for conducting credible inquiry in that diverse information environment are almost frightening, however. First, most of us are encapsulated in what has been called "filter bubbles," because of both our own searching strategies and the hidden algorithms used by search engines (disguised as "personalizing" to your location and priorities). When we relied on print resources in the library, we could almost guarantee that our patrons would at least see both sides of an issue, because the books were right next to each other on the shelf. The lateral and linked organization of the Web leads to multiple sites with the same perspective, rather than opposing views. Most searchers do not consciously seek the other side or multiple perspectives once they have discovered a Web site that confirms what they believe. They may create their own filter bubble through their searching, linking, and friending processes.

Access to Digital Resources and Impact on Inquiry

The most troubling aspect of the digital information environment in terms of the impact on inquiry is the increasing digital divide. Many students have access to a mobile technology, usually a cell phone. Yet those same students and many others may have no computer with Internet access at home and are therefore at a real disadvantage in terms of the depth and quality of inquiry that they can conduct.

A second-level digital divide is also emerging: the lack of skills to navigate, select, evaluate, interpret, and draw conclusions from the information glut. One educator summed up the problem thus: "Kids are tech savvy, but not information savvy."

Inquiry is greatly impacted by the lack of continuity and coherence in the Web environment. All information on the Web is presented with equal importance, and learners may encounter it in an order that has nothing to do with time (historical vs. current), place (Web sites from any area of the world appear on search engine results), or even synchrony with their central idea (especially if there is ambiguity in search terms). Librarians have found that this lack of coherence can be ameliorated by helping patrons use the framework of inquiry to structure the investigation and maintain focus on a main idea. Without inquiry skills, many learners lose their focus, gather superfluous or inaccurate information, or just give up and copy whatever information they find.

The multimodal nature of digital resources provides opportunities for patrons with different learning preferences and strengths, and even different languages, to engage in inquiry. What we, as librarians, cannot forget, however, are the additional challenges that these formats present. We must identify and understand the new literacies required for interpreting and evaluating digital, visual, media, photographic, and auditory information. The concept of transliteracy, or "the ability to read, write, and interact across a range of platforms" (www.transliteracy.com), must start to inform our instructional practice.

Interactivity and the Impact on Inquiry

The interactive Web 2.0 aspect of the digital world poses both opportunities and challenges to learners, librarians, and teachers, because it enables participation, collaboration, and sharing. Individuals can now produce and share their own work with the world. They can engage in online conversations and social learning, and we know from research that that deepens learning. The danger is that the participatory environment has led to a glut of information produced by authors with no authoritative knowledge and limited perspectives. Learners are challenged to hone their own evaluation skills to find high-quality digital information among the clutter. Continual interaction with too much information has led to a deterioration of thoughtfulness, "chipping away our capacity for concentration and contemplation" (Carr 2008).

TEACHING THE SKILLS NEEDED
FOR INQUIRY-BASED LEARNING

School librarians are at the epicenter of an amazing confluence of inquiry-based teaching and learning, implementation of the CCSS, and the opportunities and challenges of the digital environment. School librarians must step up to an instructional leadership role and build a path to success for every student by teaching critical inquiry skills as a part of collaborative instructional units, assessing students' ability to perform the skills that are taught, guiding and mentoring students as they pursue their investigations, and building a culture of inquiry that permeates the entire school.

What Skills We Should Teach

The question that resonates with our focus on inquiry, what should we teach? The educational context for our teaching is provided by CCSS as well as the resources, access, and interactivity of the digital world; the heart of our teaching is found in the skills required for each phase of the inquiry process.

The most often ignored aspect of teaching inquiry skills is actually teaching students to perform the steps of the skill, rather than just telling students to perform the skill. Too often, students are told to create a good inquiry question, make an inference, find the main idea, or identify point of view without being shown the steps to do that thinking. Students need to be taught the steps of any new skill explicitly, be taken through modeling and examples during guided practice, and then be given opportunities to practice the skill on their own. Although the compact nature of the Common Core, with so many skills embedded in each standard, would seem to indicate that several skills should be taught simultaneously, librarians will have the greatest impact on students' development of the skills by teaching one skill per lesson and scaffolding any missing skills that are necessary.

Connect

At the beginning of an inquiry experience, the **Connect** phase, students identify what they already know about the subject and read/explore to gain background knowledge and find intriguing ideas to pursue. When students express their *prior knowledge*, they are actually describing their existing mental model. Sometimes they have a powerful, and perhaps misinformed, mental model that closes them off to new, and especially to conflicting, information. Research has shown that students will not change faulty mental models (even after gaining more accurate information) unless they explicitly describe their existing ideas first. Librarians can help learners identify their mental models through strategic questioning.

Background information, or *contextualization*, used to be a mainstay for the beginning of all research projects, but it may be harder to sell to teachers who have heard about the horrors of Wikipedia and forbid its use or who see no benefit to students' starting with a general encyclopedia (it takes too much time for students to mess around; they just need to start researching their topic). Contextualized thinking is essential for inquiry, especially in the digital environment, where information on Web sites tends to be very specific and presented without any background or context. Students should start by reading (or viewing) background information to gather key concepts; main ideas; contrasting perspectives; controversies; and key vocabulary, persons, and dates. They should emerge from the Connect phase with interesting ideas about the inquiry topic that they would like to pursue.

Learners often have difficulty in *maintaining a focus in their inquiry*, particularly when researching online, because they get distracted by the small bits of specific information and interesting, but unrelated, sidetracks/links on Web sites. Teaching students to identify *central themes and big ideas* at the Connect phase of their inquiry helps them maintain focus later as they pursue their investigations.

Wonder

Questioning is the driving force behind inquiry. Researchers generally start with low-level, who-what-when-where questions; librarians can teach students to develop *higher-level inquiry questions* that are appropriate for the inquiry assignment, can actually be answered, and lead to expressing new understanding in the assigned assessment product (e.g., a student would develop different questions for a debate than for an ad campaign). Students must be taught how to develop questions that will lead them to pursue their topic in depth and to seek conflicting information or multiple perspectives. The challenge of questioning in the digital environment is that *complexity and alternative viewpoints* are not easily discovered. If learners are asking only descriptive or explanatory questions, then they will not explore the more complex aspects of their topic or even realize that they should pursue different perspectives.

Investigate

Ideally, learners start their investigations by *constructing search strategies*, including the key search terms, their combinations through Boolean or semi-Boolean operators, and an idea of the search engines, databases, or Web sites to be searched in addition to the online catalog. In practice, however, many learners go to Google, enter natural language search terms or whole sentences into the search box, and then compensate for the millions of hits by looking at the first few references. Without specific intervention by teachers or librarians, learners often do not know how to refine their search terms, and they almost never discover the hidden web of valuable sources not in Google, or the purchased databases of selected, high-quality information.

Sourcing, or determining the authority of sources, is absolutely essential, especially in the digital environment. Students may have a difficult time applying the *criteria for evaluating sources* in the self-publishing world of the Internet, because the identity and credentials of the creators may be difficult if not impossible to determine. To many of our students, a blog may appear as credible as an editorial from the *New York Times*, and a Web site with beautiful images may be more convincing than a more authoritative one without a lot of graphics.

Another difficult aspect of the evaluation of sources is determining the perspective that frames the information. Librarians should teach students specific signals and criteria that will help them determine the creator's perspective. In addition, students can be taught to assess perspective by *corroborating*— weighing one source against another. Librarian guidance and instruction may be necessary for students to find credible sources for corroboration.

Equally as important as teaching students to evaluate the sources that they use is teaching them to evaluate the information within the source. Librarians may begin with the *organizational tools* that help researchers locate appropriate information, like the table of contents and index. Students will be fascinated when the librarian asks them to transfer those ideas to a Web site, so that they learn to identify and use navigational tools like tabs, links, and search boxes.

Once students have learned to navigate the information source, they must learn the important inquiry skills of *evaluating the information* they find, including determining accuracy, currency, comprehensiveness, relevance to research questions, main ideas vs. supporting details, point of view, and fact vs. opinion. Critical thinking skills of interpretation and inference must also be taught. Access to information in multiple formats has led to librarians' attention to teaching the skills of *multiple literacies*. The Common Core requires students to do deep reading of complex texts; many of those literacy skills can be taught by the librarian as an integral part of inquiry investigations. Students should learn to question the text, determine the central idea, evaluate claims and evidence, analyze and interpret arguments, and compare and contrast ideas. Students must also learn to adapt many of those literacy skills to understand and interpret information presented visually, orally, graphically, or through the media.

The skills of *ethical participation* during inquiry must also be taught explicitly. Students find it too easy to cut and paste information from digital text and too difficult to track down the original author of Web information.

The result may be unethical behavior such as plagiarism. Learners are increasingly confused by the blurry lines between proprietary information and creative commons information. Mash-ups and remixing present entirely new, enticing opportunities for copyright infringement.

Construct

Construct is the phase at which learners *synthesize large amounts of specific bits of information and ideas* to form their own understandings. To do this type of thinking, learners have to *look for patterns and relationships among ideas*, even though the pieces of information may be from so many separate sources that the patterns do not emerge easily. Students can be taught how to detect patterns in the information they find and then to *draw a conclusion, form an opinion*, and *develop their own ideas* based on their own interpretations. Students can then be taught how to construct their own patterns to express their interpretations and conclusions, such as main idea and details, cause/effect, chronological sequence, or compare/contrast. The Common Core lays out an expectation that students will learn to develop a *line of argument*, which requires sophisticated interpretation and presentation of points, counterpoints, and evidence.

To help students develop the thinking processes of constructing their own ideas and conclusions, librarians can teach them to use *online organization, visualization*, and *collaboration tools*.

Express

Publication and sharing of knowledge are essential components of inquiry. The opportunities for our students to use digital tools to communicate their new ideas are bounded only by their imagination and their access to and ability to use the tools. We know that students are both motivated and engaged by the *authenticity* of these modes of communication and their applicability to their own lives. The *allure of alternative digital forms* (e.g., podcasts, wikis), however, may pressure students to create shallow presentations that focus on the glitz of the medium rather than the substance of the content. Librarians can help students use these tools to express their own ideas effectively.

Reflect

Reflection seems like a lost art in the manic digital world. The real challenge for librarians in building a culture that is supportive of inquiry is maintaining a contemplative environment (Wolf and Barzillai 2009, 33). Our libraries can be what Jaron Lanier calls "the thinking space of civilization" (West 2010). We need to build into our instructional designs opportunities for reflection, so that students regularly think about both the product and process of their inquiry experiences.

ASSESSING INQUIRY SKILLS

When we, as librarians, emphasize the explicit teaching of inquiry skills and integrate inquiry into Common Core–based collaborative units, we cannot forget to assess students' learning of the skills. To determine if students are able to apply the skills, we will want to use formative assessment, so that we can reteach or provide specific guidance to students with difficulties before the problems impact the entire inquiry investigation. An effective way to assess an inquiry skill is a graphic organizer that has been designed to walk students through the steps of the skill and allow them to show their ability to perform each step. For sample graphic-organizer assessments for each grade level aligned with the inquiry process and the Common Core, see those developed by the Office of Library Services in New York City and incorporated into the Empire State Information Fluency Continuum (http://schools.nyc.gov/Academics/LibraryServices/StandardsandCurriculum/default.htm).

BUILDING A CULTURE OF INQUIRY

Ultimately, the role of the school librarian in today's educational environment of the Common Core and digital tools and resources is to build a culture of inquiry. To do so, we must follow the wisdom of Mahatma Gandhi: "You must *be* the change you want to see in the world." The first step in empowering our students and teachers to inquire and in creating an environment in our libraries in which participation, collaboration, communication, and questioning are the norm is for us to embrace inquiry, to start with one teacher, one lesson, one collaborative unit and then build from there. Arlo Guthrie may have captured the essence of building a school-wide culture of inquiry in "Alice's Restaurant," when he sang about the power of individuals banding together around a common goal (Guthrie 1967):

> And three people do it, three, can you imagine, three people walking in singin' a bar of Alice's Restaurant and walking out. They may think it's an organization. And can you, can you imagine fifty people a day, I said fifty people a day walking in singin' a bar of Alice's Restaurant and walking out. And friends they may think it's a movement.

We can make inquiry-based learning in the digital age a movement in our libraries and our schools.

REFERENCES

Applefield, J. M., R. Huber, and M. Moallem. (2000/2001). "Constructivism in Theory and Practice: Toward a Better Understanding." *The High School Journal* 84 (2): 35–53.

Bransford, J. D., A. L. Brown, et al., eds. (2000). *How People Learn: Brain, Mind, Experience and School*. Washington, DC: National Academy Press.

Bruning, R. J., G. J. Schraw, and R. R. Ronning. (1995). *Cognitive Psychology and Instruction*. 2nd ed. Englewood Cliffs, NJ: Prentice Hall.

Carr, N. (2008). "Is Google Making Us Stupid?" *Atlantic Monthly* (July/August). Retrieved from http://www.theatlantic.com/magazine/archive/2008/07/is-google-making-us-stupid/306868/ on September 17, 2013.

Dewey, J. (1938). *Experience and Education*. New York: Simon & Schuster.

Guthrie, Arlo. (1967). "Alice's Restaurant." Retrieved from http://www.arlo.net/resources/lyrics/alices.shtml on September 17, 2013.

New York City School Library System. (2012). *Empire State Information Fluency Continuum*. Retrieved from http://schools.nyc.gov/Academics/LibraryServices/StandardsandCurriculum on September 17, 2013.

Pew Internet. (2011). *How Mobile Devices Are Changing Community Information Environments*. Retrieved from http://pewinternet.org/Reports/2011/Local-mobile-news.aspx on September 17, 2013.

Pressley, M., K. R. Harris, and M. B. Marks. (1992). "But Good Strategy Instructors Are Constructivists!" *Educational Psychology Review* 4: 3–31.

Stripling, B. K. (2003). "Inquiry-based Learning." In *Curriculum Connections Through the Library*, edited by B. K. Stripling and S. Hughes-Hassell, 3–39. Westport, CT: Libraries Unlimited.

West, J. (2010). "Toward a Human-centric Internet: Jessamyn West Interviews Jaron Lanier." *Library Journal* (February 1). Retrieved from http://www.libraryjournal.com/article/CA6716277.html on September 17, 2013.

Wolf, M., and M. Barzillai. (2009). "The Importance of Deep Reading." *Educational Leadership* 66 (6): 32–37.

Part III

Planning for Meaningful Learning

8

Evolution, Not Revolution: The Nudging Toward Inquiry Approach

Kristin Fontichiaro

INTRODUCTION

On a recent trip to Italy's Cinque Terre, I ordered what the translated menu said was shrimp in tomato sauce. When they arrived . . . Mamma Mia! These shrimp were plate-sized, with impenetrable exoskeletons, not to mention antennae, eyes, and . . . claws! There was no Maryland crab mallet, no Kennebunkport lobster-cracking tool. How should I eat these sauce-drenched, far-from-shrimpy "shrimp"? Too embarrassed to ask for help and too hungry not to eat, I picked up the "shrimp" and cracked one with my bare hands. Though my hands dripped with sauce, I unearthed the fresh meat. Messy, but delicious.

Perhaps you are feeling similar helplessness as you approach the Common Core State Standards (CCSS). You are looking at this exotic thing on your plate, wondering where your familiar tools are, worried about looking foolish if you ask for help. Sometimes, the effort of rolling up your sleeves and getting your hands dirty would be more palatable if you had confidence that it would yield meaty results.

Throughout this book, others have discussed how inquiry connects to the CCSS. But how do you actually move in that direction when your classroom colleagues are too busy to reinvent their research projects for students? In that case, focus less on the shrimp and more on eating the elephant: one bite at a time. We created the "Nudging Toward Inquiry" column in *School Library Monthly* to provide strategies for shifting the pedagogical practices of teachers and librarians from "a superficial collection of facts" (AASL 2007, Standard 1.2.1, p. 5) and into robust, multidimensional inquiry.

Today's students, surrounded by abundant, easily accessed information, need skills that supersede search and retrieve. Shifting from "find it, transcribe it, restate it" is essential. But change—particularly in pedagogy, a set of intensely personal beliefs and practices—comes slowly. Our classroom colleagues, wary of the next "transformative" program change and struggling with larger class sizes, increased testing, and unprecedented public scrutiny, may legitimately balk at a suggestion to collaboratively reenvision a research project. The time and required effort may seem insurmountable.

Rather than suggesting a revolution and receiving a polite but firm refusal, consider an evolution. Teachers may be amenable to adjusting an existing unit, and well-chosen tweaks can have a big impact on student-centered inquiry. A "nudging" philosophy does not lessen the importance of inquiry, merely the timeline.

When I was a language arts teacher, I learned from mentors who I knew could scaffold and transform fact collection into engaging projects rich with synthesis and creative thinking. When I became a librarian, however, I struggled with how to transmit this deep approach to teachers. Some research models emphasized the *doing* of research steps over the *thinking* of the research process.

The Stripling (2007) Model of Inquiry gave me clarity and guidance, marrying action steps with best practices from the broader education field about prior knowledge, questioning, and synthesis. Six stages form the model: Connect, Wonder, Investigate, Construct, Express, and Reflect. (As a mnemonic device, the initial letters of each stage spell CWICER or "quicker".) In school-based projects, as in life, researchers move back and forth between these stages as new understandings and questions arise. Because of this model's impact on my practice, I have used it to organize this chapter. As you read, I hope that you will see familiar strategies intermingled with new ones that can nudge your building's practice away from fact finding and toward meaning making.

GETTING STARTED

Identifying Standards and Clarifying Learning Objectives

Good instruction begins with good planning. It's important to identify the CCSS and other learning objectives that you want students to fulfill when doing a research project. At the secondary level, CCSS related to research are quite detailed, referencing credibility, multiple sources, citation, questioning, and more. Consider the following:

W.9-10.8: Gather relevant information from multiple authoritative print and digital sources, using advanced searches effectively; assess the usefulness of each source in answering the research question; integrate information into the text selectively to maintain the flow of ideas, avoiding plagiarism and following a standard format for citation. (CCSSI 2010, 46)

This standard is clear and specific. The team knows that your work together must address each aspect of the standard, either in a single project or spread throughout several smaller projects. You no longer need to negotiate for these elements; the CCSS do that for you.

In contrast, the elementary research standards are surprisingly vague, often referencing the need for a project without delineating its required components, as shown here:

W.3.7: Conduct short research projects that build knowledge about a topic. (CCSSI 2010, 21)

If language is vague, bring the introductory language of the English Language Arts (ELA) standards into the discussion. This language may reveal more about the *intent* of research that underpins a standard:

[Students] need the ability to gather, comprehend, evaluate, synthesize, and report on information and ideas, to conduct original research in order to answer questions or solve problems, and to analyze and create a high volume and extensive range of print and nonprint texts in media forms old and new. The need to conduct research and to produce and consume media is embedded into every aspect of today's curriculum. (CCSSI 2010, 4)

Now your planning team has a finish line in mind and can work backward to envision the activities and scaffolds students will need to reach success. It is critical to revisit these identified outcomes throughout the planning process; our natural enthusiasm can cause us to unintentionally veer away from our goals. Using CCSS as your north star keeps your planning time efficient and productive.

Bundling Standards

One challenge of CCSS and inquiry is the standards' strong focus on writing informational text. It's easy to assume that a research worksheet or "bird unit" (Loertscher, Koechlin, and Zwaan 2005), in which students restate, retell, or regurgitate, is sufficient. When a writing standard is viewed independent of the big picture, an educator might reach this conclusion. However, when we look again at the ELA introductory language cited previously, we know that the standards' *spirit* is to reach deeper. Try to couple standards together; if the classroom teacher wants students to write an informational text, marry that task with critical thinking. The efficiency of combined standards saves time for depth. Compare these examples:

Instead of this	Try this
Write a paragraph/essay describing characteristics of a mammal. *(informational only)*	Write a letter to the principal informing her about your animal. Describe the animal's characteristics and explain how each trait contributes to or diminishes the value of having that animal as a school pet. *(starts with informational text; transitions to persuasive text while requiring critical thinking)*

Framing

One challenge of student-centered research is to find a just-right balance between supported and open inquiry. In open inquiry, students have a range of choices in terms of theme, topic, work style, and presentation format—easier to find in theory than in practice. Independent researchers are made, not born; they need appropriate guidance and support as their skills mature over time. Too much openness, and students will revert back to older skills instead of stretching toward new goals. In addition, some may become frustrated and seek the "easiest way out" approach, using few sources, little imagination, and low energy investment.

Instead, consider framing the assignment. Providing a scenario—either wildly imaginative or rooted in a real-world problem—gives students an intellectual frame. Scenarios help students center their tasks within gentle guidelines, providing security without closing off options. Project- or problem-based scenarios can introduce domain-specific vocabulary (a word mentioned thirty-six times in in the CCSS ELA Standards), set constraints that push students away from fact gathering, and create the world in which the students' research makes sense and has value. A good scenario may sketch out the prologue, but the students' creativity, research, and synthesis determine the final act. The activity is framed as an invigorating challenge, not a procedural task. Consider these examples:

Instead of this	Try this

Write a biography about your assigned president.	Scientists at NASA have figured out how to bring past presidents back to life. Based on what we have talked about in class about the Great Depression that began in 1929, which president, of all the presidents, should be teleported back in time to fix it? Create a documentary film discussing the events of the Great Depression and why your president would have been a good fit.
Instead of this	*Try this*
Choose a Civil War battle. Describe the timeline of the battle, the major players, and who won.	The U.S. Postal Service would like to create a stamp recognizing a Civil War battle that most illustrated heroic actions on the battlefield. Which battle would you recommend, and why?
Describe the rituals and beliefs of ancient Egyptians.	The history museum is creating a new exhibit about death rituals and beliefs in ancient Egypt. Create a proposal for a five-case exhibit. Each case can accommodate one item plus a small plaque describing why that item had significance in Egyptian death practices. In your memo, list each item and the language you would write on the plaque.

These scenarios include varying levels of specificity. The third scenario specifies a certain number of items and that each will be accompanied by informational text; it has the most limitations. However, despite the elaborations of the scenario, the Egypt project might be an easy bridge for a traditional teacher who is used to bird units. The other two take more time, requiring students to study multiple battles or presidents before identifying a choice. If your district has a required set of technology tools, these could be added to the scenario (e.g., create a digital poster, slide deck, or animation). If you are writing a letter to the Postal Service, it should follow the conventions of a formal letter. In the presidential example, a documentary is plausible, but a diorama feels forced and unrealistic.

Scenarios tend to be more engaging than a "write about a topic" format; they can also subtly adjust the ways in which factual information is repurposed. They can be a powerful nudge in practice, either alone or in combination with one or more of Stripling's phases, discussed below.

CONNECT

What Happens in the Connect Phase?

Connect sets a foundation for questioning. For students researching familiar topics and themes, this phase should awaken their prior knowledge. For those unfamiliar with the topic, it will provide a basic overview of a topic or theme's "who, what, when, where, and why," providing an informational skeleton from which to mine initial keywords and questions.

In discussions with classroom teachers about why they provide research prompts instead of eliciting students' questions, they often reply that there is little difference between their worksheet's prompts ("When was she born? When did she die?") and the students' own. If this is the case, teachers hypothesize, why waste the time? They may have accurately diagnosed the symptom (bad questions), but not the disease (little background knowledge). Often, students ask low-level questions when they know little to nothing about a topic (Kramer and Largent 2005). Imagine being asked to brainstorm questions about Higgs-Boson. Do you have enough prior knowledge to form great questions? (Me neither.)

Nudges During the Connect Phase

When we return to novice status, as in the Higgs-Boson example, it becomes clear: a paucity of background knowledge translates to poor questions. The solution is to build up prior knowledge.

K-W-L

Many educators are familiar with the K-W-L chart created by Donna Ogle (1986), shown below. The first column calls forth prior knowledge about a topic. The students' notes here can reveal keywords for searching or reveal a paucity of working knowledge. The second step addresses Stripling's second stage, **Wonder**. The final column queries, "What have I learned?" Depending on the age of the student, this might be a list of facts, or it might be a place where students record their synthesized thoughts after reviewing their notes. Preservice educator Sandy Buczynski (personal communication 2008) points out that this K-W-L, though useful, requires students to play-act that they are interested in the topic and have genuine questions. Realistically, not all students *want* to know about the topic. Similarly, K-W-L accidentally signals to a student that his or her prior knowledge is correct and immutable. Buczyinski's version, shown here, opens up space for misconceptions while replacing "wanting" (emotional engagement) with "wondering" (intellectual engagement).

Model	K	W	L

Figure 8.1. Power House Mechanic Working on Steam Pump by Lewis Hine, 1920. Public domain. National Archives and Records Administration, Records of the Works Progress Administration (69-RH-4L-2) [VENDOR # 36]. From http://www .archives.gov/exhibits/picturing_the_century/images/port_hine_022_v36.jpg.

Ogle	What do I *know*?	What do I *want to know*?	What have I *learned*?
Buczynski adaptation	What do I *think I know*?	What do I *wonder*?	What have I *learned*?

K-W-L is useful if students have some working knowledge. If students lack knowledge, then some presearching is in order. The following activities can help connect students to content, its keywords, and its main ideas.

Using an Image, Object, or Text Sample

One often hears that today's students are visual learners. Why not jump-start a project by sharing a physical object or still image with them? A five-minute exercise can get students curious about the topic, provide some background framing, and ultimately segue into Stripling's Wonder stage.

Try showing a using the See-Think-Wonder method (Fontichiaro 2010, 2013) to awaken students' imaginations and get them thinking. Whether you give each student his or her own object or image, have students work in small groups, or engage in whole-class brainstorming, you and your students can enjoy the simple pleasures that come from looking deeply and discovering an item's secrets. We'll use the photo in figure 8.1 to try this technique.

1. Ask students, **"What do you see?"** Here, you are asking students to describe the item to you: "I see a man holding a large tool almost as big as his arm. In the background is a huge gear with bolts. He is only wearing an undershirt." Use descriptive words ("he has muscles in his arm") and avoid drawing conclusions ("he is strong"). This stage seems obvious, but it builds confidence in all learners and, as discussion of obvious characteristics gives way to minor features, students naturally segue into a deeper examination of the item.

2. Ask, **"What do you think?"** Ask for preliminary conclusions about what they think those descriptions mean and ask them to use *because* to provide evidence for their claim. In the example above, students might say, "I think he is strong *because* he has big muscles," "I think the man is poor *because* his pockets look threadbare," or "I think Lewis Hine wanted to show that the man is like a machine *because* the man is posed right in front of the big gear."

3. Ask, **"What do you wonder?"** Here is where Connect segues to Wonder (see next section). Students may generate questions such as, "Why did Hine take photographs?" "How much money did this man make?" "Did this man work alone?" "What does turning the bolt do?" "Was this photo posed?"

Use the interactive or traditional whiteboard to record student thinking (Hint: take a photo of your traditional whiteboard and upload it to your class Web site for reference), scribe on chart paper, or ask students to use a photo annotation tool like VoiceThread.com or ThingLink.com.

Try this technique with a text sample. What do students "see" in the text? What do they "think" the arguments and metaphors are meant to express? what do they "wonder" after reading the snippet?

Use an Informational Picture Book, Encyclopedia Entry, or Video

Someone wise once said, "If you want to really understand something, read a kids' book about it." In the past thirty years, the range, quality, and clarity of informational texts has skyrocketed. Informational texts—in print or eBook format—can be a powerfully efficient ways for students to "get to know" a topic and gain enough working knowledge to springboard into meaningful inquiry.

The CCSS emphasize text complexity, so one's natural instinct might be to use a complex text for this task. However, doing so might overly slow down the initial stages of inquiry, causing frustration or time lags that can put a damper on future research phases. When we adults want to learn something new, we rarely reach for the toughest tome. The proliferation of "For Dummies" and illustrated "how to" books is testimony that we gravitate toward simpler text and images when learning something new. The Connect stage should emphasize *ease* in information acquisition, so although the CCSS consider a book's linear timelines, bold headings, and other readability aids as less complex (CCSSO & NGA n.d.), this is *precisely* when students need those efficiencies. Let the intellectual challenge come later, when students are wrestling with divergent points of view, disparate data sets, or synthesis of nonaligning testimonies.

For older students who might balk at picture books, try video, an encyclopedia, or a Wikipedia entry. Remind students that all are useful starting points but could later be refuted by newer or more accurate information. Remember, too, that many Wikipedia entries are written on a high school level. Younger students may "cherry-pick" the words they recognize, skipping over difficult or domain-specific vocabulary, making their foundational knowledge similarly spotty.

The CCSS demand high performance from all, yet educators know that many students struggle with information-intense projects like research. To help level the playing field, consider how you can create opportunities at each stage for students to pool their knowledge. While students are responsible for coming up with individual information, they might share it on a wiki, Google Doc, chart paper, or other collaborative workspace. When students can compare their information to that of others, they can self-assess, acquire overlooked information, and gain additional understanding.

Connecting students to concepts is a thrilling way to start. Discovery is everywhere! Lay out a welcome mat and invite students in.

WONDER

What Happens During the Wonder Phase?

Armed with the basic informational framework created during Connect, students establish research questions that are broad and deep enough to sustain research for more than a few moments.

Nudges During the Wonder Phase

Because of Connect, students have some working knowledge about their topic or theme. Without Connect, a student assigned the okapi for an animal research project will flail and is likely to ask fishing questions to get a grasp of the topic:

- What is an okapi?
- How big is it?
- Where does it live?
- Who are its enemies?
- How many babies does it have?

These questions are certainly important, but they don't lead to deep under-standing. Levitov (2005) calls these red-light questions. Red-light questions can be answered with a single fact, statistic, or word. Often beginning with "what," "how many," "when," or "who," these questions have value as stu-dents gain foundational knowledge during the Connect phase, but truncate the inquiry journey when they are not augmented by green-light questions in the **Wonder** phase.

Following are additional examples of red-light questions:

- When was Abraham Lincoln born?
- Who signed the Declaration of Independence?
- What color are a female cardinal's feathers?

Green-light questions are more divergent. Often—but not always—beginning with words like, "How" or "Why," they often cannot be answered with a single search engine query. It may take additional reading or sources to construct an answer. Green-light questions—similar to "essential ques-tions"—help students embark on a learning journey. For the okapi research, "green-light" questions might include the following:

- How does an okapi protect itself from enemies?
- Should the okapi be on the endangered species list? Why or why not?
- What materials would you need to create a zoo habitat that an okapi would enjoy? Why?

Additional green-light questions include the following:

- How might U.S. immigration policy impact population in 2020?
- Is a bush baby a great pet for your family? Why or why not?
- Should our school move to digital textbooks? Why or why not?

To practice question design, ask students to submit anonymously two questions—one red light and one green light—and post them around the room. Invite the class on a gallery walk, giving them red and green sticker dots or pens. At each question, the student votes by placing a red or green dot next to the question (Buczynski and Fontichiaro 2009).

As during Connect, students may construct questions individually, then pool them with classmates. This encourages individual accountability but also can stimulate new potential areas to pursue. Students who are weaker in question development might be able to borrow questions from the pool in order to gain momentum for the Investigate stage. The same digital tools described in the Connect phase can be used here, as can the K-W-L chart, with students filling in the second column at this stage. In addition, educators may facilitate a conversation in which their primary role is to scribe questions on a whiteboard or digital corkboard (e.g., Padlet.com), clustering similar questions together to help students see additional inquiry paths.

INVESTIGATE

What Is the Investigate Phase?

Questions in hand, students engage in the nuts and bolts of finding and using information. Though noted as a single stage in the Stripling Model of Inquiry, the **Investigate** stage encompasses many activities. Skills necessary in this stage include the following:

- **Search and Discovery**—using keywords, tables of contents, and indexes; scanning search results lists; reiterating searches as needed; following citation chains; following links to drill more deeply into content
- **Evaluation**—developing and using "rule of thumb" guides (Abilock 2012) for determining credibility (see W.CCR.8 for grades 6–12; CCSSI 2010, 41), accuracy, utility, and appropriateness of a resource
- **Reading**—decoding and comprehending information in all formats
- **Paraphrasing**—putting information in one's own words
- **Summarizing**—discovering the main ideas of a resource and stating them in fewer words
- **Note taking**—making a personal record of a resource's salient points, as well as of one's thinking

With all these skills to work on, and so much information at hand, peripheral information can quickly distract. Students may need assistance figuring out whether new information illuminates or is outside the scope of their work. Try to have students do this work during school (not as homework), so you can support their cognitive struggles.

Be mindful that digital reading poses new comprehension questions and practices for educators. As the CCSS tests will be administered online, digital reading is an essential test preparation skill. Many studies confirm that students skim, quickly moving to another site when they do not find immediate results. CCSS testing will demand sustained focus. Limited student vocabulary on the topic also limits comprehension, so educators of younger students may wish to restrict students to online resources that are more closely aligned to their reading level or ability in order to maximize comprehension. For details on reading comprehension online, see Jabr (2013).

Circle the true sentence(s):

I am doing great.

I need the teacher's help.

I need the librarian's help.

I need computer help.

Nudges During the Investigate Phase

Dear _____,

My research question is _____.

As I work on my research, I'm getting confused about _____

_____, but I feel pretty solid about _____

_____.

I could use some help finding information about _____

_____.

My group is (select one) a strong team/struggling. We could use your help

with _____.

Signed,

_____

When research means fill-in-the-blank worksheets, there is little cognitive demand on students. Inquiry work is significantly more difficult. Mini-conferencing is an essential intervention. Especially for novice researchers, these in-process check-ins give timely feedback so that the student can backtrack and adjust. When librarians are present during this stage, they can supply a mini-lesson, an individual tutorial, a suggestion to return to an earlier inquiry phase, or a needed resource.

Exit tickets are useful throughout inquiry, but they are particularly helpful during Investigate, when students are struggling to comprehend and sift through ideas. Consider the following exit ticket for an elementary student:

For older students, exit tickets may be in letter format:

Clip exit slips to student research folders to quickly compare their self-assessments to their work (Harvey in Fontichiaro 2012) or use a Google Form as an exit ticket (Nichols in Fontichiaro 2011). Try setting up a podcasting or video recording station in the corner. Post a prompt and invite students to record themselves responding to the prompt. Prompts might focus on resources, synthesis, group work, personal effort, or other areas of concern:

- What I've learned today about using JSTOR is . . .
- Today I figured out that . . .
- One tip I've learned about working in groups is . . .
- When next year's eighth graders do research, they should remember that . . .

This "reality TV confessional" gives you not only important feedback about your students but also evidence you can share with others that information literacy is more complex than many imagine.

Be mindful that during Investigate, the teacher may feel the uncomfortable about his or her expertise. This vulnerability may explain a teacher's reluctance for embracing deeper, inquiry-oriented work. Inquiry means educators are guides, adapting on the fly to resources and challenges as they arise. It is far more difficult to predict the finish line and the time it will take to cross it. These uncertainties prey on a teacher's biggest insecurities (as well as our own!); be mindful of the power of emotion. You might offer the teacher a private tour of effective resources or ask if group work would help by minimizing the quantity of topics and resources. Group work can also gently engineer a situation in which students help each other before demanding instructional support from the teachers. An "ask three [peers] before me" policy provides another buffer: easy questions are fielded by classmates, minimizing the number of questions that can feel like pestering to the instructor.

CONSTRUCT

What Happens During the Construct Phase?

In worksheet-style research, the student's cognitive effort essentially stops once the facts have been found and are ready to be moved again into a product. There is little need to find connections between information bits: facts are shared in an episodic sequence, with little analysis or synthesis.

In inquiry-oriented work, however, students must make sense of their findings. They need time to sort, evaluate, accept, and reject information. When note cards were the prevailing method, students did this work by sorting cards into sequences, then an outline. In the cut-and-paste world, however, students sometimes skip this processing step.

Nudges to the Construct Phase

Talk with your colleagues about the difficulty of synthesis for novice researchers and the necessity of instructor support during the school day. Structure the unit so that student note taking is a separate step from sequencing, outlining, or publishing. Recognize that some teachers may not realize students are merely cutting and pasting and, in doing so, short-circuiting the cognitive experience.

Next, talk with your partner about how to model information sorting. Today's warp-speed students may be inexperienced in the thoughtful, deliberate work of rereading, evaluating, accepting or rejecting, and synthesizing information. Many have learned to cluster information in a nonlinear word web, whereas the CCSS advocate creating arguments supported by evidence, a less-familiar structure. Remind students that during the Investigate phase, they gathered information. Now they will sort that information into relevant categories. They might synthesize a group of similar notes into an argument that doesn't appear in their notes. In this case, the notes provide the evidence. Alternatively, their notes might contain arguments, which means they need evidence to support them. Do the notes contain that evidence? Do they need to go back for further investigation? Or discard the argument? In a way, notes are like LEGO bricks. Some LEGO projects require all of the bricks; some just those of a certain color or size. There are many ways to successfully assemble LEGO bricks, and the prominence throughout the CCSS of claims and arguments actually makes it easier for students to sort gathered information. Which are the major ideas? Minor ideas? It is up to the student to decide. If a decision can be justified, it can stand. Appeal to students' sense of fairness!

Consider whether reverting back to outlining—either with formal formatting or a more casual list—might help students better see the hierarchy between claims and evidence. Moving information around facilitates this for students, as it allows them to *see* the relationships. Digital resources like NoodleTools.com can mimic the note card experience while taking advantage of cloud-based, access-anywhere information storage. iPad apps can facilitate note card creation and sorting.

Also keep in mind that **Construct** can feel frustrating to students—and, by extension, to teachers. The serendipitous moments of discovery found during Investigate are gone, and it's hard to toss out scintillating information that doesn't fit the thesis or to discover that you thought you were done with research but need to go on. Resist the urge to say, "We're done with that part." At a minimum, see if the student can return outside of class time to catch up. Finding holes in one's research is often a natural result of examining what data we have. Students who struggle with Construct might need significant one-on-one time with the teacher; having a librarian also in the room can cut the waiting-for-help line in half.

EXPRESS

What Happens During the Express Phase?

This stage is probably the most common in K–12 education and therefore receives the least attention in this chapter. For decades, we have asked students to make banners, posters, dioramas, brochures, slideshows, essays, animations, drawings, models, and more to demonstrate learning. However, with technology, we can accidentally spend more time on creating a product than on understanding the content.

Nudges for the Express Phase

Authenticity is a key strategy for nudging the Express phase forward. Obviously, the most authentic product is one that expresses new understandings about a topic of the student's *choice*. Although the CCSS specify the processes students need to understand, they do not specify topics for exploration. However, district curriculum about social studies, science, and other subjects may specify a particular focus or area of study. It may be easier to nudge the *audience* by expanding the potential viewers of a student's work. When students know others will view what they do, whether online or in the hallway, there is a reason to want to show off one's best. Consider authentic *products* as well. Many traditional school products have little utility beyond the classroom. A book report has little real-world application, but a book review does. A biography poster is rare in a museum, but a display is typical. Sugarcube houses may proliferate during a castle unit, but no architect would build models with them. When we can marry research with a format students may employ in the future, we can build transferable skills.

A second nudge for **Express** is to be cautious about time. Too often, in order to have something to display or show off, the process of research is shortchanged to make time for creating. Many educators, myself included, are strong proponents of making and tinkering mindsets, but not at the cost of the tough work of critical thinking and synthesis. Take care that technology does not usurp the real cognitive challenge of learning. Especially with Web 2.0 tools, it's easy to find tools that are plug and play: enter a few links, put in a few sentences, and a delightful animation begins. It's beautiful and appealing, but it is a siren song. The tool's ease of use can trick us.

REFLECT

What Happens During the Reflect Phase?

Although **Reflect** is technically the final phase of the model, to call it such is a misnomer. Indeed, effective researchers reflect throughout the research process. As they make notes, scribble research to-do lists, fill out exit slips, and talk with friends about their progress, they are engaging in formal and informal reflective processes.

Reflective practice is essential to making learning stick (Darling-Hammond 2008). Encourage students—and yourself—to think actively about what has been learned throughout the research process and critically examine the effectiveness of our product. Unfortunately, inquiry projects can run over schedule, and it can be tempting to bypass summative reflection and just move on to the next instructional unit.

Nudging for the Reflect Phase

Consider strategies that time-shift reflection: instead of requiring a long reflective paragraph, blog post, or worksheet, try embedding quick reflective practice into the day-to-day flow of the project. Add a question to your Investigate exit slips or Google Form that prompts students to think about their process and product-in-progress. Ask older students to tweet out what they learned with hash tags like #reflectprocess or #reflectproduct, or to use Polleverywhere.com to submit quick feedback via text message. Frequent, short reflection may be more easily implemented—and therefore more effective—than waiting until end-of-project fatigue has set in.

Consider quantitative survey questions on a Google Form or Polleverywhere poll, such as these:

Right now, my work output is:
1. Awful
2. Not very good
3. Average
4. High quality
5. Very high quality

My productivity today was:
1. Awful. I need a mini-conference.
2. OK. I was on and off today, but I don't need help.
3. Very good! Most of the time, I was on task and making progress.
4. Awesome! I worked efficiently and made a lot of helpful progress.

So far, I anticipate that my score will be:
1. F

    2. D
    3. C
    4. B
    5. A

By creating brief feedback loops and repeating them several times as the project progresses, educators can easily crunch the data to find patterns about perceived confidence, accomplishment, and productivity.

CONCLUSION

As the chapters in this section show, there are clear and strong connections between inquiry learning and the CCSS. Like my giant "shrimp" in Cinque Terre, transitioning to something familiar yet new can be messy and challenging. But if you roll up your sleeves and crack it open, it can also be delicious. And the view along the way? Unforgettable.

REFERENCES

Abilock, Debbie. (2012). "True—or Not?" *Educational Leadership* 69 (6): 70–74.

American Association of School Librarians. (2007). *Standards for the 21st-Century Learner*. Retrieved from http://www.ala.org/aasl/standards-guidelines/learning -standards on July 10, 2013.

Buczynski, Sandy. Personal communication. (2008).

Buczynski, Sandy, and Kristin Fontichiaro. (2009). *Story Starters and Science Notebooking: Developing Student Thinking Through Literacy and Inquiry*. Santa Barbara, CA: Teacher Ideas Press.

Common Core State Standards Initiative (CCSSI). (2010). *Common Core State Standards for English Language Arts & Literacy in History/Social Studies, Science, and Technical Subjects*. Retrieved from http://www.corestandards.org/assets /CCSSI_ELA%20Standards.pdf on July 1, 2013.

Council of Chief State School Officers (CCSSO) and National Governors Association (NGA). (n.d.) "Supplemental Information for Appendix A of the Common Core State Standards for English Language Arts and Literacy: New Research on Text Complexity." Retrieved from http:/www.corestandards.org/assets /E0813_Appendix_A_New_Research_on_Text_Complexity.pdf on July 15, 2013.

Darling-Hammond, Linda. (2008). *Powerful Learning: What We Know About Teaching for Understanding*. San Francisco: Jossey-Bass.

Fontichiaro, Kristin. (2010). *Go Straight to the Source*. Ann Arbor, MI: Cherry Lake.

Fontichiaro, Kristin. (2011). "Nudging Toward Inquiry: Formative Assessment." *School Library Monthly* 27 (6): 11–12.

Fontichiaro, Kristin. (2012). "Formative Assessment Using Feedback." *School Library Monthly* 28 (7): 51–52.

Fontichiaro, Kristin. (2013). *Find Out Firsthand: Using Primary Sources*. Ann Arbor, MI: Cherry Lake.

Jabr, Ferris. (2013). "Do e-Readers Inhibit Reading Comprehension?" *Salon*, April 14. Retrieved from http://www.salon.com/2013/04/14/do_e_readers_inhibit_reading_comprehension_partner/ on July 15, 2013.

Kramer, Kym, and Connie Largent. (2005). "Sift and Sort: The Answers Are in the Questions!" *School Library Media Activities Monthly* 21 (8): 33–37.

Levitov, Deborah. (2005). "Red Light, Green Light: Guiding Questions." *School Library Media Activities Monthly* 22 (2): 25.

Loertscher, David V., Carol Koechlin, and Sandi Zwaan. (2005). *Ban Those Bird Units! 15 Models for Teaching and Learning in Information-rich and Technology-rich Environments*. Salt Lake City, UT: Hi Willow Research and Publishing.

Ogle, Donna M. (1986). "K-W-L: A teaching Model That Develops Active Reading of Expository Text." *The Reading Teacher* 39 (6): 564–570. Retrieved from http://jstor.org/stable/20199156 on July 15, 2013.

Stripling, Barbara. (2007). "Assessing Information Fluency: Gathering Evidence of Student Learning." *School Library Media Activities Monthly* 28 (8): 25–29.

9

Designing Learning Plans for Inquiry and the Common Core

Violet H. Harada

The previous chapters emphasized some of the following elements in creating effective learning experiences:

- Inquiry is a powerful approach to learning that matters to students.
- The Common Core and AASL standards complement and extend learning that is deep and rigorous.
- School librarians can be critical teaching partners in shaping and facilitating learning that stimulates rather than stifles real learning.

This chapter focuses on designing learning plans that incorporate these essential features.

INQUIRY AS A FRAME FOR THINKING AND LEARNING

The seed for authentic learning begins with a need or want to know (Stripling 2008). This curiosity to "learn more" propels students to ask questions they care about, define tough problems, retrieve and examine evidence, analyze assumptions and ideas, and tolerate ambiguity as a natural part of any inquiry (Richardson 2013, 12). Students view the world from various perspectives, ranging from the artistic and scientific, to the historic and literary (Moreillon, Luhtala, and Russo 2011; Stripling 2008).

DESIGNING THE UNIT/PROJECT

Educational researchers suggest that twenty-first-century students should engage with fewer topics and focus on learning how to learn, self-assess their knowledge and intellectual development, and use their minds to deal with complex and ambiguous challenges (Alberti 2013; Richardson 2013; Reeves 2011; Jacobs 2010). This type of learning links themes and thinking across grades and disciplines. It demands "rigorous pursuit of conceptual understanding, procedural skill, and application" (Alberti 2013, 26).

Start with Concepts

Units and projects should center on big ideas that are intriguing and abstract (Donham 2010). They have universal meaning that can be applied in many settings and extend beyond schooling. They demand analyzing, interpreting, and asking more questions. There is a difference between simple topics and enduring concepts. The first focuses on a subject or an event that can usually be described by collecting and organizing facts; the second is not explicitly stated and requires analysis and inference. Following are some examples:

Topic	Concept
Recycling	Waste management, sustainability
Monk seals	Wildlife endangerment
Rain forests	Planet ecology
Holocaust	Prejudice and genocide

Focus on Essential Questions

Essential questions emerge from the concepts being studied; they help students make sense of complex ideas and knowledge. These questions have no easy answers and often require examination from multiple perspectives. They are central to understanding a key issue or theme and are generative because they lead to more questions. They can be categorized according to purpose (Dahlgren and Oberg (2001). Examples include the following:

- Relational questions: How is _____ related to _____?
- Value-oriented questions: How can you assess the value or importance of _____?
- Solution-oriented questions: Can you propose a _____ to this problem?

McKenzie rightfully says that these types of questions are "essential technology for those who venture onto the Information Highway" (online).

Develop Critical Thinking Skills

Meaningful learning challenges students to effectively seek, manage, make sense of, and present information. The Common Core State Standards (CCSS) require that students experiment with arguments and counterarguments, check on the validity of evidence found, and identify additional evidence needed (Callison 2013). These are examples of critical skills:

- Raise vital questions and problems and formulate them clearly and precisely.
- Retrieve and analyze evidence from multiple primary and secondary sources.
- Test for the value and validity of information as meaningful evidence.
- Search for evidence, facts, or knowledge by identifying relevant sources and gather objective, subjective, historical, and current data from those sources.
- Analyze assumptions and biases.
- Draw inferences or conclusions that are supported or justified by evidence.
- Recognize differences and similarities among ideas or situations.
- Arrive at well-reasoned conclusions and solutions and test them against relevant criteria and standards.
- Consider alternative systems of thought—assess assumptions, implications, and practical consequences.
- Use collective knowledge to create, conclude, and communicate.

Crosswalk the Standards

By blending the AASL *Standards for the 21st-Century Learner* and the CCSS, we have a richer and stronger foundation for what students learn and how they learn it. The Common Core emphasizes building knowledge through content-rich nonfiction (and literature), reading and writing that is grounded in evidence, and regular practice with close reading of complex texts that introduce students to academic and technical language (Alberti 2013). The AASL standards focus on inquiry that leads to deeper, more all-encompassing instructional design (Fontichiaro 2009). Importantly, the AASL standards contribute the need to nurture dispositions that are critical for learning anywhere, anytime.

According to Moreillon, Luhtala, and Russo (2011), the Common Core relates directly to the AASL standards in the following specific areas:

- research to build and present knowledge
- production and distribution of writing
- range of reading and level of text complexity
- key ideas and details
- craft and structure
- comprehension and collaboration
- interpretation of linear models

By integrating the two sets of standards, then, educators lay a common ground for student success.

Design Lessons Using a Backward Mapping Approach

Wiggins and McTighe (1998) popularized the term "backward design" to describe this important concept in curriculum planning, which requires the instructional planner to identify the outcomes first and the means by which outcomes will be measured before creating the activities themselves. This is counter to common practice, in which instructors begin by creating lesson procedures and then tacking on objectives (Harada and Yoshina 2010). The following points are critical to keep in mind when designing lessons that are effective learning plans:

- **Learning goals answer the question, "What's important for the learner to know?"** The goals should clearly state the intended outcomes in language that the learner will understand. They must reflect skills or dispositions embodied in the AASL and Common Core standards.
- **Assessment criteria answer the question, "How does the learner know how well he or she performed?"** The criteria must be specific and measurable. They indicate what the student must demonstrate as a result of the learning experience.
- **Learning plans answer the question, "How do we design the learning experience to help learners achieve the desired goals?"** The plan should be constructed so that goals and criteria for assessment are transparent and clear to the student. It should provide for direct instruction as well as opportunities for modeling. Important, there should be time for guided practice and feedback.
- **Self-reflection answers the question, "What have I learned, and how well did I learn it?"** Assessment for learning has to be a vital part of the process if we wish to empower students to take charge of their learning and develop lifelong habits of self-improvement.

The self-checklist in figure 9.1 summarizes the points made in this chapter.

SUMMARY

Although "planning is the less visible part of the teaching and learning process . . . it serves as the blueprint for student learning" (Stripling and Harada 2012, 6). Effective learning does not happen by chance in classrooms and libraries. It requires thoughtfully crafted plans that view the experience as a holistic adventure for the learner. It invites metacognition and demonstration of conceptual knowledge and skills. In part IV, librarian leaders from various states have contributed examples of inquiry-framed learning plans that engage students in rigorous and meaningful discoveries.

UNIT—INQUIRY BASED	
MAJOR ELEMENTS	√ if done
Concepts Address a broad theme or issue Require demonstration of higher order thinking Present universal meanings and allow for applications in many settings or situations	
Essential questions Emerge from the concepts addressed Extend beyond collecting facts to interpreting and creating personal meaning Generate more questions	
Critical thinking skills (examples) Formulate thoughtful questions Retrieve and analyze evidence from multiple sources Test for value and validity of information Analyze assumptions and biases Arrive at well-reasoned conclusions and solutions	
Standards *Standards for the 21st-Century Learner*: target specific skills, dispositions, responsibilities, and/or self-assessment strategies that reflect an inquiry approach to learning *Common Core State Standards*: target specific strands, topics, and standards that address higher order skills in reading, writing, and/or speaking and listening	

LESSON	
MAJOR ELEMENTS	√ if done
Learning goals Clearly state outcome intended Target the learner in terms of language he or she understands	
Assessment criteria Demonstrate intended outcome in specific, measurable behavior Target the learner in terms of language he or she understands	
Learning plans Introduce the learning goals and assessment criteria Directly teach the targeted skill or concept Model, provide examples of the skill or concept Allow for guided practice and feedback of the skill or concept Engage students in self-assessing for learning	
Self-reflection Assess the impact of the lesson on students based on observation and evidence Identify strengths and areas for possible improvement	

Figure 9.1. Self-Checklist for Units and Lessons

REFERENCES

Alberti, Sandra. (2013). "Making the Shifts." *Educational Leadership* 70, no. 4 (December/January): 24–27.

Callison, Daniel. (2013). "Inquiry and Common Core: Argument Processes, Part 1." *School Library Monthly* 29 (6) (March): 20–22.

Dahlgren, Madeleine Abrandt, and Gunilla Oberg. (2001). "Questioning to Learn and Learning to Question: Structure and Function of Problem-based Learning Scenarios in Environmental Science Education." *Higher Education* 44 (3) (April): 263–282.

Donham, Jean. (2010). "Deep Learning through Concept-based Inquiry." *School Library Monthly* I (1) (September/October): 8–11.

Fontichiaro, Kristin. (2009). "Nudging toward Inquiry: Re-envisioning Existing Research Projects." *School Library Monthly* 26 (1) (September): 17–19.

Harada, Violet H., and Joan M. Yoshina. (2010). *Assessing for Learning: Librarians and Teachers as Partners*. 2nd ed. Santa Barbara, CA: Libraries Unlimited.

Jacobs, Heidi Hayes, ed. (2010). *Curriculum 21: Essential Education for a Changing World*. Alexandria, VA: ASCD.

McKenzie, Jamie. (n.d.). "The Question IS the Answer." *From Now On*. Retrieved from http://fno.org/oct97/question.html on April 1, 2013.

Moreillon, Judi, Michelle Luhtala, and Christina T. Russo. (2011). "Learning That Sticks: Engaged Educators + Engaged Learners." *School Library Monthly* 28 (1) (September/October): 17–20.

Reeves, Anne R. (2011). *Where Great Teaching Begins: Planning for Student Thinking and Learning*. Alexandria, VA: ASCD.

Richardson, Will. (2013). "Students First, Not Stuff." *Educational Leadership* 70 (6) (March): 10–14.

Stripling, Barbara. (2008). "Inquiry: Inquiring Minds Want to Know." *School Library Media Activities Monthly* 25 (1) (September): 50–52.

Stripling, Barbara K., and Violet H. Harada. (2012). "Designing Learning Experiences for Deeper Understanding." *School Library Monthly* 29 (3) (December): 5–12.

Wiggins, Grant, and Jay McTighe. (1998). *Understanding by Design*. Alexandria, VA: ASCD.

Part IV

Exemplars of Learning Plans

Throughout the exemplars you will note AASL's learning standards, which were excerpted from *Standards for the 21st-Century Learner* by the American Association of School Librarians, a division of the American Library Association, copyright © 2007 American Library Association. Available for download at www.ala.org/aasl /standards. Used with permission. It is recommended that you download the standards to reference while using this section.

Plan 1:
Just Why Does My Iowa Animal Live There? (Kindergarten)

Shannon McClintock Miller with Lynne Caltrider,
Brooke Gadberry, and Christa McClintock

DESCRIBING THE CONTEXT

Subjects integrated: Science, Language Arts, Information and Technology Literacy

Duration of project: Four to six weeks

SUMMARIZING THE PROJECT

A favorite topic in kindergarten is the study of animals. Young learners possess some background knowledge about animals that they bring to the discussion, and they love learning about new animals and facts. The focus on animals specific to Iowa came from questions the students were asking, such as, "Do whales live in the Mississippi River?" The students and kindergarten team, consisting of Lynne Caltrider, Brooke Gadberry, and Christa McClintock, decided that they would focus on animals found in their state.

The teachers and librarian used Barbara Stripling's inquiry model with the students. In the Wonder phase of the model, the students and teachers brainstormed a list of the Iowa animals they knew. They used a page found on the Iowa DNR (Department of Natural Resources) Web site about Iowa wildlife to further the conversation. The students

From *Inquiry and the Common Core: Librarians and Teachers Designing Teaching for Learning.* Violet H. Harada and Sharon Coatney, Editors. Santa Barbara, CA: Libraries Unlimited. Copyright © 2014.

were curious about where the various animals lived in Iowa, so they used Google Maps as well as maps from the DNR Web site to locate the different parts of the state. Working together, students and teachers formulated the essential question, "Why does your animal live where it lives in Iowa?" This big question spawned a stream of more specific questions, such as, "Why does the Blue Spotted Salamander migrate across the road every year in Dallas County? Why do bald eagles live along the major rivers in Iowa?"

As the students progressed in the unit, they developed more questions and made predictions. They learned about their animals through online resources such as eBooks within MackinVIA, *Encyclopaedia Britannica*, and Web sites (National Geographic Kids and Animal Planet). The online resources that were used at Van Meter were bookmarked and organized using Symbaloo, a free online social bookmarking Web site and app. Each grade level's resources have been organized in separate Symbaloo "Web mixes" that contain links to appropriate and relevant Web sites, databases, eBooks, and Web 2.0 tools. The Kindergarten Symbaloo allowed students to easily access their resources from the library, classroom, and home. Students also utilized their fluency center during reading time to search for more information using the classroom computers, laptops, and iPads. With all of these tools available, the kindergartners felt empowered to follow their own sense of wonder and investigate new things.

To help students document their investigations, they received Iowa Animal Report Packets, in which they could record what they uncovered about the animal group, habitat, food, adaptations, babies, and other interesting facts, as well as a photo album. In addition, the librarian created an online newsletter using the Web 2.0 Smore. The Iowa Animal Research Project Smore was used to gather resources and make them accessible to the students from both school and home. The Smore could be shared online through e-mail and social media tools such as Facebook and Twitter, embedded onto the Van Meter Library Voice blog, and also printed offline. Using this tool, the kindergarteners were motivated to expand their investigation by finding information in different places and developing new questions. Prior to this project, students had been taught how to locate information within the library and online using MackinVIA (eBook and e-resource portal) during their 65-minute library/technology class every four days. These skills proved to be critical as students navigated through the materials and resources. Along with the reports, students also created models of their animals using diverse materials and technology applications such as Animoto, Tux Paint, and eBooks.

The project became an exciting family affair. At the onset, students shared letters with their parents describing the goals of the project and inviting their families to join the adventure. Even the assessment involved the parents. The nine-question checklist required students and parents to evaluate the projects by using smiley and frown faces. Students shared their reports and models at the end of the project. The instructional team videotaped the students and used the tape in a culminating project that they put together.

After the students displayed their reports and models in the school hallway, they created a class eBook with the assistance of the librarian. Using Tux Paint, they each created one page with an illustration of their animals and words to describe where their animals lived in Iowa and why. They saved their illustrated pages and uploaded them into FlipSnack. They then used Camtasia Relay to capture their voices while going through the eBook in FlipSnack. Students also created word clouds using Wordle.net to display key details or facts about their Iowa animals. Each Wordle was also saved as a PDF document and uploaded into FlipSnack using Camtasia Relay. The librarian added these eBooks to the library's digital collection.

Resource links:
- Iowa Animal Research Project Smore, https://www.smore.com/rydj
- Iowa's Wildlife, Iowa Department of Natural Resources, http://www .iowadnr.gov/Education/IowasWildlife.aspx
- Van Meter Kindergarten Symbaloo, Van Meter Community School, http:// www.symbaloo.com/mix/vanmeterkindergarten

Librarian blogs (Contact Shannon Miller at shannon.miller@vmbull dogs.com for more information on her blogs.):
- "Our kindergartners are starting their Iowa animal research—the first steps we are taking this week." April 9, 2013.
- "Look, Mrs. Miller. We are researching our Iowa animals in the library today!" April 15, 2013.
- "Our little kindergarten researchers show 'wonder and investigation' in their Iowa animal research project . . . and with a special little visitor too!" May 12, 2013.
- "Learning together in Iowa and Colorado all about the animals in our states." May 19, 2013.
- "Our kindergartners' last day . . . but they left their mark with our animal research project." May 21, 2013.

Tech tools:
- Animoto [for video slideshows], http://animoto.com
- Flipsnack [to make flipbooks], http://www.flipsnack.com/
- Smore [to create online newsletters] , https://www.smore.com/
- Symbaloo [online book marking social network tool], http://www.symbaloo.com/
- Tux Paint [to create illustrations with text], http://tuxpaint.org/
- Worldle [for word clouds], http://www.wordle.net/

BUILDING AN INQUIRY FOCUS

Concepts addressed
- Animal habitats
- Animal survival

Essential question investigated
- Why does your animal live where it lives in Iowa?

Critical skills taught
- Locating information about selected animals in the following:
  - library's new animal neighborhoods (category based library)
  - MackinVIA Group (for eBooks) setup entitled "K Animal eBooks and Research"
  - *Encyclopaedia Britannica Online*
  - Web sites (National Geographic Kids and Animal Planet) from the Symbaloo Web mix
- Using text features and visual clues to efficiently find information.
- Forming questions throughout the research process.
- Collaborating with parents to complete the Iowa Animal Report and a model of the animal.
- Using technology to communicate knowledge gained about animals living in Iowa.

CONNECTING THE STANDARDS

AASL *Standards for the 21st-Century Learner*

1. Inquire, think critically, and gain knowledge.
Indicators 1.1.1, 2.1.4

SAMPLE LESSONS

Lesson focus: Identifying and using main ideas/details to create word clouds about why animals live where they do in Iowa

Lesson resources:
- Iowa Animal Report Packet
- Wordle, http://www.wordle.net/

Duration: Two thirty-minute sessions. The first session is in the morning's literacy block, and the second session is in the afternoon during the library/ tech time. Note: All students will have completed Iowa Animal Reports with them. They will complete the "My Iowa Animal Lives Here!" note card during the morning literacy block time and bring it with them to the library for the afternoon session. They will also be using MacBooks during library time.

Designing for Learning

Learning outcomes desired: I can
- use text features and visual clues to locate key details or facts.
- write these key details or facts on "My Iowa Animal Lives Here!" note card.
- use key details or facts from my note card to create a word cloud of my Iowa animal.
- save "My Iowa Animal Lives Here!" word cloud on the desktop to use for our flipbook/eBook.

Assessing for learning: I will
- write down important facts about my animal by looking at pictures and other text features.
- identify at least three facts or details about why my animal lives where it does in Iowa.
- create a word cloud using my facts on my animal by using Wordle.net.

Learning plan to achieve outcomes

Session 1: Creating Note Cards

Introduce

- Connect with prior knowledge by explaining: "I want you to think about the information you learned about the Iowa animal you chose to research. You searched for information about its animal group, habitat, adaptations, life cycle, and many other interesting facts. I am so proud of the Animal Research packets that you have completed throughout your project."
- Link to the new task by saying, "Today we are going to reflect and create a note card that lists at least three things that you learned about your Iowa animal. What were the most interesting facts that you found out?"
- Remind them about writing mechanics: Ask students to keep in mind spelling words correctly and beginning each sentence with an uppercase letter, as well as ending each sentence with the correct punctuation.

Model

- Introduce the task by explaining: "I am going to show you what to include on your note card. First, put the name of your Iowa animal in the middle of the Iowa state shape. Next, list a fact in each of the three fact boxes."
- Model the task: Demonstrate how to develop a note card using a think-aloud procedure. Encourage students to think of the following questions to guide their note taking:
  - Where does my animal live?
  - What does my animal eat?
  - What does my animal do to protect itself from danger?
  - What is my animal called when it is a baby?
  - Why does my animal live where it lives?

Practice

- Create the note cards: Students work independently to complete their note cards. Remind them to put their names on the cards.
- Provide feedback: As students work, circulate to monitor their progress. Encourage students to do their best, remember finger spaces, and take their time.

Assess

- Examine finished notes: Assess the completed note cards. Confer with individual students who may have inaccurately identified main ideas and details.

Session 2: Creating Word Clouds

Introduce

- Tap prior knowledge by recalling: "Remember when we created word clouds about ourselves? We used Wordle on the computers and I printed them off for you to keep."
- Set the stage by elaborating: "Today you are going to create a Wordle about your Iowa animal and why it lives where it lives. This morning you used My Animal Report to write down your name, your Iowa animal, and at least three things about why your animal lives where it lives. Now, let's use that information to create your Wordle."
- Engage and challenge: Review use of Wordle by asking, "What are some things we need to remember when creating our Wordle? (Examples of responses: Type in the words correctly; type the word in multiple times if we want a word larger than the others; we can also change the layout and color.) Also ask, "Where can we find the link to Wordle?" (Van Meter students would find it in the Kindergarten Symbaloo.)

Model

- Directly teach: Model the following steps using computer projections on the big screen:
  - First, go to the Kindergarten Symbaloo. Find the Wordle tile at the top. It is yellow and has "Wordle" on it. Remember that Wordle starts with a W.
  - Click on the Wordle tile. This takes you to the Wordle Web site.
  - Once you are in Wordle, push "Create your own."
  - Take your "My Iowa Animal Lives Here" note card and type all of the words into Wordle. Put a space between each word and spell the words correctly.
  - If you want to make the word bigger, type the word more than once. For example, if you want the word "Cougar" to be bigger, type it three times. Then it will be three times as big as the other words.
  - If you want the words to be connected together, use the "~" button. For example, if you have Blue Spotted Salamander and you want the words to stay together, you must type "Blue~Spotted~Salamander" without any spaces between the words.

- Once you have the words from your note card typed into Wordle, click on "Create." This will create your Wordle.
- You can change the way the words are laid out on the page under "Layout" and you can also select colors from the buttons on the top of the Wordle.
- When your Wordle looks the way you would like it to, I will take a screen shot using "Command+Shift+4" to save on the desktop. That screen shot will then be used in the class flippable eBook.

Practice

- Create word clouds: Students find Wordle on the Kindergarten Symbaloo and create their word clouds following the instructions provided by you. They make sure to use all the words on their note cards.
- Provide feedback: You and the teacher provide assistance as students work on their word clouds.

Assess

- Confer with students: As students complete their word clouds, assess the products as you take screen shots of them. Informally ask students to self-check if they have included all the information from their note cards. This provides an opportunity to see if students truly understand where in Iowa their animals live and why location is important to animals (habitat).

Reflecting on Student Outcomes

What happened, and why?

We also connected via Skype with a class of seventh and eighth graders in Colorado so our kindergartners could share what they had learned about their Iowa animals. The Colorado students were studying animals in their state, so it was a fun and valuable connection to exchange information about our respective states and the special animals living in them. It gave our kindergartners such a feeling of ownership—they were so proud to teach older students something the older youngsters didn't know.

It was very rewarding to watch kindergartners embrace and enjoy this project. From the first conversation that we had as a class about animals that live around us, to the end when we were sharing with students in another state, their excitement was contagious. Every student was successful.

Upon reflection, we could have used a little more time on the technology-based parts, including the Tux Paint illustrations and the flippable eBooks. With the extra time, we could have given more responsibility to the students. For example, they could have learned how to take the screen shots of their Tux Paint illustrations and saved them on the zip drive. We believe that with more instruction and practice, they would have been able to handle these tasks successfully.

How did this influence our next actions?

We are considering the following possibilities for next year. First, our kindergartners already work with third-grade buddies each week. We are considering ways that the buddies might assist the younger students with technology-based projects like this one.

Second, by observing what the kindergartners accomplished this year and the enthusiasm they felt in sharing their findings with both peers and the Colorado students, we realize that their work should be shared with the entire school community. With this in mind, we would like to sponsor an "Iowa Animal Day" on which we would invite the entire school community to become involved, including other classrooms, teachers, parents, and grandparents. And why not share this globally? We would like to use Web 2.0 tools such as Google Hangout, Twitter, and Facebook to present the project to a world audience!

Plan 2:
Who Is the Best President? (Grade 1)

Judi Paradis

DESCRIBING THE CONTEXT

Subjects integrated: Social Studies, English Language Arts, Mathematics

Duration of project: One to two weeks

SUMMARIZING THE PROJECT

As part of the social studies curriculum, students in grade 1 learn about notable U.S. presidents. They also read biographies to begin learning about important people in the United States.

In this unit, we first invited the students to share what they knew about the duties of the president of the United States. We followed this with some exploratory reading on presidents to have the students validate their prior knowledge and expand on the president's duties. Students then collaborated with the teacher and librarian to develop a list of traits that a president must demonstrate in performing well. From a list of possible presidents to investigate, students then selected their favorites. They read simple biographies about two important presidents. Assuming the role of information detectives, the students determined whether these individuals possessed the necessary traits. Finally, the students "voted" for the president they thought did the job best and wrote a short paragraph providing evidence from their readings in support of their votes. To showcase their work, the class created a bar graph displaying the final votes, and they used a presentation program (e.g., VoiceThread, StoryKit or Photo Story) to report their findings, which they shared online with their families and also presented at our monthly all-school meeting.

BUILDING AN INQUIRY FOCUS

Concepts addressed
- Qualities of a leader
  - Responsibilities of a U.S. president
  - Traits an individual must have to carry out the duties of a president
- Graphic presentation of information
  - Using bar graphs to depict results of a vote

Essential questions investigated
- What are the duties of the U.S. president?
- What makes a good president?
- What traits should a president have to do this important job?
- How can I use evidence from a text to prove something is true?

Critical skills taught
- Generating a list of traits
- Finding evidence in a text to support an opinion
- Comparing two individuals and identifying similarities and differences
- Writing a paragraph supporting an opinion with evidence from a text
- Creating a bar graph to communicate findings

CONNECTING THE STANDARDS

AASL *Standards for the 21st-Century Learner*

1. Inquire, think critically, and gain knowledge.
Indicators 1.1.1, 1.1.6

2. Draw conclusions, make informed decisions, apply knowledge to new situations, and create new knowledge.
Indicators 2.1.3, 2.1.6, 2.4.1

3. Share knowledge and participate ethically and productively as members of our democratic society.
Indicators 3.3.4, 3.3.6

Common Core State Standards

CC.1.RI.3>>English Language Arts>>Reading Informational>>Key Ideas and Detail >> 3. Describe the connection between two individuals, events, ideas, or pieces of information in a text.

CC.1.RI.8>>English Language Arts>>Reading Informational>> Integration of Knowledge and Ideas>>8. Identify the reasons an author gives to support points in a text.

CC.1.RI.9>>English Language Arts>>Reading Informational>>
Integration of Knowledge and Ideas >> 9. Identify basic similarities in
and differences between two texts on the same topic (e.g., in illustrations, descriptions, or procedures).

SAMPLE LESSON

Lesson focus: Identifying the tasks and traits of an effective president

Resources:
- Online subscription databases (e.g., article on the President from *World Book Student Encyclopedia*)
- Buller, Jon. *Smart About the Presidents.* New York: Grosset and Dunlap, 2004
- Steir, Catherine. *If I Ran for President.* Morton Grove, IL: Albert Whitman Press, 2007

Duration: One 45-minute lesson

Designing for Learning

Learning outcomes desired: I can
- explain the work the U.S. president does.
- help to create a list of identifying words that describe a good president.

Assessing for learning: I will
- identify the different jobs of the president by listening to a book and/or article about the president's job.
- work with a group to brainstorm a list of describing words for a good president.
- explain how I could find evidence to show whether or not a president did this job well.

Learning plan to achieve outcomes

Introduce

- Open session: Show the students a photograph of President Obama and ask them to identify him.
- Tap prior knowledge: Ask the students if they know what he does and record their suggestions.
- Anticipate the next activity: Inform students that we are going to see if we understand his job by reading a book that tells what the president is supposed to do.

Model/Practice (Part 1)

- Explain the task: Before reading the book, inform students that they will help to create a list of jobs that the president must do.
- Read aloud: Begin the reading and alert students that you are going to stop when you come to a place that tells about something the president does. Model this procedure.
- Practice active listening: As you continue to read the book about the president's work, stop often and ask students if they can name any more jobs for the president. As the jobs are identified, add them to a chart of the president's work.

Model/Practice (Part 2)

- Explain the new task: Inform students that they will now help to create "describing words" that describe a good president.
- Model creating traits: Demonstrate how to do this by selecting a specific task from the list and use a think-aloud strategy to share some words that would describe someone who would be good at this task. For example, if the president has to make sure that everyone follows the laws, he should be "fair."
- Form teams: Organize the students in pairs or groups of three. Go through the list of tasks and invite the groups to identify describing words for each task. As various groups respond, add commonly expressed traits to the list.
- Anticipate the next activity: Once the list of adjectives is created, challenge students to think about how we might find out if a president has the traits they listed. Introduce the idea of reading a biography to find evidence in the next phase of the project.

Assess

- Review and discuss: Look over the completed list of presidential jobs and traits with the students. To be sure the students understand which tasks are appropriate for a president, ask the following types of questions:
  - Can the president decide what you will do during your school vacation?
  - Can the president decide how much money to spend on building our army?
- Select important traits: As students leave, remind them that we are going to be looking for the traits we identified in our work on presidents. In preparation for the next phase of their investigation, ask the students to come up to the board and place sticky notes with their names on them next to the traits they think are the most important.

Reflecting on Student Outcomes

What happened, and why?

All students were familiar with President Obama and understood that there were other presidents before him. When asked what he did, many responded with very general answers (e.g., "He is in charge of America"). Modeling how to read for information was important to show students how to identify more specific work accomplished by the president. It was critical to guide the discussion with cues and prompts.

When we created the list of the traits possessed by an effective president, it was important to begin with a discussion about describing words and to model the first one. It also helped to have students work in smaller groups of two or three to brainstorm words. When the children reported out, it was easy for everyone to see the traits most commonly identified.

How did this influence our next actions?

The next steps in this project involved having students read or listen to biographies of two important presidents and look for the traits we had identified in our first lesson. Before we began reading the biographies, we carefully reviewed the list we had created in the first lesson. We reminded students about how we stopped to record information when we found something that presidents did and to also model this process again. We reinforced that students would need this information to vote intelligently for the best president and to write their paragraphs supporting their choices.

Plan 3:
Amazing Animals:
How They Survive (Grade 2)

Chelsea Sims

DESCRIBING THE CONTEXT

Subjects integrated: Science, Language Arts

Duration of project: Three weeks

SUMMARIZING THE PROJECT

The inquiry process is new but in many ways familiar to second-grade students, who are constantly wondering about the world around them. A topic of great interest to many students is animals—a natural fit for a formal introduction to research skills. Combining a language arts unit that called for writing informative pieces and a science unit in which students investigated how living things survive in their habitats, this collaborative unit built on reading, writing, and information literacy skills developed throughout the school year.

In the Wonder stage, students chose an animal of interest to them from resources available in the library and brainstormed questions as a class. A graphic organizer was created based on several of the more universal student-created questions that closely related to the essential questions of the unit. Lessons on locating information in the library had been previously completed during 25-minute library class periods as part of a fixed schedule, and lessons on text features had been taught separately by the classroom teacher and during library classes. Students used language arts and science class time to complete their reading, note taking, and finally writing to express their findings. Student writing was shared in a display near the classroom, and selections were also posted on the teacher's Web site.

BUILDING AN INQUIRY FOCUS

Concept addressed
- Interdependence: living things must interact with their surroundings to survive.

Essential question investigated
- How does an animal's body help it survive in its habitat?

Critical skills taught
- Locating informational books in the library by call number and section; information can be organized to help learners make meaning
- Forming questions on a focused topic
- Using text features to find information efficiently

CONNECTING THE STANDARDS

AASL *Standards for the 21st Century Learner*

2. Draw conclusions, make informed decisions, apply knowledge to new situations, and create new knowledge.
Indicators 2.1.2, 2.2.1

4. Pursue personal and aesthetic growth.
Indicator 4.3.2

Common Core State Standards

CC.2.W.7>>English Language Arts>>Writing>>Research to Build and Present Knowledge>>7. Participate in shared research and writing projects (e.g., read a number of books on a single topic to produce a report; record science observations).

CC.2.W.8>>English Language Arts>>Writing>> Research to Build and Present Knowledge>>8. Recall information from experiences or gather information from provided sources to answer a question.

SAMPLE LESSON

Lesson focus: Using text features to make inferences

Resources: Digital images, informational texts selected by students

Duration: One 25-minute library class period followed by a 30-minute language arts block

Designing for Learning

Learning outcomes desired: I can
- use text features to locate key facts or information in text.
- ask questions about objects, living things, and our environment to get information or solve problems.
- draw or write my observations and conclusions.

Assessing for learning: I will
- locate and identify a picture and caption in a nonfiction book.
- use a picture and caption to create a relevant question or record a key fact.

Learning plan to achieve outcomes

Introduce
- Open the inquiry by saying, "Today we will look at how animals' bodies can help them survive."
- Challenge with questions: "Our body parts do different things to help us live. What does our mouth help us do? Our nose? How does smell help us survive? What about our skin? Would we be good at living outside if we didn't have clothes? What do animals use to help them live outside?"

Model
- Engage interest: Show digital images of animals projected for the class.
- Think aloud while viewing an image: "When I look at this bird, I think about its wings. I wonder what its wings help it do. I know the bird lives in a tall tree and that wings let it fly. So that makes me think, or *infer*, that maybe its wings help it survive so it can fly to find food and stay safe. I also think about its claws, or talons. I wonder what the talons do to help it to survive. I could *infer* that maybe it needs talons to pick up food from the ground or help it land on tall trees."
- Continue sharing and thinking aloud: "Let's look at another picture. What do you notice? What parts of its body do you think will help it survive? What habitat would these body parts allow an animal to live in?"

- Model the use of an organizer: "Let's practice writing our answers on a graphic organizer. You already have the name of your own animal in the middle diamond. Find the square with the question 'What does the animal look like?' Let's write our description of the animal here. Find the square with the question 'How does the animal's body help it survive in its habitat?' Let's write what we think, or infer, in this box. Later, we will check another source to make sure we are correct, and change our answer if we are not."

Practice

- Explain the task by saying: "You will try this activity on your own in the books you had already chosen about your animal. Last time we practiced using the table of contents and headings to help us find important information in a nonfiction book. Remember, authors and illustrators use text features to help us learn more information. Today, you are going to find a picture with a caption in order to learn more about your animal."
- Infer from a picture with a caption: "Describe the animal. What do you wonder about the animal? Look at the picture and caption and think about what you know about other animals and how their bodies help them live where they do. Can you make an inference, or a good guess, about how you think this animal uses its body to help it survive in its habitat? Write your ideas on your graphic organizer."
- Complete organizers: Students work on using text features to research the animals they have selected and complete the organizers. Circulate as students work and provide assistance as needed.

Assess

- Study the completed graphic organizers to see if students were able to accurately describe their animals and infer about how the animals use their bodies to survive in particular habitats.

Reflecting on Student Outcomes

What happened, and why?

Students had trouble staying focused during the discussion part of the lesson—the set of expectations and skills obviously needed more explanation and practice. During the modeling stage, students were very excited to ask their own questions and share what they already knew about the animals in the pictures. When students were ready to practice on their own, most students had no trouble coming up with questions and making inferences about their animals and what their bodies might help them to do. Of course, some animals were easier to make inferences about than others—how a frog's webbed feet helped it swim was easier to determine than how a platypus's bill helps it to eat in a river. A few students were only able to report basic things about the animal, for example, sharks have sharp teeth. With some prompting and more modeling, I was able to redirect most students to come up with interesting ideas and inferences based on the images and captions that they read and viewed.

How did this influence my next actions?

Because students came up with so many great ideas on their own, I took a few extra minutes at the end of class for students to share what they discovered with each other. Many were interested in other animals and asked if they could research other animals as well. This led to an interesting discussion about researchers learning "deeply" or just learning a little bit. I realized that questioning and inferring skills are very closely related—if students ask questions about their animals first, with some prompting, they can often make inferences about the answers on their own. For example, one student asked why cheetahs had spots. With some of my own questions and referring back to the image, he was able to infer that the spots help it to hide in the tall grass of the savannah. Realizing this, I added a section to the graphic organizer for one or two of my students' questions in addition to the questions we came up with as a group. In previous sessions like this one, I had found that students had trouble coming up with questions; but this particular group of students was more able to come up with things they wondered about and therefore made inferences more quickly. Perhaps this happened because I spent more time modeling my own thinking and forming of questions.

Plan 4:
What's Our History?
Our Sugar Plantation Past (Grade 3)

Debora Lum

DESCRIBING THE CONTENT

Subjects integrated: Social Studies, Language Arts

Duration of project: One quarter

SUMMARIZING THE PROJECT

Our community of Waipahu has a unique and interesting history in Hawaii. It was originally built around the sugar plantation economy with laborers from both the Far East and Europe. The sugar company shut down in the mid-1990s, and today Waipahu is a suburban community.

Susan Nakagawa, a third-grade teacher, and I collaborated on a project to engage young students in raising questions about the community's history and to seek information that they might share with families. The project began with students taking a gallery walk through archival photos, and it blossomed into the students studying additional archival materials, e-mailing staff at a sugar company on a neighboring island, and interviewing community residents. Our students also partnered with older students in the Academy of Travel, Tourism and Telecommunications at Waipahu High School. They ultimately produced multi-media artifacts from their findings that we edited and incorporated into CD products that were distributed to all the families.

BUILDING AN INQUIRY FOCUS

Concept addressed
- Change and continuity

Essential questions investigated
- What is a sugar plantation? What kind of work do people perform on a plantation?
- What was life like on a plantation? How did the company help its workers?
- How has our community changed over the years? Why did this happen?
- What things are still the same even with the changes?

Critical skills taught
- Finding reliable, credible resources on Waipahu's sugar plantation community
- Reflecting on the research process to help problem solve the next steps
- Demonstrating critical listening skills
- Practicing interviewing skills (face to face and via telephone)
- Searching the local newspapers using keywords
- Designing a multimedia page with Hyperstudio 5

Differentiated skills taught based on information needs and resources
- Writing letters to request information
- E-mailing

CONNECTING THE STANDARDS

AASL *Standards for the 21st-Century Learner*

1. Inquiry, think critically, and gain knowledge.
Indicators 1.1.1, 1.1.3, 1.1.6

2. Draw conclusions, make informed decisions, apply knowledge to new situations, and create new knowledge.
Indicators 2.3.1, 2.4.1, 2.4.3

3. Share new knowledge and participate ethically and productively as members of our democratic society.
Indicators 3.1.1, 3.1.3, 3.1.6

4. Pursue personal and aesthetic growth.
Indicators 4.2.1, 4.4.1, 4.4.2

159

SAMPLE LESSON

Lesson focus: Developing student connections to the Waipahu sugar plantation community through a critical examination of archival photographs

Resources:

- Photographs courtesy of the Hawaii State Archives, Waipahu Zippy's Restaurant
- Scott, Edward B. *The Saga of the Sandwich Islands.* Lake Tahoe: Sierra-Tahoe Publishing Co., 1968
- Baker, Ray Jerome. *Hawaiian Yesterdays: Historical Photographs.* Honolulu: Mutual Publishing Co., 1982

Duration: One 45–60 minute session

Designing for Learning

Learning outcomes desired: I can

- identify clues about life during the sugar plantation days by closely studying photographs.
- ask questions about the sugar plantation days that I want to explore after seeing the photographs.

Assessing for learning

- I will be able to create at least two questions about life during the plantation days by closely studying the photographs.

Learning plan to achieve outcomes

Introduce

- Read aloud: Prior to the gallery walk, do a read-aloud of Leo Lionni's *Frederick*. During the postdiscussion, point out that the mice remind us that a community or a group living together help each other survive.
- Invite wonder by asking: "What are some things people need to survive?" (Responses might include food, shelter, clothing, rules/laws so people get along, jobs.)
- Connect to the story: Frederick in Lionni's picture book adds something else to the community that is also important. Ask: "What are other important things in a community?" (Responses might include poetry, art, music, games.)
- Connect to the project: Relate the picture book to the community the students live in—Waipahu.
- Explain: "What things looked like in the past is not what we see today. Where we now live was once part of a sugar cane field, part of a sugar plantation community. To help you return to those earlier days, the library will become a walking gallery with large photographs of what Waipahu's sugar plantation community was like."

- Engage students: Have the students consider the following types of questions on the gallery walk:
  - What did the community look like?
  - Who lived in the community?
  - How did the people work together?
  - How did the community meet people's needs?

Model

- Conduct a gallery walk: Take the students on a photo tour of Waipahu's sugar plantation days. At the start of the tour, inform the students that they will have a chance to look more closely at the photos that interest them.
- Model: On the tour, focus on a particular photograph and invite students to look closely at it.
- Facilitate discussion: Guide the discussion with questions like the following:
  - Ask: What do you see? (Possible responses: A man standing next to the sugar cane; the sugar cane looks taller than the man.)
  - Point out that the photo is trying to show us how tall the cane grows, but do we really know how tall it is? (Different responses possible.) Why? (One student points out that we don't know how tall the man is. He could be short.)
  - Ask: What questions might we have about sugar cane? (Possible responses: How big is sugar cane? How much sugar does a sugar cane plant make?)
- Flag use of notes: Direct students to a pad of sticky notes near each display board. Students will write their names and questions about what they see in the photos on the sticky notes.
- Provide more tips: Before allowing them to begin the tour, remind students to pay careful attention to the background (sugar fields, rice fields, town), the equipment, and the people (what they are doing and what they are wearing).

Practice

- Participate in the gallery walk: Students identify at least one photograph that they are curious about.
- Observe and question: They carefully study the photographs and develop questions based on them.
- Record: They write their questions on sticky notes and attach them to the photographs.

Assess

Note: Prior to this session, the teacher had asked her students for questions they had about Waipahu's plantation community.

- Assess questions: The teacher and librarian compare the quality of the students' questions before and after the gallery walk.
- Share questions: They also ask students to share some of their questions with the rest of the class.

Reflecting on Student Outcomes

What happened, and why?

As a result of what they saw, the children's questions after the gallery walk reflected a deeper interest and curiosity about the Waipahu plantation community. Instead of asking about the kinds of animals and pets the people had, they were asking about water buffalos in rice paddies, how sugar was made, and how the people got along on the plantation. They wanted to know more about the equipment, trains, and cars in the photographs. This was great!

How did this influence our next actions?

As instructors, we compared the two sets of questions (pre and post); however, we should have included the students in this conversation to help them develop "good" questions in the future. Involving them in this self-assessment would have helped the students realize that having background knowledge aids in developing questions for deeper understanding.

We shaped the unit based on the types of questions that the students raised. Key activities included the following:

- connecting children with guest speakers and resources
- introducing lessons on keyword searching to retrieve information from local newspaper sites
- teaching students to share their research process reflections to help them determine next steps

Since we first developed this unit in 2001, it has become an annual activity for third-grade classes. Senior citizens who grew up on the Waipahu sugar plantation have volunteered to share their experiences and personal artifacts. Their contributions have added special value to the photo gallery walk and the entire project.

Plan 5:
Water for a Thirsty Planet
(Grade 5)

Suzy Rabbat

DESCRIBING THE CONTEXT

Subjects integrated: Science, Global Issues, Language Arts: Opinion Writing

Duration of project: One month

SUMMARIZING THE PROJECT

Although 70 percent of the earth's surface is covered with water, much of it is undrinkable. The water that is drinkable is not evenly distributed around the globe. In some places, finding drinking water is a constant daily problem. In addition, overuse, contamination, and global climate change continue to have a great impact on the world's drinking water.

In this project, students broadened their awareness of the world's water problems and explored various ways scientists are working to solve them. They investigated methods for accessing safe drinking water in countries where clean water is scarce. These methods included rainwater harvesting and the use of fog nets, and Lifestraws (personal water filters). Students shared their new knowledge through a series of public service announcements that were posted on the school Web site and broadcast on the daily school news. The PSAs raised the awareness of the school community regarding the importance of preserving natural resources and working together to improve the lives of others. Before taking a look at how people accessed water around the world, students began by developing an understanding of how they accessed drinking water in their community.

BUILDING AN INQUIRY FOCUS

Concepts addressed
- Global issues: water supply
- Preserving natural resources for present and future use

Essential questions investigated
- How do problems lead to discovery?
- How does *where you live* impact *how you live*?
- Would you rather get your drinking water from a municipal water tower or a private well?

Critical skills taught
- Reading critically to understand a process
- Organizing information so that it is useful in communicating your message
- Analyzing evidence from the text to support a claim
- Arriving at a well-reasoned conclusion
- Reflecting on personal understanding

CONNECTING THE STANDARDS

AASL *Standards for the 21st Century Learner*

1. Inquire, think critically, and gain knowledge.
Indicators 1.1.1, 1.1.9

2. Draw conclusions, make informed decisions, apply knowledge to new situations, and create new knowledge.
Indicators 2.1.2, 2.1.3

3. Share knowledge and participate ethically and productively as members of our democratic society.
Indicators 3.1.3, 3.1.5

Common Core State Standards

CC.5.RI.1>>English Language Arts>>Reading Informational>>Key Ideas and Details>>1. Quote accurately from a text when explaining what the text says explicitly and when drawing inferences from the text.

CC.5.RI.8>>English Language Arts>>Reading Informational>> Integration of Knowledge and Ideas>>8. Explain how an author uses reasons and evidence to support particular points in a text, identifying which reasons and evidence support which point(s).

CC.5.W.1>>English Language Arts>>Writing>>Text Types and Purposes>>1.Write opinion pieces on topics or texts, supporting a point of view with reasons and information.

CC.5.W.7>>English Language Arts>>Writing>>Research to Build and Present Knowledge>>7. Conduct short research projects that use several sources to build knowledge through investigations of different aspects of a topic.

CC.5.W.9>>English Language Arts>>Writing>>Research to Build and Present Knowledge>> 9. Draw evidence from literary or informational texts to support analysis, reflection, and research.

SAMPLE LESSON

Lesson focus: Critically reading informational text and taking notes

Resources:
- Municipal Water Tower:
  - EPA Kids Water Treatment Process, http://water.epa.gov/learn/kids /drinkingwater/watertreatmentplant_index.cfm
  - Brunelle, Lynn. *Turn on the Faucet*. San Diego, CA: Blackbirch Press, 2004
- Private Wells
  - USGS Water Science School—Groundwater: Wells, http://ga.water.usgs .gov/edu/earthgwwells.html
  - USGS Water Science School—Contamination in U.S. Private Wells, http:// ga.water.usgs.gov/edu/gw-well-contamination.html

Duration: Three one-hour sessions: two sessions to gather information and one session to reach a personal conclusion and complete the written analysis and synthesis of the research findings

Designing for Learning

Learning outcomes desired: I can
- read critically to identify the differences between two methods people use to access drinking water: from a municipal water tower and from a private well.
- weigh evidence from my research to support my opinion.

Assessing for learning: I will
- read to identify and understand important attributes in drinking water.
- locate evidence from the texts to address each attribute.
- organize and analyze the evidence in order to determine which water source I would prefer.

Learning plan to achieve outcomes

Introduce

- Invite curiosity by asking: "When you turn on the faucet to get a glass of water, have you ever wondered how the water gets to your kitchen sink? What body of water is used to supply your drinking water? How does it get from the source to your home? What kind of process does it go through to remove impurities? How do you know it's safe to drink?"
- Introduce new information: Explain that two of the most common ways people access drinking water in the United States are through a municipal water tower or a private well.
- Explain the learning goal: "You will be asked to decide on your preferred way to access drinking water, but first it is important to understand how both systems provide water to homeowners. We'll do this by learning about municipal water towers and private wells using a strategy called critical reading."
- Focus on critical reading: Emphasize that critical reading is an important skill that helps the reader uncover all the important ideas presented in the text. In order to analyze information, stress that students must first develop an understanding of the information. Elaborate that reading critically requires
  - dividing the text into small chunks,
  - reading slowly,
  - rereading to check understanding,
  - questioning what was read, and
  - connecting the ideas to other information read.

Model

- Introduce a sample: Begin with an article or book excerpt that explains how a municipal water tower works. In addition to projecting the text on a screen for all to see, provide hard copies for students to mark as you model the skill of critical reading.
- Set the purpose for reading: "We are reading to understand how this method provides access to drinking water. We want to find out how a water tower works. There may be additional interesting information in the article, but we will focus on understanding how the water gets from the water source to the tower, and ultimately, to the kitchen faucet."

- Demonstrate: Read the first two or three paragraphs aloud. Stop to determine if there is any information that would help students understand how the water tower works. Explain, "This portion of the text explains that the water is treated in a treatment plant to remove sediment and bacteria before it is pumped into the tower. This ensures that the water is safe to drink."
- Think aloud: "Knowing that my water is safe to drink is important in making my decision. I'm going to underline this portion of the text—please do the same on your copy. In the margin, I will write the word, *safety*, as a reminder that this portion of the text talks about purifying the water so it is safe to drink."
- Explain: "A graphic organizer, like the matrix below, can be used to organize notes in a way that makes it easy to weigh the evidence when making a decision."

Attribute	Municipal Water Tower	Private Well	Reflections
Safety	Water is tested and processed to remove impurities.		

- Continue reading the next few paragraphs aloud: Model the process of critical reading by thinking aloud. Example: "This portion of text mentions that some water towers are shaped or painted to represent something that is unique to the town. For example, the water tower in Rosemont, IL, is painted to resemble a rose. This may be interesting, but it doesn't supply the information needed to address the essential question. I won't include it in my notes."
- Engage students in discussion: As you move through the article, engage students in deciding which information is relevant and how to record this on the graphic organizer. Solicit suggestions for labeling each attribute based on the content presented. By completing the article, students will have identified several important concepts related to water accessed from a municipal water tower.
- Provide a second resource: During the second research session, provide copies of the second resource that explains how people access water through a private well. Model the critical reading of the first few paragraphs by reading and thinking aloud. Perhaps the text will begin by explaining that homeowners need to supply their own pumps to bring the well water to their homes. Help students infer that the pump runs on electricity. If there is a power failure, this may result in no access to water. Guide students in scanning their notes to determine where to record this information on the graphic organizer. The facts in the second text will not necessarily be presented in the same order as in the first text.

- Introduce metacognition: The fourth column in the graphic organizer encourages students to capture their thoughts about the information they have gathered. Students may also use this space to record questions they still have, helping them identify the gaps in their understanding. This metacognitive practice sets the stage for synthesizing and analyzing the evidence to support their claims.

Attribute	Municipal Water Tower	Private Well	Reflections
Safety	Water is tested and processed to remove impurities.	Well water may become contaminated by chemicals from fertilizers.	If I had a well, how would I know if my water was contaminated? Can I trust that the water from the municipal water tower is safe to drink?
Dependability	The water tower can hold enough water to supply the town for several days.	If there is a power failure, the pump cannot bring water to the house unless we have a back-up generator. If there's a drought, your well may run dry.	It would be hard to be without water, even for a short time. What do people do when the well dries up?

Practice

- Provide pointers for practice: "As you read to understand about water from a private well, you will continue to apply the skill of critical reading." Tips to keep in mind:
  - "Look for information that addresses the same attributes we found when reading about the municipal water tower. You may also find information that is unique to a private well but important in making your decision. Be sure to include this in the graphic organizer. As a result, your graphic organizer may not have information recorded in all fields."
  - "As you compare your notes on both water sources, remember to record your thoughts, reactions, and questions in the reflection column."

- Provide feedback: Circulate as students continue reading and taking notes. Having combed through the resources prior to the session, you will have a clear idea of the attributes and related information students will find in these selected resources. This will guide you in steering students to portions of the text they may need to re-read.

Assess

- Weigh the evidence by asking: "What are the attributes you feel strongly about, for example, safety, cost, dependability?"
- Summarize: "Write a paragraph summarizing your research. State your claim in the topic sentence. Cite at least three pieces of evidence from the texts to support your claim."

Note: The focus of this lesson is to identify evidence that supports a claim. It does not matter which method students prefer. What is important is the evidence they provide to support their answers.

Reflecting on Student Outcomes

What happened, and why?

By providing limited preselected resources, students focused on close reading and locating relevant information from the text, rather than skimming several sources. Although most students were able to provide evidence from the texts to support their claim, some of the notes on the graphic organizers showed incorrect information or misinterpretation of what was read. Since students have not had extensive practice with this reading strategy, I feel additional support and scaffolding is needed.

How did this influence my next actions?

When modeling critical reading using the first resource, students benefited from discussing the text, their understandings, and their reactions. When left to read and analyze the second resource, this rich discussion was missing. In the future, I would encourage students to read the second text independently and collaborate on the note-taking process. If I post the graphic organizer in Google Docs or on a wiki, students will be able to share their findings and reactions with a team of researchers. In the end, each would be responsible for stating his or her claim and providing evidence; however, the exchange of ideas during the research process would strengthen students' understanding and clarify their thinking.

In addition, the information presented in the resources would have been easier for students to process if they had some background knowledge about surface water and ground water. This distinction wasn't made when we introduced the topic. We realized that this explanation would have provided a context for understanding some of the risks and benefits associated with a water tower and a private well.

Plan 6:
Geography: Bringing the World Home (Grade 6)

Elizabeth Gartley

DESCRIBING THE CONTEXT

Subjects integrated: World Geography, English Language Arts

Duration of project: Four to five 45-minute sessions (including introduction, research sessions, and share/museum walk)

SUMMARIZING THE PROJECT

This project was designed to align with the state social studies frameworks for sixth-grade world geography in a diverse, urban school. The school has a large immigrant population, with two-thirds of the students speaking a first language other than English, which creates a rich, international school culture. This was a collaborative project involving the school librarian, a classroom teacher, and a staff member who served as a U.S. Peace Corps volunteer in Samoa. Our objective was to move beyond the typical country project by having students dig for deeper and personally meaningful facts.

In the introductory lesson, students developed questions based on the presentation of a guest speaker (in this case a former Peace Corps volunteer staff member). The student-generated questions informed their investigations into the daily lives and work of people in countries around the world. The essential question that framed the research was,

"How does where you live affect how you live?" In subsequent lessons, students imagined that they lived and worked in a self-selected country and shared their findings through exhibits displayed in the library for the school community to view and enjoy.

BUILDING AN INQUIRY FOCUS

Concepts addressed
- Human interaction with the environment
- Movement (of people, goods, and ideas)
- Culture shock

Other related concepts aligned with the social studies curriculum frameworks:
- Location (absolute and relative)
- Place (physical and man-made characteristics of a place, such as a town or city)
- Regions
- Demographic terms (ethnic group, religious group, linguistic group)
- Standard of living

Essential questions investigated
- What is it like to live and work in another country and culture?
- How does where we live affect how we live?

Critical skills taught
- Using prior and background knowledge to contextualize new learning
- Developing questions to investigate that require going beyond superficial facts
- Considering global perspectives and interpreting information within a cultural context

CONNECTING THE STANDARDS

AASL *Standards for the 21st-Century Learner*

1. Inquire, think critically, and gain knowledge.
Indicators 1.1.2, 1.1.3, 1.2.1, 1.3.4

2. Draw conclusions, make informed decisions, apply knowledge to new situations, and create new knowledge.
Indicators 2.3.2, 2.4.4

4. Pursue personal and aesthetic growth.
Indicators 4.1.5, 4.4.4

SAMPLE LESSON

Lesson focus: Developing and refining questions relevant to life and work in another country

Resources: Guest speaker and artifacts from the guest speaker's country

Duration: One 45-minute class period

Designing for Learning

Learning outcomes desired
- I can ask questions that are connected to life and work in another country after listening to our speaker.

Assessing for learning
- I will write at least two questions regarding life and work in another country based on the presentation of our guest speaker.

Learning plan to achieve outcomes

Introduce

- Inquire and connect: Engage students' interest by asking the following types of questions:
  - Who has visited or traveled to another country?
  - Who came to the United States from another country?
  - Who has family that emigrated from outside the United States?
  - How do we think life in the United States is different from life in other countries around the world?
  - How might where you live impact how you live?
- The instructor will record student responses and ideas on a whiteboard or newsprint for future reference.
- Explain the project goal: Inform students that they will choose a country to study from a list of developing countries around the world. They are encouraged to select a country of which they have little to no prior background knowledge. In this project, students will imagine that they are living and working in the chosen country, and will investigate how the location affects lifestyles there. They will create museum displays and share these final products with classmates and the wider school community.
- Set the context for the next activity: Inform students that they will be hearing a guest speaker talk about his or her experience living and working overseas. Challenge them to listen carefully and jot down questions they might have as they listen to the speaker. Emphasize that the questions they develop will guide their research on the countries.
- Introduce the essential question: Present and discuss the essential question with the students: "How does where you live impact how you live?"

Model

- Invite preliminary questions: Introduce the guest speaker, his or her country, and the topic. Engage students in generating preliminary questions for the speaker and the country of focus (Examples: Why did you go there? What was your job? What food do the people eat there?). Record student responses.
- Prepare for active listening: The speaker will share experiences of life and work overseas, touching on world geography themes such as absolute and relative location, region, housing, food, and transportation, and other topics as appropriate. This portion of the presentation may include pictures, artifacts, dress/clothing, music, or other available items. Role-play something the speaker might say. Demonstrate how you might listen carefully and jot down facts and questions based on the speaker's presentation.

Practice

- Practice active listening: Students listen to the guest speaker, take brief notes, and jot down questions based on the presentation.
- Revisit preliminary questions: Students review initial questions and responses with the instructor and speaker. They reflect on the following:
  - What have we learned?
  - Which questions were answered?
  - What new questions do we have?
- Record student responses.
- Extend and expand on questions: As a group, generate two or three new sample questions (Examples: How did you cope without Internet or TV? Was it hard to get used to life in [your country]? How hot or cold does it get there?). To ensure quality thinking, discuss the relevance and appropriateness of the questions.
- Generate and record new questions: Have students individually write down two new questions about the presentation regarding life and work in another country.

Assess

- Share and comment on new questions: Engage students in sharing some of the new questions before collecting them for a more formal assessment. Reinforce that these questions will be saved and used to guide research. Recommended: transfer or rewrite questions onto a poster or newsprint.
- Next phase: Students will select a country to begin their independent investigations during the next class session.

Reflecting on Student Outcomes

What happened, and why?

The students enjoyed the lesson, and I was impressed with the quality and variety of their questions (Examples: Would you rather live in the United States or Samoa? Would you do it again? Why did you join the Peace Corps? What sports do they play in Samoa? What are everyday activities for people living in Samoa? Did you play with the kids? What is the hottest/coldest it gets there?).

In keeping with inquiry-based learning and our essential question (How does where you live affect how you live?), even seemingly simple questions, such as "What is the hottest/coldest it gets there?" led to further research and insights. I explained that Samoa has a tropical climate, and most houses have roofs to protect people from rain and sun, but no walls (to allow the breeze to come through). Naturally, this revelation led to more questions about privacy and culture. However, this connection and style of investigation did not come naturally to students. Generating their own researchable questions was a new experience for the students, and many became anxious about including the "right" information. We also had to work closely with students because they became frustrated when they encountered (real or perceived) dead ends during the research process.

How did this influence our next actions?

The students were accustomed to having project elements explicitly outlined and were somewhat overwhelmed and intimidated by the independence of a student-driven project. As a result, many students became easily frustrated and fixated on minor points. As the project progressed, we had to repeatedly reinforce and review the guiding questions. We also provided encouragement and feedback throughout the project, both in the library and in the classroom. In future projects, we plan to more strongly emphasize the purpose of developing questions in the early phase of research. We are also aware that we need to anticipate and deal with concerns that students experience in conducting more independent investigations.

Plan 7:
Zombie Apocalypse:
The Invasion of an Infectious
Disease (Grade 7)

Elizabeth Schau and Chelsea Sims
with Lynda Johnson, Ben Mosher,
Andrew Smith, and Scott Stimmel

DESCRIBING THE CONTEXT

Subjects integrated: Science, Information Literacy, and Language Arts

Duration of project: Three weeks

SUMMARIZING THE PROJECT

This annual collaborative research project on infectious diseases had been losing its luster with our students. To spice it up and nudge it toward inquiry, we collaborated with Science 7 teachers Lynda Johnson, Ben Mosher, Andrew Smith, and Scott Stimmel. We decided to give the project a new spin: students would take on the role of expert pathologists—the only ones left on Earth!

The project began with breaking news about a worldwide outbreak of a disease that caused zombielike symptoms. The disease spread so quickly and with such devastating effect that the scientists who had gathered to research the problem had all perished, leaving only the scientists in our seventh-grade classrooms to solve the crisis. In this role, students each researched one well-known disease and developed a presentation to share with their colleagues. Once their expertise had been shared, groups created recommendations for further study based on which well-known diseases seemed to be most similar to the unknown "zombie" disease. This scenario allowed students to address many of the same concepts, questions, and information literacy skills that the traditional project did, but with much more student interest and an "authentic" problem to solve. Presentations were contained within the classrooms, but in the future, we plan to have students share across classes and with the other junior high schools in the district.

BUILDING AN INQUIRY FOCUS

Concept addressed
- Global infectious diseases
  - There are differences in how people contract a disease.
  - Microbes cause many infectious diseases.
  - There are many ways to reduce the risk of contracting diseases.

Essential questions investigated
- How do diseases spread?
- How is public health impacted?
- How can the spread of disease be treated and/or prevented?

Critical skills taught
- Retrieving, evaluating, analyzing, and using information from print and online sources
- Synthesizing information from multiple sources to answer questions
- Using text features to find information efficiently
- Identifying and recording key information in organized notes
- Making well-reasoned conclusions and suggesting data-supported solutions to problems
- Sharing information to enhance knowledge

CONNECTING THE STANDARDS

AASL *Standards for the 21st-Century Learner*

1. Inquire, think critically, and gain knowledge.
Indicators 1.1.1, 1.1.8, 1.1.9, 1.4.1, 1.4.3

2. Draw conclusions, make informed decisions, apply knowledge to new situations, and create new knowledge.
Indicators 2.1.1, 2.1.2, 2.1.5, 2.1.6

3. Share knowledge and participate ethically and productively as members of our democratic society.
Indicators 3.1.1, 3.1.4, 3.1.6

Common Core State Standards

CC.6-8.RST.7>>English Language Arts/Science and Technical Subjects >>Reading Science and Technical>>Integration of Knowledge and Ideas>>7. Integrate quantitative or technical information expressed in words in a text with a version of that information expressed visually (e.g., in a flowchart, diagram, model, graph or table).

CC.6-8.RST.8>>English Language Arts/Science and Technical Subjects >>Reading Science and Technical>>Integration of Knowledge and Ideas>>8. Distinguish among facts, reasoned judgment based on research findings, and speculation in a text.

Iowa State Standards

21st Century Skills (Grades 6–8)
- Communicate clearly.
- Create a plan for the use of digital tools and resources to investigate a real world issue.
- Locate, organize, analyze, evaluate and synthesize information from a variety of sources and media and use this information in a legal and ethical manner.
- Use technological tools to select data and organize it into a format that is easily understood by others.
- Develop possible solutions or a complete product to demonstrate knowledge and skills.
- Use technology efficiently and in a manner that does not harm them or others.

Science (Grade 6–8)
- Select and use appropriate tools and techniques to gather, analyze, and interpret data.
- Incorporate mathematics in scientific inquiry.
- Think critically and logically to make the relationship between evidence and explanations.
- Disease is a breakdown in structures or functions of an organism. Some diseases are the result of intrinsic failures of the system. Others are the result of damage by infection caused by other organisms.

SAMPLE LESSON

Lesson focus: Identifying main ideas and supporting details from text-based resources using a two-column organizer for notes

Resources: Encyclopedia article, two-column notes organizer

Duration: One 45-minute lesson

Designing for Learning

Learning outcomes desired: I can
- state the central idea in a text.
- provide a summary of the text.
- gather information from multiple sources.
- quote or paraphrase information while avoiding plagiarism.
- analyze the main ideas and supporting details in diverse media and formats.
- use a standard format for citations.

Assessing for learning: I will
- identify and state the main idea in an informational text.
- paraphrase information while avoiding plagiarism when gathering information from multiple sources.

Learning plan to achieve outcomes

Introduce

- Set the stage by explaining, "Scientists always begin their research by reviewing the materials that already exist from the data generated by the hard work of others. We will learn what we can about this unknown disease from what the scientists before us published in a (fake) encyclopedia article titled 'Z-X227.' Scientists also need to be able to remember what they have learned and be able to compare it to existing data. One method of recording our new knowledge is through two-column note taking. This format will help us organize what we learn and enable us to easily find and review what we have written for later comparison."

Model

- Introduce the learning resources: Each student will have a copy of the teacher-created encyclopedia article that was modeled after the specialized encyclopedia that students will use independently the next day in the unit. Project the article and the two-column notes format on the interactive whiteboard so all students can view and participate in the modeling of the note taking.
- Think aloud and model: Review the SQR method (modified from SQ3R).
  - Survey: Look over the article, survey, skim, notice important text features such as headings, captions, and bold words.
  - Question: Determine the main ideas or big questions using the headings. In this step, remind students of the unit's essential questions and what scientists need to know when studying an infectious disease.
    - Model using the section headings to fill in the first column of the two-column notes.
    - Point out that these headings produce a clear structure for organizing new learning and relate well to the essential questions.
  - Read: Read aloud the first small section of the text and challenge the class to select one word that best summarizes the main idea of that section.
    - Discuss additional key facts in the section and model through think-aloud if each fact should be included or not.
    - Seek student input on putting key facts in one's own words and why this is important.
- Continue modeling: Repeat the same process with another section of the article. Record notes on the projected organizer for students to include in their own research packets.

Practice

- Organize teams: Assign small groups of students (lab teams) the remaining sections of the article. Each team focuses on a different section. Students work together to read, analyze, and determine the key facts in the assigned section.
- Provide feedback: The teacher and you confer with each group to make suggestions and ask questions during this guided practice session.

Assess

- Share findings: The class regroups to share what each lab team found and recorded. Groups record their notes on the projected form.
- Provide feedback: Teachers and students make suggestions for rewording, additions, or removal of unnecessary facts.
- Plan ahead: Announce that students will use the same format and process to record notes on their own topic using various print and online sources. The same headings from the original article will be used multiple times, reinforcing the essential questions for the unit.

Reflecting on Student Outcomes

What happened, and why?

Students were excited to learn about this new disease that was currently causing a "Zombie Apocalypse." This created sustained attention throughout the lesson. The shorter paragraphs allowed for clear large group demonstration. The longer paragraphs challenged students to discuss the information in their lab teams and decide on the information necessary for further study. Given the diverse abilities of the students, we realized that the first audience for the notes had to be the individual note taker. Some students used more sophisticated language; others broke terms down into simpler language they could understand. For example, one student was able to use the word "transmission" in her notes, but another student used the phrase "spread of disease" to comprehend the term. In inclusive classes with special education students and struggling readers, we created a note-taking guide with fill-in-the-blank phrases to help them focus on the most important ideas and not get bogged down in the details. As students recorded information about the big ideas of treatment and prevention, they also discussed human rights, ethics, and morality (all in the name of zombies). Students left the class with completed notes on a new topic. They were ready to use the same methodology and strategy when they began studying their individual topics in the following session.

How did this influence our next actions?

This session guided our lesson on the following day. We activated prior knowledge of the fake zombie disease as well as the two-column note-taking strategy we had used as a group. Students used their notes from the previous session as a model for their individual efforts. Students were much more independent after receiving their individual topics than they would have been without the previous day's extensive modeling. While many of the headings remained the same, some well-known diseases had headings specific to the topic. For example, "stages and progress" was more pertinent to some diseases than others. In the future, we will consider adding other headings such as "diagnosis" and "history" in the fake zombie article to make sure we fully address the big ideas surrounding research on infectious diseases. We may also integrate a similar lesson earlier in the school year to set the framework for two-column note taking and the construction of meaning from informational text.

Plan 8:
Just One: The Holocaust Story of Ilse Sara Ury (Grade 8)

Ronda Hassig

DESCRIBING THE CONTEXT

Subjects integrated: English Language Arts: Communication Arts/Reading and Social Studies

Duration of project: Four sessions

SUMMARIZING THE PROJECT

Students often have a difficult time contemplating the sheer number of victims who died in the Holocaust—six million Jews. This number goes right over their heads, and it doesn't even include the countless millions of other victims. It is important for students to realize that each one of those six million people must be understood as one person, one human being. "Just One" is a project focusing on themes of guilt and culpability. Students learn the different levels of responsibility identified by noted Holocaust historian Raoul Hilberg, including the roles of perpetrator, collaborator, beneficiary, and bystander. Students then analyze several primary source documents that deal with the life and death of one Holocaust victim—Ilse Ury, a German Jewish author who wrote children's stories. As they analyze the sources, the students retrieve and

From *Inquiry and the Common Core: Librarians and Teachers Designing Teaching for Learning.* Violet H. Harada and Sharon Coatney, Editors. Santa Barbara, CA: Libraries Unlimited. Copyright © 2014.

ponder the *who*, *what*, *where*, *why*, and *when* of the documents and organize the documents in chronological order. Finally, they revisit the evidence in these documents, decide what level of culpability each of the document's participants deserves, and justify their conclusions. Students' responses must be thoughtfully supported from the primary sources.

Note: Peter Mehlbach, a teacher in the international baccalaureate program in Lakewood, Colorado, created the original lesson. I have adapted it with his approval.

BUILDING AN INQUIRY FOCUS

Concepts addressed
- Identifying prejudice and injustice: role of responsibility in the Holocaust
- Combating prejudice and injustice: importance of the individual and his or her actions

Essential questions investigated
- How can the actions of one individual make a difference?
- Do all actions have a consequence?
- To what extent should one take personal action in a catastrophe such as the Holocaust or other genocides?

CONNECTING THE STANDARDS

AASL *Standards for the 21st-Century Learner*

1. Inquire, think critically, and gain knowledge.
Indicators 1.1.1, 1.1.6, 1.1.9, 1.2.1, 1.4.4

2. Draw conclusions, make informed decisions, apply knowledge to new situations, and create new knowledge.
Indicators 2.1.1, 2.1.3, 2.1.5, 2.3.1, 2.4.1, 2.4.3

3. Share knowledge and participate ethically and productively as members of our democratic society.
Indicators 3.1.1, 3.1.3, 3.1.5, 3.2.2, 3.2.3

Common Core State Standards

CC.8.RI.2>>English Language Arts>>Reading Informational>>Key Ideas and Details>>2. Determine a central idea of a text and analyze its development over the course of the text, including its relationship to supporting ideas; provide an objective summary of the text.

CC.8.RI.3>>English Language Arts>>Reading Informational>>Key Ideas and Details>>3. Analyze how a text makes connections among and distinctions between individuals, ideas, or events (e.g., through comparisons, analogies, or categories).

CC.8.RI.6>>English Language Arts>>Reading Informational>>Craft and Structure>>6. Determine an author's point of view or purpose in a text and analyze how the author acknowledges and responds to conflicting evidence or viewpoints.

CC.8.RL.1>>English Language Arts>>Reading Literature>>Key Ideas and Details>>1. Cite the textual evidence that most strongly supports an analysis of what the text says explicitly as well as inferences drawn from the text.

CC.8.W.1>>English Language Arts>>Writing>>Text Types and Purposes>>1. Write arguments to support claims with clear reasons and relevant evidence.

CC.8.W.2d>>English Language Arts>>Writing>>Text Types and Purposes>>2d. Use precise language and domain-specific vocabulary to inform about or explain the topic.

CC.8.SL.1>>English Language Arts>>Speaking and Listening>>Comprehension and Collaboration>>1. Engage effectively in a range of collaborative discussions (one-on-one, in groups, and teacher-led) with diverse partners on grade 8 topics, texts, and issues, building on others' ideas and expressing their own clearly.

CC.8.SL.2>>English Language Arts>>Speaking and Listening>>Comprehension and Collaboration>>2. Analyze the purpose of information presented in diverse media and formats (e.g., visually, quantitatively, orally) and evaluate the motives (e.g., social, commercial, political) behind its presentation.

CC.6-8.RH.2>>English Language Arts>>Reading History>>Key Ideas and Details>>2. Determine the central ideas or information of a primary or secondary source; provide an accurate summary of the source distinct from prior knowledge or opinions.

CC.6-8.RH.4>>English Language Arts>>Reading History>>Craft and Structure>>4. Determine the meaning of words and phrases as they are used in a text, including vocabulary specific to domains related to history/social studies.

CC.6-8.RH.6>>English Language Arts>>Reading History>>Craft and Structure>>6. Identify aspects of a text that reveal an author's point of view or purpose (e.g., loaded language, inclusion or avoidance of particular facts).

CC.6-8.RH.8>>English Language Arts>>Reading History>>Integration of Knowledge and Ideas>>8. Distinguish among fact, opinion, and reasoned judgment in a text.

CC.6-8.WHST.1b>>English Language Arts>>Writing History>>Text Types and Purposes>>1b. Support claim(s) with logical reasoning and relevant, accurate data and evidence that demonstrate an understanding of the topic or text, using credible sources.

CC.6-8.WHST.9>>English Language Arts>>Writing History>>Research to Build and Present Knowledge>>9. Draw evidence from informational texts to support analysis reflection, and research.

SAMPLE LESSONS

Lesson focus: Identifying and analyzing the concept of responsibility in the Holocaust. *Note:* Prior to these sessions, students have done background readings and discussions on the Holocaust.

Resources:
- Raoul Hilberg's Responsibility Classifications in *Perpetrators, Victims, and Bystanders: the Jewish Catastrophe 1933–1945*
- Primary source documents including:
- Document 1—Ordinance from Gestapo—Berlin, 1 October, 1942
- Document 2—To the Mayor of the Reich Capital—Berlin, 15 March, 1943
- Document 3—Report Concerning Evacuated Jews—Berlin, 3 April, 1943
- Document 4—Central Finance Office—Berlin, 20 April, 1943
- Document 5—Transport List—12 January, 1943
- Document 6—Cover Letter for Transport List—12 January, 1943

Duration: Four 45-minute class periods.

Designing for Learning

Learning outcomes desired: I will:
- identify and apply Raoul Hilberg's classifications of responsibility.
- analyze each primary source document for *who, what, where, why,* and *when* and include the meaning and purpose of the document.
- assess responsibility based on evidence within the documents.
- communicate findings in writing and discussions.

Assessing for learning: I will accurately:
- describe the contents of a primary document in terms of the subject and situation presented in it.
- identify the role of the author or producer of the document according to Hilberg's classifications of responsibility.
- explain the purpose of the document and justify the levels of responsibility of different parties involved in the Holocaust.

Learning plan to achieve outcomes

Introduce

[Session 1]

- Introduce theme: Post two statements heard throughout Germany when World War II was over:

  I'm not a Nazi!
  I had no idea there were camps!

- Post and introduce new vocabulary: Introduce the word *culpability* as a noun that means *guilt or blame that is deserved, blameworthiness.* Inquire: "Can you think of a synonym for this word (e.g., *responsibility, blame, liability, accountability,* and *fault*)? Write this word in your notes and refer back to it throughout this lesson."
- Organize group work: Divide students into five teams and distribute chart paper. Each team has one of the following terms and definitions on the charts: *perpetrator, victim, collaborator, beneficiary,* or *bystander.* Briefly share background information on political historian Raoul Hilberg's classification of these terms. Each team must discuss and report out the meaning of their term to the other groups. They must also provide an example of their word in connection with the Holocaust. They record their work on chart paper. As each team reports, all students also complete their personal charts on these terms.
- Introduce a victim of the Holocaust: Present Ilse Sara Ury, a German Jewish author who was known as the Dr. Seuss of Germany. Explain that Sara wasn't her real middle name—the Nazis made Jewish women include "Sara" in their names and made men include "Israel" in their names.

Model

[Session 2]

- Organize resources: Have five tables set up with a primary source document on each table. Students remain in the same teams from the earlier activity. Each document specifically refers to Ilse Ury, who perished at Auschwitz in January 1943.
- Explain the graphic organizer: Each student has a graphic organizer that includes the titles and dates of the five documents being studied. There are spaces for notes on *who*, *what*, *where*, *why*, and *when* as well as the meaning and purpose of each document.
- Describe the process: Individuals will rotate through all five tables. Encourage students to help one another as they analyze the documents and make needed inferences. At the end, everyone will have studied each of the documents.

Practice

[Session 3]

- Analyze the documents: In the case of Ilse Ury, students analyze the actions of people mentioned in the primary source documents and determine their roles according to Hilberg's classification: perpetrator, victim, collaborator, beneficiary, and bystander. The individual also assesses the level of the participant's responsibility as follows:

    1—Not responsible
    2—Minimally responsible
    3—Responsible
    4—Very responsible

- Support decisions: Using evidence from the documents, students justify their responses and cite where the evidence came from in the documents. They work on this individually in the library.
- Provide feedback: As students work, instructors circulate to provide encouragement and support.

Assess

[Session 4]

- Share responses: Reconvene the class and discuss student responses.
- Revisit and reflect on the theme: Return to the two original statements introduced at the beginning of the lesson:

    I'm not a Nazi!
    I had no idea there were camps!

- Reflect on what students have learned about culpability and individual responsibility in the face of injustice.

Note: In this unit, we also connected the Holocaust to issues of intolerance and injustice that were closer to home for our students. For example, we brought up the issue of bullying and asked students what we should do when we see bullying going on in our school. What is our responsibility?

Reflecting on Student Outcomes

What happened, and why?

The first lesson began with the vocabulary and two quotes that were unfamiliar to the students. Once students learned about Hilberg's classification of roles and shared their understandings with one another, they were intrigued about where this was all going. When we finished the roles and examples, we watched a slide presentation on Ilse Ury that was based on information found on the Internet and in one of Ury's books that had been published recently in English. I wanted students to know enough about Ury that they would want to find out what happened to her.

When students returned the next day, it was time to analyze the documents. I had them move from source to source so they had a chance to get up and move around. I kept them in their teams because I felt that they could help each other with the information they were gathering. The communication arts/reading teacher and her aide assisted as we circulated to prompt and help students. The students needed more time to really look at the sources. For the next activity, I carefully explained the task before the students found a quiet spot in the library to assign a role and the level of responsibility to each of the people in the primary source documents. They also wrote their justifications based on the documents and cited their evidence.

How did this influence our next actions?

We moved to the second activity too quickly. In the future, I would allow two sessions to analyze sources. The students might also have an additional session to work on their justifications for role and level assessments. We could follow this by reflecting together and discussing the essential questions. Of all the roles, the students seemed to struggle most with the role of the bystander. I would definitely spend more time discussing this with them to ensure that they understood how seemingly small acts of abuse often contribute to the big ones. This was also the first lesson that I assessed based on the Common Core standards. The CA/reading teacher wanted to use the RI (Reading Informational) standards for assessment, and we were challenged to connect them to the work we had done with the students.

Plan 9:
Understanding Communities Through Oral Histories (Grades 9–12)

Sandy Yamamoto

DESCRIBING THE CONTEXT

Subjects integrated: History, Language Arts

Duration of project: Two months

SUMMARIZING THE PROJECT

Our perceptions, experiences, and knowledge of events and the world around us provide valuable perspectives on history. Stories from family, friends and neighbors reflect unique insights into the development, change, and continuity of a community.

In this project, students conducted oral history research in their own neighborhood, which had evolved from an agricultural and rural center into a rapidly growing "second city." This research involved utilizing various sources, especially interviews with community members. Students created multimedia presentations based on their findings, which they then shared with community members at a special event held on campus. The project not only allowed students to practice and refine their research, information literacy, and communication skills, but also provided them with an opportunity to reach out across generational and cultural distances to touch their family and community members.

BUILDING AN INQUIRY FOCUS

Concept addressed
- Change, continuity, and causality: recording oral histories to interpret historical events and how they impact people's lives in a community

Essential questions investigated
- What defines a community?
- How do individuals and events shape a community's history?
- How does the past influence present-day perspectives?
- How can oral histories contribute to our understanding and appreciation of the past?

Critical skills taught
- Practicing skills in historical inquiry
- Applying skills in interpersonal communication
- Identifying, contacting, and interviewing community members
- Evaluating a range of primary resources
- Analyzing and synthesizing information

CONNECTING THE STANDARDS

AASL *Standards for the 21st-Century Learner*

1. Inquire, think critically, and gain knowledge.
Indicators 1.1.1, 1.1.3, 1.1.5, 1.1.6, 1.2.1

2. Draw conclusions, make informed decisions, apply knowledge to new situations, and create new knowledge.
Indicator 2.1.4

3. Share knowledge and participate ethically and productively as members of our democratic society.
Indicators 3.1.4, 3.1.5

Common Core State Standards

CC.11-12.RH.2>>English Language Arts>>Reading History>>Key Ideas and Details>>2. Determine the central ideas or information of a primary source; provide an accurate summary that makes clear the relationships among the key details and ideas.

CC.11-12.RH.8>>English Language Arts>>Reading History>> Integration of Knowledge and Ideas>>8. Evaluate an author's premises, claims, and evidence by corroborating or challenging them with other information.

> **CC.11-12.RH.9**>>English Language Arts>>Reading History>> Integration of Knowledge and Ideas>>9. Integrate information from diverse sources, both primary and secondary, into a coherent understanding of an idea or event, noting discrepancies among sources.

SAMPLE LESSON

Lesson focus: Developing interviewing skills

Resources: Community resource persons who have already been identified and contacted by students

Duration: One 60-minute session in library to introduce interviewing skills (another session may be needed depending on students' prior experience and skill level); interviews as out-of-class assignments, ranging from 30 to 60 minutes each

Designing for Learning

Learning outcomes desired
- I can demonstrate effective strategies to open, conduct, and conclude an interview with a community resource person.

Assessing for learning: During an interview, I will courteously and clearly
- introduce myself and my purpose.
- ask questions in an organized fashion.
- clarify questions that confuse the interviewee.
- allow "think time" for the interviewee to respond.
- listen carefully and jot down notes without being distracting.
- thank the interviewee for participating.

Learning plan to achieve outcomes

Introduce

- Connect with students and invite wondering: "Do your family members reminisce about the past? What do you learn about your family from these stories? What could these stories tell us about our community?"
- Engage students: Facilitate discussion in small then large groups using the above questions.

Model

- Introduce the concept: Ask, "What are oral histories? How can they and other primary sources help us to learn more about our community?"
- Tap prior knowledge: Brainstorm steps to prepare and conduct interviews.
- Connect prior knowledge to new information: Connect students' responses to interviewing guidelines prepared by librarian and teacher.
- Instruct: Provide explanation and guidelines for students to conduct an interview with a family or community member who can provide personal perspective and historical information relating to the topic selected by the student. The instructions should address preparation (e.g., contacting, generating questions, recording), etiquette (e.g., dress, behavior, language), and forms (evaluation and permission). Each person interviewed (interviewee) will do an evaluation on the interviewer.
- Introduce questioning: Brainstorm possible questions for the interview. Ask, "What do you need to find out? How and what can the interviewee provide to support your topic?" Encourage students to list as many questions as possible to create a database of questions. A chart like the one below can help students organize their questions.

Sample: Question Organizer

Question Focus	Questions
Personal Background	1. When and where were you born? 2. Who were your parents? What were they like? 3. Who are your brothers and sisters? 4. What ethnic background are you? 5. What family events did you celebrate?
Education	1. Where did you go to school? 2. What was school like? 3. Which subjects did you enjoy? Dislike? Excel in? 4. Do you remember any funny or memorable moments from school?
Housing	1. What was your house like? 2. What kind of neighborhood did you live in? 3. Who were your neighbors, and what were they like? 4. How many houses were in the neighborhood? Were they all alike? 5. How has housing changed over time in the neighborhood?

Lifestyle	1. What did you do for fun growing up in this neighborhood?
	2. How did neighbors relate to or connect with one another?
	3. Were there any community practices that stand out in your memory?
	4. How has the lifestyle changed over time since you've lived there?
	5. How have people in the community impacted the lifestyle?
Geography	1. What were the physical surroundings like when you were growing up?
	2. What was the population like? What was the community makeup?
	3. How did the ethnic makeup influence the community?
	4. What were some of the landmarks and important buildings in the community?
	5. How has the area changed and developed over the last 30 years?

- Obtain feedback from peers: Students exchange questions for feedback.
- Demonstrate: Stage a mock interview (librarian and teacher).
- Check for understanding: Invite students to provide critical feedback on the effectiveness of the mock interview based on guidelines similar to the sample rubric below.

Sample: Rubric to Assess Interview

Excellent	Good	Needs Improvement	Unsatisfactory
The student:	The student:	The student:	The student:
❐ Prepared in-depth questions which showed knowledge of the topic.	❐ Prepared general questions that suggested some knowledge of the topic.	❐ Prepared some general questions that didn't suggest knowledge of the topic.	❐ Did not prepare any questions prior to the interview.
❐ Never interrupted or rushed me during the interview.	❐ Rarely interrupted or rushed me during the interview.	❐ Rarely interrupted or rushed me.	❐ Interrupted or rushed me during the interview.
❐ Listened carefully.	❐ Listened carefully.	❐ Asked one or two follow-up questions.	❐ Didn't ask any follow-up questions.
❐ Asked several relevant follow-up questions based on my responses.	❐ Asked a few follow-up questions based on my responses.	❐ Asked questions that indicated he/she didn't listen carefully to my responses.	

> ### Practice
> - Organize for practice: Place students in pairs to practice interviewing skills.
> - Explain the activity: One pair observes and critiques the other pair on their interview skills; pairs switch roles when the first group is done. Students may want to video or tape the interview to practice using technology.
>
> ### Assess
> - Assess performance: Each pair completes a team exit slip that addresses what they did well and what they might improve on for the actual interviews. If students recorded the practice interviews, pairs might view the recordings and assess their performance.

Reflecting on Student Outcomes

> ### What happened, and why?
>
> Although we planned for one session on how to conduct interviews as a source of gathering primary information, we found that this was a totally new experience for all of the students. They had never been asked in previous classes to consider interviews as a form of acquiring valid and valuable information. We had to deconstruct the interview process and teach students how to properly greet people, how to conduct the interview itself, even what to wear to an interview and how to write thank-you letters. We also had to show them how to approach and contact people and prepare for the interview.
>
> As an added activity to support the importance of oral history, we invited a local storyteller to share interesting tales from the past in our community. This really increased the interest of the students—they commented that they had always wondered where certain local urban legends got their start.
>
> ### How did this influence our next actions?
>
> We realized that students needed more guided practice in performing the tasks required in effective interviews. They also needed more opportunities to exchange peer feedback in role-playing situations and more feedback from the community resource people actually interviewed. To support these various activities, we refined the guidelines and created feedback forms. Working on this project made us more cognizant of student needs (weaknesses or gaps in prior knowledge) and the importance of breaking down skills and creating more relevant tools that students could use to improve practice.

Plan 10:
Immigration Reform:
Resource Evaluation—Discerning
Purpose and Point of View (Grade 11)

Michelle Luhtala with Evan Remley
and Robert Stevenson

DESCRIBING THE CONTEXT

Subjects integrated: Social Studies, English Language Arts, Information and Communications Technologies

Duration of project: Three weeks

SUMMARIZING THE PROJECT

American studies is an interdisciplinary course including both U.S. history and junior English. It is a double class, taught by a team of two teachers, and it meets two class periods daily. In this unit, students examined immigration from both historical and personal perspectives. They explored different phases of immigration in the United States, each of which produced varied, yet distinctive stakeholder experiences and shaped the cultural identity of the nation. Their essential questions were, "How has U.S. policy and/or social institutions shaped the immigrant experience? In what ways have these elements impeded or helped the quest for status?" These questions prompted students to identify critical issues, conduct research, develop a thesis, write a persuasive paper, and reflect on their learning throughout the process.

Students were instructed to research two historical periods of immigration and provide an analysis of a particular policy or social institution and how it shaped the experience of certain immigrant groups. Students referred to a variety of evidence in their analysis, including anecdotes, statistics, policies, and expert analysis. Students then developed a two-clause thesis (dependent clause, independent clause) that encapsulated the sum of their research and analysis. They formed a theory on how a specific aspect of immigration affected a targeted group of people and then argued that thesis using their collected evidence. Teachers offered students exemplars as models and provided a list of suggested themes to consider.

As a critical component of this substantive research project, students located, evaluated, synthesized, and incorporated online news articles into their finished product. The teachers and librarian discovered that Millennial students sometimes approached this research process backward. Rather than using resources to inform their opinion, they found resources that aligned with their existing opinions. In order to ensure that students used the research process to build on prior knowledge and synthesize new learning that morphed into original ideas, it was important that students practiced critical resource evaluation. Given the abundance of "news" resources available, particularly with the increase of paywall-protected news reporting, it has become increasingly difficult for students to distinguish between factual, biased, and anecdotal information.

In this assignment, students demonstrated close reading of opinion pieces, prompting them to carefully examine literary craft and structure to infer the author's point of view. Students then compared an array of perspectives on a given topic to inspire their own inquiry about that topic. Without this valuable skill, students were likely to take biased articles at face value. Treating them as factual evidence might have mistakenly led students to develop weak, flawed, or incurious reasoning. While this specific lesson featured an article on immigration reform, the close reading activity is replicable with different content and for different reading levels.

BUILDING AN INQUIRY FOCUS

Concepts addressed
- Historical interpretation—dealing with questioning facts, analyzing events, testing hypotheses, and understanding points of view in order to make informed decisions
- Connections between the past and the present—developing a better understanding of the world, avoiding the mistakes of the past, and using past actions to guide current and future decisions
- Text complexity—discerning point of view in and the purpose of informational texts as a prerequisite to effective research
- Text analysis—inferring author purpose and point of view through examination of textual structure and organization

Essential questions investigated
- How has U.S. policy and/or social institutions shaped the immigrant experience? In what ways have these elements impeded or helped the quest for status?
- Why did the author write this?
- How does the writing itself reveal the author's purpose?

Critical skills taught
- Identifying clues in the craft and structure of informational texts that point to the author's purpose and point of view
- Explaining how literary choices can change the meaning of a message in informational texts
- Reading text closely and critically
- Inferring point of view and bias in informational texts

CONNECTING THE STANDARDS

AASL *Standards for the 21st-Century Learner*

1. Inquire, think critically, and gain knowledge.
   Indicators 1.1.5, 1.1.6, 1.1.7, 1.2.1, 1.2.4

2. Draw conclusions, make informed decisions, apply knowledge to new situations, and create new knowledge.
   Indicators 2.1.1, 2.1.2, 2.3.3

4. Pursue personal and aesthetic growth.
   Indicator 4.2.3

Common Core State Standards

CC.11-12.RI.1>>English Language Arts>>Reading for Informational Text>>Key Ideas and Details>>1. Cite strong and thorough textual evidence to support analysis of what the text says explicitly as well as inferences drawn from the text, including determining where the text leaves matters uncertain.

CC.11-12.RI.2>>English Language Arts>>Reading for Informational Text>>Key Ideas and Details>>2. Determine two or more central ideas of a text and analyze their development over the course of the text, including how they interact and build on one another to provide a complex analysis; provide an objective summary of the text.

CC.11-12.RI.3>>English Language Arts>>Reading for Informational Text>>Key Ideas and Details>>3. Analyze a complex set of ideas or sequence of events and explain how specific individuals, ideas, or events interact and develop over the course of the text.

CC.11-12.RI.4>>English Language Arts>>Reading for Informational Text>>Craft and Structure>>4. Determine the meaning of words and phrases as they are used in a text, including figurative, connotative, and technical meanings; analyze how an author uses and refines the meaning of a key term or terms over the course of a text (e.g., how Madison defines faction in Federalist No. 10).

CC.11-12.RI.5>>English Language Arts>>Reading for Informational Text>>Craft and Structure>>5. Analyze and evaluate the effectiveness of the structure an author uses in his or her exposition or argument, including whether the structure makes points clear, convincing, and engaging.

CC.11-12.RI.6>>English Language Arts>>Reading for Informational Text>>Craft and Structure>>6. Determine an author's point of view or purpose in a text in which the rhetoric is particularly effective, analyzing how style and content contribute to the power, persuasiveness or beauty of the text.

CC.11-12.RI.7>>English Language Arts>>Reading for Informational Text>>Integration of Knowledge and Ideas>>7. Integrate and evaluate multiple sources of information presented in different media or formats (e.g., visually, quantitatively) as well as in words in order to address a question or solve a problem.

CC.11-12.RI.10>> English Language Arts>>Reading for Informational Text>>Range of Reading and Level of Text Complexity>>10. By the end of grade 11, read and comprehend literary nonfiction in the grades 11-CCR text complexity band proficiently, with scaffolding as needed at the high end of the range. By the end of grade 12, read and comprehend literary nonfiction at the high end of the grades 11-CCR text complexity band independently and proficiently.

SAMPLE LESSON

Lesson focus: Using text features to make inferences about author purpose and point of view

Resources: Student-selected articles in addition to the following:

Please contact Michelle Luhtala at luhtala.michelle@gmail.com for more information about these resources.

Duration: One 50-minute period for instruction with guided practice, then student-directed research and resource evaluation performed either independently or with guidance, depending on students' ability and motivation

Designing for Learning

Learning outcomes desired: I can
- identify criteria to study informational text that will help me determine its relevance for my research.
- infer author's purpose and point of view when reading informational text.
- factor information about an author's professional profile in deducing the purpose of his or her writing.

Assessing for learning: I will
- match 12 qualifiers for resource evaluation with a corresponding descriptive question.
- accurately answer detailed questions about assigned informational texts to practice discerning point of view and purpose.
- identify purpose and point of view in multiple sources of information in order to address a question or solve a problem.

Learning plan to achieve outcomes

Introduce

- Link to prior activities: Begin by saying, "Over the past few days, we have been exploring research topics by examining news articles and using them to formulate research questions around themes."
- Introduce purpose and relevance of lesson: Continue, "There are many reasons for writing articles and different types of articles. Increasingly, newspapers make their opinion articles (e.g., blogs, columns) accessible free of charge online, while keeping their journalistic news reporting behind a paywall, making them accessible for subscribers only. Balanced research includes factual, opinion-laden, and anecdotal resources, but it is essential to distinguish among the three. Today's activities will help you understand what to look for when making those distinctions."

Model

- Jump-start thinking: Begin with a matching exercise ("Be Judgmental") in which students identify qualifiers to assess both objective and subjective writing (e.g., relevance, currency, reliability, authority).
- Engage in discussion: Display screenshots of three articles via a projector or give students hard copy handouts. There should be one factual, one opinion, and one anecdotal article. Ask students if the specific article is an opinion, anecdote, fact, or something else. Challenge students to explain their answers. Through the ensuing discussion, students should arrive at the understanding that there is not always a clear-cut answer to these questions—that students must carefully examine articles to make that determination, and that even after careful analysis the answers are still subject to interpretation.

Note: This is a great opportunity to use a student response system or an online polling tool if students have access to mobile technology (refer to slide presentation on "Resource Evaluation" for more details).

Practice

- Instruct and guide: Introduce the next activity that requires close examination of an author's literary craft to discern his or her point of view. Review the practice activity for close reading, "*New York Times* Room for Debate: Understanding Immigration Reform." Read the directions together. Ask students to respond to the numbered questions on page 2 by analyzing the corresponding footnoted text in the passage below.
- Guide: "Find footnote #1. What word does it follow? Read the first question on page 2. Write your response in the space provided. Share your response with the class. Do you understand how this works? Are there any questions? Please complete the remaining nine questions on your own."
- Transition to independent practice: Say, "Keeping your initial research questions in mind, it is now time for you to locate your own resources, explain their purpose, and identify any existing bias. As you move from the exploration to the investigation phases of your research process, and you begin to develop expertise on your topic, the scope of your research needs will shift from broad overviews to deeply focused sources. Keep in mind the criteria highlighted in this lesson's introductory activity, 'Be Judgmental,' as you gather sources. Read closely for purpose and point of view just as we did with the *New York Times* exercise. Document your process by completing the Note-Taking Template and use the corresponding rubric to assess your work."
- Provide feedback: As students begin their independent work, circulate and confer with individual students about their selections and review the alignment between line of inquiry and selected resources. Focus on critical reading, point of view, and bias. Where applicable, ask students to identify specific evidence of subjectivity in the text.

Assess

- Assess work: Both instructors and students use the completed Note-Taking Template and the accompanying rubric to measure learning and students' ability to apply this lesson to new materials.

Reflecting on Student Outcomes

What happened, and why?

This lesson took more time than anticipated. The introductory activity, "Be Judgmental," which appeared to be a simple vocabulary matching activity, actually required a comprehensive review of correct responses, because they were foundational to resource evaluation and were prerequisite to identifying bias and subjectivity in informational texts. The slide presentation ("Resource Evaluation") was very popular, because students liked the interactive aspect of using "Poll Everywhere" to answer questions; however, this activity took time as well.

Students moved quickly through the *New York Times* activity once they understood how it worked. Reviewing correct responses took time, because this activity focused on discerning an author's point of view or purpose by analyzing the use of rhetoric and evaluating how style and content contributed to the power, persuasiveness, or beauty of the text.

The "Note-Taking Template" and the rubric also slowed students down. This was actually a good problem, because it forced students to evaluate resources through several lenses: overall meaning, salient points, purpose, and point of view. Providing separate fields for these elements challenged students to carefully examine each resource. This strengthened their understanding of the symbiosis between inquiry and new learning.

How did this influence our next actions?

Since this lesson required more time than originally anticipated, we decided that we had to break it into smaller modules and administer some of the content online. In short, we flipped the lesson. We piloted a 10-question Moodle Quiz that is available at http://bit.ly/moodlequiz. It still needs work, but we will keep tweaking it until we get it right.

Plan 11:
Human Impact on Earth's Systems (Grades 11–12)

Fran Glick

DESCRIBING THE CONTEXT

Subjects integrated: English, Science

Duration of project: Three weeks

SUMMARIZING THE PROJECT

Writing is a key element in demonstrating understanding, asserting and defending a position, and communicating the results of the research process. As students strive to become career and college ready, they must consider the task, purpose, product, and intended audience in their writing. They must engage in the research process and report their findings in light of the task and with sufficient evidence to present and defend a position.

As an extension of students' work in science regarding the impact of human population growth on natural resources, they researched the increased need for energy sources and its impact on the natural world. They explored the use of new methods to gather sources of energy and the controversy that has developed around their use.

From *Inquiry and the Common Core: Librarians and Teachers Designing Teaching for Learning.* Violet H. Harada and Sharon Coatney, Editors. Santa Barbara, CA: Libraries Unlimited. Copyright © 2014.

In this project, the students were assigned specific roles to examine the issue of hydrofracking (or "fracking") from multiple perspectives. Working in cooperative teams, they investigated the issue from one of the following perspectives: environmental activist, area resident, legislator, or lobbyist for a pro-fracking energy company. At the conclusion of their research, students constructed an oral and written argument supported by evidence to address energy and resource extraction and the associated economic, social, environmental, and geopolitical costs and risks as well as benefits. Students created public service announcements in multimedia formats to communicate the results of their research and the risk/reward ratios. Colleagues and teachers evaluated student work during a showcase for the school community.

BUILDING AN INQUIRY FOCUS

Concepts addressed
- Resource extraction
- Risk and benefits of energy consumption
- Human impact on earth's systems
- Demand for energy sources

Essential questions investigated
- How do new technologies impact energy acquisition?
  ○ What is hydrofracking or fracking?
  ○ What views currently exist regarding this form of energy extraction?
  ○ Why is this issue controversial?

Critical skills taught
- Evaluating, analyzing, and synthesizing information in primary and secondary sources in many formats
- Applying group collaboration and communication skills
- Examining evidence on current issues to support an opinion
- Presenting information with focus on the following: line of reasoning, organization, development, style, task, purpose, and audience
- Demonstrating an understanding of reasoning and relevance and the need for sufficient evidence

CONNECTING THE STANDARDS

CC.11-12.WHST.1b>>English Language Arts>>Writing History>>Text Types and Purposes>>1b. Develop claim(s) and counterclaims fairly and thoroughly, supplying the most relevant evidence for each while pointing out the strengths and limitations of both in a manner that anticipates the audience's knowledge level, concerns, values, and possible biases.

SAMPLE LESSONS

Lesson focus:

- Refining and extending comprehension skills by selecting, reading, analyzing, and evaluating a variety of print and electronic texts
- Defending and rationalizing the development and use of a proposed technology
- Developing an understanding of the cultural, social, economic, and political effects of technology
- Justifying the contention that individual citizens have to make informed decisions about the development and use of technology

Resources:

- Online subscription resources, e.g., SIRS Issues Researcher, Gale Cengage, Opposing Viewpoints
- News footage: http://www.youtube.com/watch?v=oMboTKOWeAs&feature=youtu.be
- National news sources

Duration: Three 50-minute class periods for initial research; two 50-minute periods for PSA planning and creation

Designing for Learning

Learning outcomes desired: I can

- analyze controversial issues in order to generate and communicate possible solutions.
- integrate and evaluate content presented in diverse formats and media, including visually and quantitatively, as well as in words.
- delineate and evaluate the argument and specific claims in a text, including the validity of the reasoning as well as the relevance and sufficiency of the evidence.

Assessing for learning: I will

- delineate between fact and opinion as I research information about the issue.
- identify information that supports or contradicts my argument or stand.

- connect ideas by sorting the information in an ordering scheme using a cluster/idea map.
- demonstrate ethical use of intellectual property and responsible and safe use of the technologies.
- maintain inquiry logs that reflect on my attention to the task, relevance of resources, and my progress throughout the investigation.

Learning plan to achieve outcomes

Sessions 1–3: Initial Research

Introduce

- Set the context/tap prior knowledge: Ask students to summarize the information they have gained in their study of resource extraction. Explain that they will be challenged to assume the role of someone on one side of the issue.

Model

- Introduce point of view: Using one of the articles that clearly demonstrates one side of the issue, discuss that issues are often presented based upon viewpoint.
- Explain team tasks: Share with the students that by working in cooperative teams they will examine the issue from an assigned perspective: environmental activist, area resident, legislator, or lobbyist for pro-fracking energy company.

Practice

- Retrieve and evaluate information: Collect relevant information from the assigned perspective; remind students to do the following:
  - Evaluate sources of information as you find them.
  - Use the inquiry log to reflect on choices and track the inquiry journey.
  - Read deeply from pertinent resources and apply reading strategies to construct meaning. Thoughtful analysis of information gathered requires application of critical reading skills. Students must read deeply in order to extract the information needed to frame and support a position.
  - Apply the following strategic reading behaviors: sorting and classifying; sifting information, presenting a coherent argument, drawing conclusions, and summarizing. Students may find that they have not gathered sufficient information through this analysis.
- Retrieve and evaluate information: Use different strategies and tools for note taking and documentation as follows:
  - Use cluster/idea maps to visualize relationships between ideas.
  - Organize both physical and mental workspaces to avoid frustration and anxiety and the loss of important documents, resources, and time.
  - Demonstrate digital citizenship and avoid plagiarism by paraphrasing or quoting information, and by citing your sources in a Works Cited list.

- Assess progress: Carefully study research notes based on the following questions:
  - Have I gathered sufficient details about my topic?
  - Do I have enough details to answer each of my subsidiary questions?
  - Do I have additional information that would be of value to my audience?
  - Is there any unrelated information I should eliminate?
  - Have I gathered sufficient details to persuade my audience?

Sessions 4–5: Creating PSAs

- Communicate findings: In teams, create a PSA that reflects a stance from the assigned perspective on the topic:
  - Review and select arguments that best present the assigned viewpoint.
  - Create a storyboard for the PSA to assemble the most compelling arguments.
  - Use a Web 2.0 or other multimedia tool to create the PSA.

Assess

- Assess the process: The student research process is evaluated by examination of student graphic organizers and inquiry logs.
- Assess the product: Teachers and peers review the PSAs using a rubric.

Reflecting on Student Outcomes

What happened, and why?

As students started this project, they demonstrated enthusiasm for its relevance and the opportunity to examine a controversial topic framed in the context of course content and a research experience.

It was a challenge for the students to shift their thinking from simply presenting a topic to that of examining a topic through the context of a stakeholder. Students had to be reminded to use the facts to support the stance of the stakeholder they were assigned. This element caused some confusion for the students and some frustration when their personal opinions were not in line with the position they were challenged to represent. It required them to think deeply and objectively in order to present a point of view supported by facts.

As the students used their findings to create the PSAs, they were reenergized by the task. They enjoyed the opportunity to use multimedia tools to communicate their viewpoints and understandings. Overall, students were challenged by this assignment but persisted, to complete quality products.

How did this influence my next actions?

In the future I would invest more time in direct instruction, modeling, and discussion to help students use claims to support opinions. I would shape lessons around the following essential skills in order to prevent some of the confusion the students faced:

- Approaching all issues from the point of view of a skeptical reader
- Using formal logic and other rhetorical devices
- Ordering the arguments for maximum effect

Plan 12:
Creating Twenty-first–Century Superheroes (Grades 11–12)

Joan Upell

DESCRIBING THE CONTEXT

Subjects integrated: English, U.S. History, World History

Duration of project: Six weeks

SUMMARIZING THE PROJECT

Throughout American history, comic book superheroes such as Captain America have emerged during times of great turmoil in the world. As a conclusion to a unit on the history of the comic book as literature, students worked in teams to research a current global issue and create a superhero who had the twenty-first-century skills to solve it. Each group designed a comic book splash page using original or computer-generated artwork to introduce their superhero and his or her twenty-first-century mission via a public wiki and class presentation. (Note: Based on the golden era of comic books, a splash page is the first, one-panel page used to introduce the superhero's name, story, setting, and special powers or objects, and includes the creator's name.) Student work was peer reviewed via a class-generated rubric. Students used their superhero creations and knowledge to conduct mini-classes for students in grades K–12 during the school's Fine Arts Day.

BUILDING AN INQUIRY FOCUS

Concepts addressed
- Literature as a reflection of human experience
  - Role of fictional superhero in literature
  - Role of superhero during time of world crisis
- Global issues in context
  - Impact on communities and families
  - Diverse interpretations of global issues

Essential questions investigated
- What are the characteristics of a superhero?
- What is a global issue?
- Which global issues impact my community?
- What purpose might a superhero serve in relation to a global issue?

Critical skills taught
- Evaluating, analyzing, and synthesizing information in primary and secondary sources in all formats
- Applying group collaboration and communication skills
- Applying creative thinking and interpretation to historical and current issues
- Identifying opposing viewpoints in context of history, culture, and literature

CONNECTING THE STANDARDS

AASL *Standards for the 21st-Century Learner*

1. Inquire, think critically, and gain knowledge.
Indicators 1.2.2, 1.3.1

2. Draw conclusions, make informed decisions, apply knowledge to new situations, and create new knowledge.
Indicators 2.1.3, 2.1.5, 2.3.2

3. Share knowledge and participate ethically and productively as members of our democratic society.
Indicators 3.1.5, 3.2.3, 3.4.2

Common Core State Standards

CC.11-12.W.7>>English Language Arts>> Writing>>Research to Build and Present Knowledge>>7. Conduct short as well as more sustained research projects to answer a question (including a self-generated question) or solve a problem; narrow or broaden the inquiry when appropriate; synthesize multiple sources on the subject, demonstrating understanding of the subject under investigation.

CC.11-12.W.9>>English Language Arts>>Writing>>Research to Build and Present Knowledge>>9. Draw evidence from literary or informational texts to support analysis, reflection, and research.

CC.11-12.RI.7>>English Language Arts>>Reading Informational>> Integration of Knowledge and Ideas>>7. Integrate and evaluate multiple sources of information presented in different media or formats (e.g., visually, quantitatively) as well as in words in order to address a question or solve a problem.

CC.11-12.SL.1>>English Language Arts>>Speaking and Listening>> Comprehension and Collaboration>>1. Initiate and participate effectively in a range of collaborative discussions (one-on- one, in groups, and teacher-led) with diverse partners on grades 11–12 topics, texts, and issues, building on others' ideas and expressing their own clearly and persuasively.

CC.11-12.SL.1.c>>English Language Arts>>Speaking and Listening>> Comprehension and Collaboration>>1c. Propel conversations by posing and responding to questions that probe reasoning and evidence; ensure a hearing for a full range of positions on a topic or issue; clarify, verify, or challenge ideas and conclusions; and promote divergent and creative perspectives.

CC11-12.RH/SS.2>>Reading Standards for History>>2. Determine the central ideas or information of a primary or secondary source; provide an accurate summary that makes clear the relationships among the key details and ideas.

SAMPLE LESSONS

Lesson focus: Identify and summarize a global issue with possible opposing viewpoints

Resources:
- Krensky, Stephen. *Comic Book Century: The History of American Comic Books*. Minneapolis, MN: Learner Books, 2008
- Online subscription resources, e.g., SIRS Issues Researcher or EBSCO Points of View

Duration: Three 50-minute class periods for initial research

Designing for Learning

Learning outcomes desired: I can
- locate and evaluate information on a self-selected global issue.
- explain the issue from more than one point of view.

Assessing for learning: I will work with my group members to
- brainstorm possible global issues to investigate.
- explore resources to narrow choices.
- select two or three issues to discuss and narrow to final choice.
- evaluate and summarize information from multiple resources.
- contribute to group discussion regarding points of view related to the issue.
- determine if more information on selected issue is needed.

Learning plan to achieve outcomes

Introduce

- Connect new project to prior work: Discuss final project through review of Captain America, World War II, and the applicable global issue.
- Questions to initiate the discussion: "What was occurring in Europe in 1940–1941 when Captain America made his first appearance? How did the creators of Captain America portray his mission to the reader?"

Model

- Brainstorm: As a class, brainstorm current global issues and select one as a search example to demonstrate possible resources to use. A search example might be childhood hunger.
- Select resources: Using the search example, identify several resources discussing the issue in the United States, Europe, and Africa.
- Engage through questioning: "Are the underlying causes the same in each area of the world? What role does the economy play in this issue? Are natural disasters an important factor?"

- Encourage deeper thinking: Discuss possible viewpoints on the sample issue. Brainstorm what additional details might be needed before a superhero could be created to solve the issue.

Practice

Possible foci for the sessions might be the following:

- Session 1: brainstorm issues and narrow to two or three to explore
- Session 2: select one issue; study it in depth
- Session 3: use collected information to discuss the issue from different viewpoints; decide if more information is needed

Assess

- Self-reflect: Student groups post selected issue, summarized information, and viewpoint discussion to a wiki page, noting what went well and what additional steps might be necessary to develop a superhero.
- Critique postings: Students and instructors assess the content of the postings using the following criteria:
  ○ Clear explanation of the issue
  ○ Clear statement of the group's viewpoint
  ○ Evidence for viewpoint directly referenced from resources
  ○ Reflection on next steps

Reflecting on Student Outcomes

What happened, and why?

Students wanted to immediately jump into creating their superheroes without developing background information on their global issue. We worked with individual groups to help them summarize their global issue, identify the possible local impact, and cite evidence supporting their point of view on the selected issue.

How did this influence our next actions?

Focusing first on the search for global issue information in the subscription databases guided students in narrowing their issue choices. This step provided essential background information. Expanding their search to the open Internet and all other library resources then led them to dig deeper for specific details. We believe that the project could easily be expanded to the creation of an entire story or episode rather than just the beginning splash page, and we may consider doing this in a future project.

Plan 13:
The Cloning Wars
(Grades 11–12)

Carolyn Kirio

DESCRIBING THE CONTEXT

Subjects integrated: Biology/Human Physiology, American Problems

Duration of project: Two months

SUMMARIZING THE PROJECT

With the constant medical and technical advances in genetics, there is also a need for global regulation of genetic research and practice. Guidelines need to be established and monitored to ensure that bio-medical research is ethical at the same time that practices are purposeful and provide useful, reliable medical test results. One of the controversial issues in genetics has been cloning. The issue poses moral and religious concerns. There are many scientific and technical reasons for and against advancing the practice that must be considered.

In this project, students became aware of these controversies and weighed evidence found through their research to individually decide whether cloning should be endorsed. They developed multimedia presentations in which they took a stand on the positive and negative impacts of cloning and its implications. The students ultimately shared their findings at a statewide summit, where they debated the issue with

From *Inquiry and the Common Core: Librarians and Teachers Designing Teaching for Learning.* Violet H. Harada and Sharon Coatney, Editors. Santa Barbara, CA: Libraries Unlimited. Copyright © 2014.

other high school students and worked collectively to draft broad regulatory guidelines for cloning practices. They presented their work before a community panel of scientists, legislators, and other policy makers for consideration and feedback.

BUILDING AN INQUIRY FOCUS

Concepts addressed
- Medicine and science—comparing perspectives on controversial topics in medicine and science
- Nature of science—understanding that science, technology, and society are interrelated

Essential questions investigated
- What is cloning, and why is it controversial?
- How do different stakeholders in our community view this research?
- What is my position on cloning? How can I support my position?
- How can I effectively communicate my ideas and my stand to others?
- How can I work with others to improve and influence current cloning practices?

Critical skills taught
- Gathering and analyzing information from multiple sources on the issue of cloning
- Identifying both positive and negative implications of cloning
- Assuming a stand on the issue and organizing evidence to support my stand
- Communicating ideas and positions clearly and effectively to a wider audience
- Engaging in a decision-making process to reach consensus on policies to regulate cloning
- Presenting and receiving feedback through participation in an authentic assessment to evaluate the learning experience

CONNECTING THE STANDARDS

AASL *Standards for the 21st-Century Learner*

1. Inquire, think critically, and gain knowledge.
  Indicators 1.1.1, 1.1.5

2. Draw conclusions, make informed decisions, apply knowledge to new situations, and create new knowledge.
  Indicators 2.1.3, 2.2.3, 2.4.2

3. Share knowledge and participate ethically and productively as members of our democratic society.
   Indicator 3.3.3

Common Core State Standards

CC.11-12.RI.7>>English Language Arts>>Reading Informational>> Integration of Knowledge and Ideas>>7. Integrate and evaluate multiple sources of information presented in different media or formats as well as in words in order to address a question or solve a problem.

CC.11-12.W.1>>English Language Arts>>Writing>>Text Types and Purposes>>1. Write arguments to support claims in analysis of substantive topics or texts, using valid reasoning and relevant and sufficient evidence.

SAMPLE LESSONS

Lesson focus: Develop a persuasive argument on the issue of cloning

Resources: Range of current online textual and multimedia resources

Duration: Two 60-minute sessions in library. Session 1: introduce the organization of a persuasive argument, continue work in the classroom, and as homework draft and revise position papers that serve as the foundation for the multimedia presentations. Session 2: teach the multimedia software to be used in the presentations; provide pointers on selecting the appropriate research findings to include in the presentation, communicating information to a wider audience and constructing effective visual aids.

Designing for Learning

Learning outcomes desired: I can
- synthesize and organize my research notes to prepare a persuasive essay and presentation on the issue of cloning.
- create a multimedia presentation to effectively communicate my ideas and findings to a wider audience.
- collaborate with other learners in creating guidelines that will be shared with experts in the field to receive authentic feedback and suggestions for continued improvement.

Assessing for learning:

- I will use my notes to
  - clearly and succinctly state my stand.
  - identify major points or reasons to support my stand.
  - support my points or reasons with relevant evidence from a range of reliable resources.
- I will present my research using multimedia to
  - clearly communicate my stand to a wider audience.
  - identify major points or reasons to persuade others to support my stand.
  - support my points or reasons with relevant evidence from a range of reliable resources.
- I will work with others to collaboratively create a document that
  - clearly outlines proposed cloning guidelines.
  - identifies major points or reasons for change and implementation.
  - supports my points or reasons based on relevant information shared by summit participants.

Learning plan to achieve outcomes:

Session 1: Building Persuasive Arguments

Introduce

- Connect with prior knowledge: Review with students the steps they have taken thus far to collect information from a range of resources. Have students bring their notes to this session.

Model

- Model the process: Demonstrate how you might take notes on a sample topic and complete a graphic organizer devised for students to use. The treelike organizer includes a box for the stand being taken. This box is connected to additional boxes for major points or reasons. In turn, these main reasons branch out to boxes for supporting evidence.

Practice

- Allow for application: Have students use their own notes to complete an organizer.
- Provide timely feedback: The teacher and you circulate to assist students as they work.

Assess

- Exchange views on progress: Reconvene the group and discuss students' progress as well as the difficulties they encountered.
- Identify the need for next steps: Discuss and identify assistance the students feel they need as they continue with their drafts.

Session 2: Creating Multimedia Presentations

Introduce

- Connect with prior knowledge: Review with students the criteria they are expected to follow in creating their presentations. Examples of the criteria include the following:
  - Attention gainers should be enlightening and educational (hook your audience from the beginning, foreshadow your presentation, and keep the audience engaged).
  - Each slide should be designed for brevity and clarity. Hone it down to no more than three talking points per slide (this is not a teleprompter; please do not type out your entire script).
  - Keep transitions basic and avoid distracting animations or sound effects (e.g., sounds of a typewriter, laser or gunshot effects).
  - Graphics should be meaningful; they should enhance or further clarify your ideas (this is not a time for scrap booking or collage making; keep to the point).
- Introduce targets for the session: Provide directions for the multimedia software being used. *Note:* We used Microsoft PowerPoint and Go Animate!

Model

- Model the process: Demonstrate how to select the most appropriate information for the presentation. Critical questions include the following:
  - What is my main idea or point of view?
  - What is important for my audience to see, know, and understand?
  - Are the facts that I have selected essential in supporting my stance and position on cloning?
  - Is this information new, and will it educate my audience?
- Introduce the assessment tool: Before examining a sample product and assessing its quality, go over a "check-bric" that the instructors have devised for analyzing the content and technical quality of the product. The "check-bric" combines a checklist and a rubric and includes the criteria and questions that have been discussed in these sessions.
- Demonstrate critiquing: Introduce a sample product and facilitate a discussion on how it might be improved. Select a sample that might earn a rating of "approaching." Using the check-bric as a tool for reflection and feedback, solicit ideas from the students about best ways to improve the product.

Practice

- Draft presentations: Have students begin the creation of their presentations using the software.
- Provide timely feedback: The teacher and you circulate to assist students as they work.

Reflecting on Student Outcomes

What happened, and why?

Many students discovered that they had not collected sufficient evidence to justify their reasons. When they used the organizer in the first session, they suddenly realized that they had informally thought of reasons, but not consciously sought information to justify their reasons. While the students had amassed a good deal of miscellaneous facts, they were not always sufficiently focused in their initial searches. They required additional help in identifying which reasons were most critical and conducting additional searches to find convincing evidence to support those specific reasons.

Many students also found that they had difficulty paraphrasing and stating effective points found in their research. Finally, creating the presentation was more difficult than they had originally anticipated. Overall, many first drafts reflected an unclear rationale and an uneven progression of supporting ideas.

How did this influence our next actions?

We realized that we had to provide more modeling and discussion for a project of this nature, which required deep and critical reading and persuasive writing that had to be based on documented evidence. The students also needed more time to search for information that justified their reasons. We had to assure students that conducting research was not a linear process—that going back and forth to strengthen the final product was a natural part of the learning cycle. We tried to accommodate these various learning needs as students continued to refine their drafts.

In addition, we discovered that students had to practice their presentations for feedback on clarity and understanding. We built in sharing with a friend and parent as part of the process. This feedback provided students with constructive and positive criticism on the presentation of ideas and the effective communication of their stand to others. The practice resulted in students demonstrating confidence and poise in presenting their findings at the summit.

Index

About the Editors and Contributors

Elodie Arellano is a tenth-grade social studies teacher at Kapolei High. She has a master's degree in library and information science from the University of Hawaii and hopes to secure a librarian post in the near future. She has collaboratively planned and implemented many history and civics projects with the librarian and with other teachers in the social studies department.

Lynne Caltrider is a kindergarten teacher at Van Meter Community School in Iowa. She is discovering that kindergartners are not too young to embrace inquiry and critical thinking in their learning. With the other teachers at Van Meter, she is seeking creative ways to make the Common Core standards both rigorous and relevant to students.

Sharon Coatney is a retired school librarian from Kansas. She is Senior Acquisitions Editor at LU/Linworth and is the editor of *The Many Faces of School Library Leadership* (Libraries Unlimited, 2010) and a coauthor with Blanche Wools and Ann Weeks of *The School Library Manager*, 5th edition (Libraries Unlimited, 2013).

Jean Donham is Professor of School Library Studies at the University of Northern Iowa. Her experience includes serving in building- and district-level positions in school librarianship as well as directing the library at Cornell College, a selective liberal arts college. She is the author of *Enhancing Teaching and Learning: A Leadership Guide for School Librarians*.

Kristin Fontichiaro is a clinical assistant professor at the University of Michigan School of Information. She has written or edited several books for children, educators, and librarians, including *Growing Schools: Librarians as Professional Developers* (edited with Debbie Abilock and Violet H. Harada; Libraries Unlimited, 2012) and the makerspace-focused *Makers as*

Innovators series for kids (Cherry Lake Publishing, 2013). She was named a 2012 Mover and Shaker by *Library Journal*.

Brooke Gadberry is currently a K–2 instructional strategist and Title 1 teacher at Van Meter Elementary School, located in Van Meter, Iowa. She previously taught kindergarten in Kentucky and implemented the Common Core within her school district. She is very passionate about creating life-long learners through discovery and technology-based learning.

Elizabeth Gartley is the Library Media Specialist at Melrose High School in Melrose, Massachusetts. Her work has also appeared on the American Association of School Librarians lesson plan database.

Fran Glick is the Supervisor of Instructional Technology and Library Media in Baltimore County Public Schools. She was a contributor to the AASL publication *Standards for the 21st-Century Learner in Action*.

Violet H. Harada is a professor emeritus at the University of Hawaii. For the past twenty years, she has coordinated the school library specialization for the Library and Information Science Program. She has jointly authored and edited seven books and countless articles on the instructional role of school librarians as twenty-first-century partners in learning with teachers. She has also shared her work at various state, national, and international conferences.

Ronda Hassig is a middle school library media specialist in Overland Park, Kansas. She has just renewed her national board certification and is a Kansas master teacher. She has received the ALA National Sara Jaffarian Award for the Humanities and the AASL/Highsmith Collaborative School Library Media Award.

Lynda Johnson is a teacher at South East Junior High in Iowa City, Iowa.

Carolyn Kirio is the librarian at Kapolei Middle School in Hawaii. She is a National Board Certified Librarian and is currently working on her PhD in educational technology at the University of Hawaii. She is joint author of *Collaborating for Project-Based Learning in Grades 9–12* (Linworth, 2008).

Deborah D. Levitov, PhD, is managing editor of *School Library Monthly*. She was a school librarian and coordinator of Library Media Services for Lincoln Public Schools for a total of twenty-seven years. She has contributed to the magazines *Knowledge Quest*, *School Library Monthly*, and *Teacher Librarian*; edited the book *Activism and the School Librarian* (Libraries Unlimited 2012); and contributed the chapter "The School Librarian as an

Advocacy Leader" in *The Many Faces of School Library Leadership* (Libraries Unlimited 2010).

Michelle Luhtala is the department chair of New Canaan (CT) High School Library and facilitates a professional learning community at edWeb.net/ emergingtech. She is a member of the American Association of School Librarians' (AASL) Board of Directors, and a contributing author to Libraries Unlimited's *Growing Schools: Librarians as Professional Developers*. She blogs at Bibliotech.me.

Debora Lum is a retired librarian whose last position was at Waikele Elementary School in Hawaii, where she created an inquiry-focused instructional program in collaboration with her teachers. She has served as president of the Hawaii Association of School Librarians (HASL) and is currently serving as cofacilitator for the L4L initiative for HASL.

Leslie K. Maniotes, NBCT, MEd, PhD, is an educational leader in the Denver Public Schools. A National Board Certified Teacher with over a decade of classroom experience, Maniotes is a Teacher Effectiveness Coach and has served as a K–12 literacy specialist in rural and urban Title I schools. She is a nationally reputed educational consultant on the guided inquiry approach, leading teams to improve learning and inquiry design through integrating workshops and coaching. She is coauthor of *Guided Inquiry: Learning in the 21st Century* (Libraries Unlimited, 2007) and *Guided Inquiry Design: A Framework for Inquiry in Your School* (Libraries Unlimited, 2012).

Christa McClintock is a kindergarten teacher at Van Meter Community School in Iowa. She has been actively working with her teaching colleagues and librarian to engage young students in inquiry-based research and to integrate the Common Core standards into the curriculum.

Shannon McClintock Miller is the district teacher librarian and technology integration specialist at Van Meter Community School in Van Meter, Iowa. Over the last five years, Shannon has learned about, supported, and embraced her school community's connections to the Common Core. She has integrated technology, wonderful digital and print resources, and inquiry-based learning throughout the curriculum by collaborating with the teachers, students, administrators, and parents.

Judi Moreillon is an assistant professor in the School of Library and Information Studies at Texas Woman's University. She has served as a school librarian at every instructional level. Judi is the author of professional books for school librarians that support classroom-library coteaching in the areas of reading comprehension and inquiry learning.

Ben Mosher teaches seventh- and eighth-grade science at South East Junior High School in Iowa City. His current interests include incorporating differentiated instruction methods into his classroom and developing inquiry-based projects that meet Common Core standards.

Olga M. Nesi was a middle school librarian for eleven years, prior to which she was a classroom teacher for six years. She is currently a library coordinator in a large city school district. Her book *Getting Beyond Interesting—Teaching Students the Vocabulary of Appeal to Discuss Their Reading* was published by Libraries Unlimited in 2012.

Judi Paradis is the library media specialist at Plympton Elementary School, Massachusetts. She is particularly interested in using the library as a literacy center and as a cultural center in her school. Judi enjoys working with her teachers on project-based learning. She is active in the Massachusetts School Library Association, currently serving as president-elect.

Suzy Rabbat is a National Board Certified Teacher and school library media consultant in the Chicago area. She created the concept for Cherry Lake's Information Explorer series and authored several books in the series.

Evan Remley is a twelve-year veteran of the English department of New Canaan High School in New Canaan, CT. He has focused his work on in-tegrating online course platforms to support Common Core standards and develop student inquiry with twenty-first-century skills. He holds a MEd in curriculum and instruction from Harvard University and a BA in English literature from Trinity College.

Elizabeth Schau is a teacher librarian at South East Junior High in Iowa City, Iowa. She is always looking for opportunities to collaborate and incorporate inquiry into the student learning experience.

Chelsea Sims is a teacher librarian at Hills Elementary and South East Junior High in Iowa City, Iowa. She is enthusiastic about inquiry learning and the opportunity for teacher librarians to collaborate in the implementation of Common Core standards across disciplines.

Andrew Smith is a teacher at South East Junior High in Iowa City, Iowa.

Robert Stevenson is the department chair of the social studies department at New Canaan High School, where he helped develop the district's new teacher evaluation and professional leadership framework and align it with Connecticut's Common Core standards.

Scott Stimmel teaches seventh-grade science at South East Junior High, which is a part of the Iowa City Community School District. Scott collaborated with teacher librarians at South East to develop the Zombie Apocalypse Infectious Disease Research Project.

Barbara Stripling is an Assistant Professor of Practice in the School of Information Studies, Syracuse University. She received her doctorate in information management from Syracuse University in May 2011 and has written or edited numerous books and articles. Stripling is a former president of the American Association of School Librarians and is the 2013–2014 President of the American Library Association.

Joan Upell is currently a school library coordinator for the South Dakota State Library, a division of the South Dakota Department of Education. In her position she coteaches and collaborates with school librarians and other educators across the state on the implementation of the Common Core State Standards. This professional development includes online courses, webinars, conference workshops, and School Library Boot Camp.

Sandy Yamamoto is the librarian at Kapolei High School in Hawaii. She is a National Board Certified Librarian and works closely with her teachers in building professional learning communities to implement school reform initiatives and mentor new teachers. She is joint author of *Collaborating for Project-Based Learning in Grades 9–12* (Linworth, 2008).